The History of The Philadelphia Mafia

Before Bruno

The History of The Philadelphia Mafia

Book Two: 1931–1946

Celeste A. Morello

Library of Congress Control Number: 2001126376.

ISBN: 0-9677334-21 (Volume 2)

Cover designs by CAM and Frank J. Szerbin with photographs from The Philadelphia Police, *The Philadelphia Record*, *The Public Ledger*, and *The Evening Bulletin* from the 1930s.

Contents

Photographs and Maps

Homicide & other Criminal Data

Introduction

The word, "gangster" usually stirs and causes an immediate image in our minds of a slick fellow in a pin-striped suit carrying a gun and riding on the sideboard of a fleeing car. Somehow, Americans have embraced this criminal type as their own, a product of United States culture—yet, Americans have never associated any foreign ethnicity to the urban gangster of the 1920s through 1940s. Likewise, in the contemporary news media and on film, the gangster has no foreign accent in his speech, affects no behaviors or gestures of a foreign culture and did not seem to be alien to native American values in any way because the gangster was portrayed as a romantic, mysterious figure, too attractive to deny as a "bad man." In short, the gangster represented American ingenuity, risk-taking and capitalism despite that the gangster was also a pioneer in crime.

This classic gangster image related to the period in U.S. immigration history when the development of such criminals arose within the American urban ghettos with those born in eastern or southern Europe. This criminal type among the newly arrived or temporarily settled arose just before the years of the Great War, an appropriate time to mature criminally for the illegal advantages presented during Prohibition (1920-1933). There were gangsters in gangs which were wholly or partly comprised of members of their own ethnicity. But traditionally, early crime historians in the 1970s such as Humbert S. Nelli and Mark H. Haller, and earlier sociological works by Donald Cressey and Daniel Bell[1] only note foreign nativity as a fact in the criminal's biography, not necessarily as a condition or element in the gangster typology or gang model. Hence, the gangster evolved on U.S. soil regardless of one's background in Europe, Appalachia or in the "Wild West."

This volume in the *Before Bruno* series examines the genesis and evolution of the Italian-born male who interpreted and processed his experiences in the U.S.'s urban areas into a form of deviance identified as part of the gangster culture. It was a fluid lifestyle of moving in and out of mainstream society, with the gangster found in circumstances suitable for himself, not for the family or community, as with Sicilian American Mafiosi. This time frame also included an evolutionary stage in U.S. crime history of when the Italian gangster not only was recruited by Sicilian American Mafiosi into the Mafia here, but was converted into a new criminal type, the La Cosa Nostra member, a synthesized version of the Italian gangster who was influenced by Mafiosi custom, tradition and behavior.

John Avena and Joseph Bruno, the LCN bosses of the Philadelphia-South Jersey Family from 1931 to 1946 typify this transition in crime history. In marked difference to Salvatore Sabella, Avena's Mafioso predecessor, Avena and Bruno were born in eastern Sicily where the Mafia was unknown; Avena and Bruno learned about the Mafia in the U.S. and moreover, they chose Mafia involvement. These bosses' lives also exemplified points of reference to negate the "Ethnic Succession Theory"[2] in criminology which alluded to a socio-economic disadvantage within certain immigrant groups. To proponents of the "Ethnic Succession Theory," the impoverished immigrant on the margins of U.S. society naturally gravitated to illegal acts because he had no other choice at the time, given his station. Avena and Bruno are not only exceptions to this theory, but stronger historical data deflates such a generalized concept overall. The importance of Avena's and Bruno's years as bosses rests upon a basis in illegal activities that survived into the twenty-first century: gambling, narcotics, infiltration into the food, clothing, construction and waste industries, and political corruption climaxed during the 1931 to 1946 period in Philadelphia. What also made this time more significant was that the LCN along with the Jewish Mob had great impact upon Philadelphians during the Depression, New Deal Era and World War II years through the criminal justice and political systems.

Time and distance allow for acceptable revisionist history in areas where the subjects of crime and criminals were previously too offensive to credit, as well as to dignify. Book 1's historiography, methodology and notes on the sources mentioned the challenges in obtaining consistently reliable data on the American Mafia and its members; the same applies to Book 2. Integrating new findings and correcting old information continues again, with an examination of violent crime within the Italian communities in Philadelphia. The birth of the Italian gangster in this city is also discussed by enhancing his three dimensional qualities criminologically and through interpretation of the historical sources. The recurrent theme begun in Book I on the Philadelphia Sicilian American Mafia and La Cosa Nostra as a case study and how differently local and state law enforcement responded to these groups was taken into account in order to fully appreciate the environment in which these criminal activities flourished. The reader will notice that no photographs were taken of Philadelphia mobsters' bullet-riddled bodies—for several reasons. And there was very little publicly printed on Philadelphia's Mafia and LCN members to assure citizens that the law was effected upon these bad men. This was Philadelphia in the 1930s and 1940s, not Chicago or New York! One need not expect power conflicts between gangsters and politicians, or between gangsters and police! No prosecutors in Philadelphia used LCN members as "stepping stones" to further their careers. All of the forces of influence in Philadelphia, whether criminal or not, worked well in concert towards common goals, thereby justifying the "City of Brotherly Love's" true definition.

Angelo Bruno moved and grew with gangsters during this time. He "became a man," i.e., was initiated into the LCN with John Avena, and he learned who did what and how and for whom. These were times when the emotions spent on a national depression and Second World War left most Philadelphians in a state of uncertainty. Yet Philadelphia's gangsters and many in the underworld lived with the "here and now" attitude that separated them from mainstream society and allowed them to cunningly draw the confidence from the unsuspecting in the not so victimless of crimes as narcotics and gambling.

It was a time to prey insidiously upon others in more criminally creative ways.

And it began with these men who established this practice before 1959, when the Philadelphia's LCN boss was Angelo Bruno.

• • • • • • • • • •

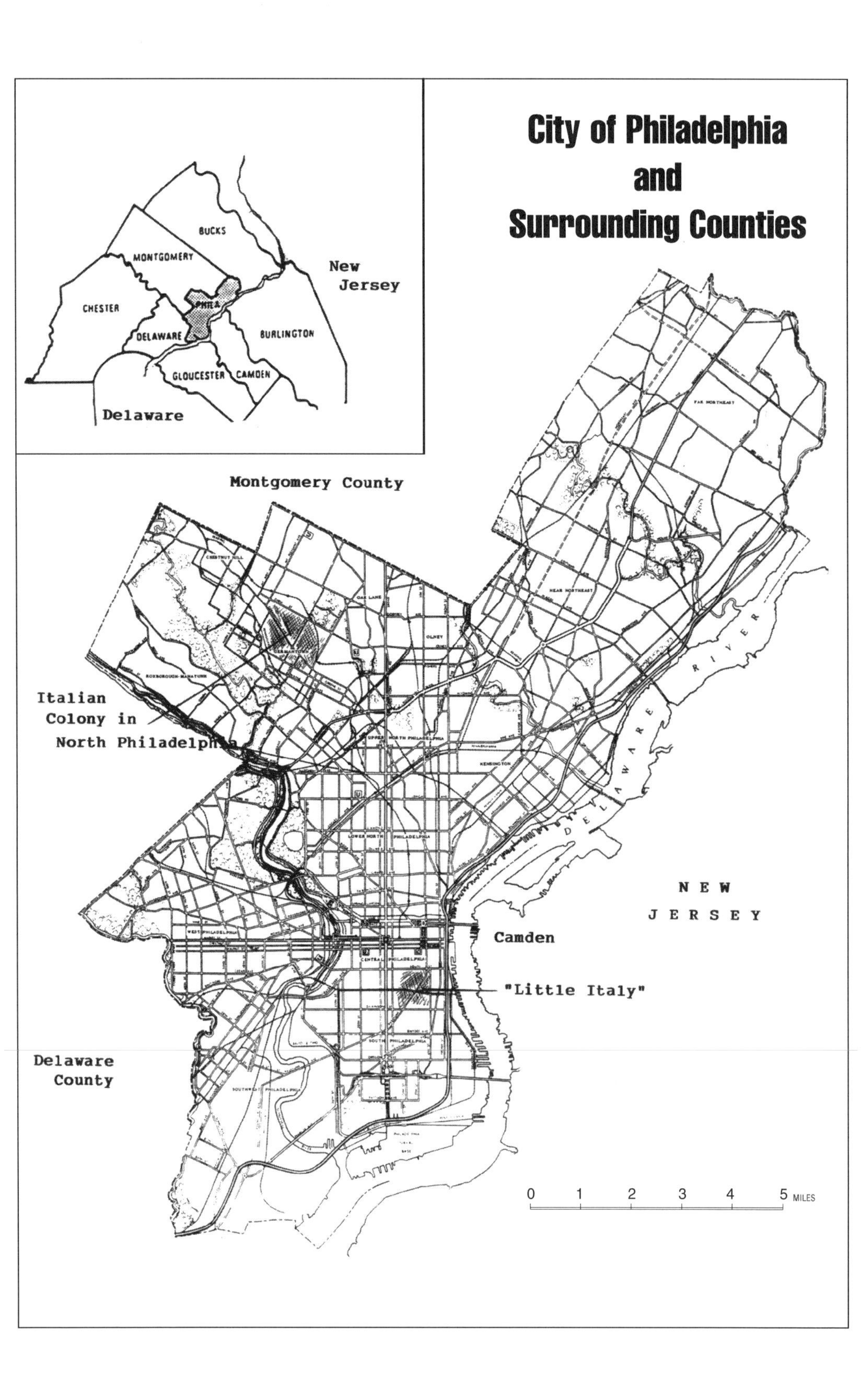
City of Philadelphia
and
Surrounding Counties
BUCKS
MONTGOMERY
New
Jersey
CHESTER
PHILA
DELAWARE
BURLINGTON
GLOUCESTER
CAMDEN
Delaware
Montgomery County
Italian
Colony in
North Philadelphia
DELAWARE RIVER
NEW
JERSEY
Camden
"Little Italy"
Delaware
County
0
1
2
3
4
5 MILES

Chapter 1
Killings Among Italians in Philadelphia

There was perhaps no better way to assess the great difficulty in settlement in Philadelphia by those of Italian ancestry during the migration period from 1880 to 1930 than by a review of why there had been so many Italians taking the lives of their fellow countrymen. The reasons for killing one of their own ranged from jealousy and anger, which were without much premeditation, to retribution and revenge or to send a warning, all with intentions to end lives. Rarely were deaths attributed to self-defense or to robbery. Even rarer were the killings of Italian females by Italian males that would have been critically calculated. Killings occurred at any area within Philadelphia where there were groups of Italians, usually in the national parishes of their Roman Catholic churches. And the causes of death were typically from gun shot wounds because the majority of the foreign-born newcomers customarily carried firearms to protect their only material assets which they carried on their persons.[1]

This summary of findings though, should not suggest a definitive conclusion. This case of the Italians in Phildelphia was causal and somewhat predictable for poor, unskilled immigrants trying to adjust to the complexities of a Victorian culture in an industrialized urban venue. Yet many other immigrant groups experienced the same stimuli in the same environment at the same time without reacting as the Italians.[2] Without trying to resolve why some ethnic groups seemed inherently more violent than others, the example of another large immigrant group in Philadelphia, the Irish Catholics, may offer some basis for comparison. Crime historian Roger Lane described the "violent expression of aggression" first seen in this city in the Irish Catholic communities arising after the arrivals from famine-ravished Ireland in the mid-nineteenth century. Ethnicity, religion, class and economics had initially detained the Irish Catholics from attaining a higher social status at that time,[3] but the "aggression" was usually from external forces, such as from Protestant nativist or labor groups. In contrast to these Irish Catholics in Philadelphia, the Italians' aggression was projected internally and not in the direction to fend off any political or economically-based entity. Also unlike the Irish, the Italians did not test Philadelphia's social institutions during their attempts at settlement in the 1880s through the early twentieth century. The Italians, Roman Catholic and unlettered in English, may have been indeed frustrated by some local social problems; but there seemed to have been more unspoken reasons for such grievous intraethnic hostility. Research of Philadelphia's earliest Italian immigrants and residents reflected a much longer time frame for Italian-on-Italian violence, as well as for a perturbingly higher rate of incidents of deaths than the Irish Catholics. Among the first recorded homicides were those found by sociologist Richard N. Juliani in his epic work, *Building Little Italy: Philadelphia's Italians Before Mass Migration.* In an Italian-on-Italian death publicized in

Philadelphia in 1843, there was a stabbing over an insult to the assailant's region in Italy. Juliani commented that, "Italians in Philadelphia...were sometimes a nuisance to each other," on the isolated world of the immigrant in the lower class. He also noticed that by the 1860s that Italians and crime were tied together more publicly in newspapers that featured some thefts by Italians though "without violence" and then more fatalities from stabbings by Italians using the uncommon "stiletto," which further reinforced the negative image of the entire group of ethnic Italians with crime in Philadelphia.[4]

Lane's research on Philadelphia's Italians of the late nineteenth century produced findings that they "succeeded the mid-century Irish as the most violent people... their murder rate for some time far exceeding the blacks."[5] Lane used the list of indictments as his source. However, Volume 1 of the Philadelphia Police's "Murder Squad" only lists twenty-four violent deaths involving Italians for the years 1892 to 1899 without any annual figures in which to reckon ratios. (See chart on page 11.) Lane added that the 1891–1900 decade closed with an Italian-on-Italian homicide rate that was higher than any other Caucasian group in the city.[6] If one were to doubt the police homicide records, or to speculate that there was purposeful inflation of the figures, there could be no dispute to show bias or any anti-Italian sentiment among Philadelphia's police and municipal courts in the 1890s as there had been with the Irish Catholics in the 1840s. Neither Juliani nor Lane noted such prejudices, however subtle, from their research despite that contemporary thought in the 1890s harbored some bias against the Italians.[7] The same matter-of-fact attitude is evident in the homicide records without any suggestion of anti-ethnic hostility.

Violent, suspicious and accidental killings within the Italian colonies in Philadelphia were significant for other social reasons as well. Lane attributed the high numbers of deaths to the usual urban stresses arising from living as a member in a "low status or even marginal" place in Philadelphia society.[8] Furthermore, Lane examined the number of suicides among Italians in Philadelphia in the 1890s and found the figure to be 6.4 deaths per 100,000 citizens, unusually high for a single group considering Lane's suicide figure to have been 12.2 for all Philadelphians during the same decade.[9] The police's records on homicide from 1901 to the first half of 1909 have been lost, yet Lane found "the truly astonishing homicide conviction rate" for defendants of Italian ancestry to measure 26.5 per 100,000. But where Lane found the intraethnic Italian homicide rate to fall by 1908 to 1915,[10] the Philadelphia detectives reported some distressing figures of violent deaths involving those of Italian descent as seen on the chart on page 11. In some years before 1920, the ratio was one violent death involving an Italian for every five or six homicides by others; in 1913 and the war years of 1917 and 1918, the Italian-on-Italian figure produced a startling 1:3 homicide ratio.

Before 1915, the main sites for these Italian-on-Italian deaths were in North Philadelphia's Germantown section, and in the quadrant of South Philadelphia, south of South Street, east of Broad Street and above Washington Avenue-sites where Italian national parishes drew immigrants and where the Italian tongue could be heard. The time frame for this surge in violent deaths, though, could never have been worse for those who were quarrelsome, easily offended, drunk or just very angry at their world of all males, low salaries and lots of idle time for mischief. Up to mid-1910, Philadelphia police wrote detailed "Remarks" such as this March 20, 1910 entry to explain their detective work as well as what happened:

> Tell from 14th Dist. says 7^{00} this P.M. during a quarrell [sic] at 4905 Wayne Avenue Socooso

PHILADELPHIA HOMICIDES AMONG THOSE OF ITALIAN OR SICILIAN ANCESTRY.*

YEAR	TOTAL # HOMICIDES**	ITALIAN-ON-NON-ITALIAN	NON-ITALIAN-ON-ITALIAN	ITALIAN-ON-ITALIAN
1892	not available	0	0	1
1893	"	0	1	2
1894	"	1	0	1
1895	"	0	0	4
1896	"	0	1	2
1897	"	1	0	4
1898	"	1	1	0
1899	"	1	0	3
1900 to 1908	"			
1909	45+(incomplete)	1	1	6
1910	76	5	1	12
1911	70	2	0	14
1912	91	1	1	10
1913	71	2	0	18
1914	64	5	0	12
1915	69	2	1	9
1916	88	4	1	12
1917	82	8	0	19
1918	119	2	3	21
1919	104	2	0	17
1920	111	3	0	13
1921	108	0	0	20
1922	130	0	3	21
1923	163	2	2	17
1924	119	3	3	11
1925	163	1	5	20
1926	153	3	1	11
1927	161	4	1	9
1928	175	3	2	20
1929	168	2	0	11
1930	155	3	2	8

Estimated margin of error: ± 2 recorded homicides.

* Surnames were identified as Italian based on language reference and the notes of the police detectives.

** These include all recorded deaths arising from domestic disputes, accidents, robberies, assaults, arguments and self-defense. The "vendetta" deaths noted, as well as where "unknown person or persons" appeared were presumed among this ethnic group.

Note: Not all deaths may have been recorded by the police.

Source: Philadelphia Police Homicide Unit, Volumes 1, 3 to 9.

> Eiulino 45 Yrs. Res. 4905 Wayne Ave. was Shot in right side and removed to Germantown Hospital in Serious condition by Donato Masciemareno 24 Yrs. 5 ft. 7 in. 160 lbs. Dark Complex Black hair smooth face Dark cloths Black Shirt and tie Black soft hat may go to Norristown watch Deptors [sic] Ferries and Freight. Dets. Palma and Fox.[11]

By the spring of 1910, the detectives began to note "Fugitive" and "escape" more often after an Italian was the assailant; "Unknown party" or "Unknown person"[12] often suggested Italians, given the circumstances, as in this February 17, 1910 case:

> Tell 2rd [sic] Dist. says Arrest an Italian 25 Yrs. 5 ft. 7 in Lt. complexion brown hair smooth face Lt brown suit Lt soft hat for shooting a man this P.M. who may die Notify Doctors and Hospitals may apply for treatment for Gun Shot wound About 9^{30} this P.M. while 2 Unknown men were Shooting at Each other on Christian St. West of 7 ...Luigi Placigo 25 Yrs. Res. 761 S. 7th st. while walking on street was shot in the Breast taken, to Penna. Hospital in Serious Condition 3^{45} this A.M. Officers arrested 2 men for this shooting Det. Clear and O'Sullivan on Case.

As discouraging as it may have been for anyone of Italian or Sicilian background during these years when the Black Hand was active in Little Italy, few murders were attributed to this criminal group of extortionists. In 1910, Little Italy's intraethnic crime and violence spree continued with a variety of intriguing deaths that ranged from nine year old Giachino [sic] Camise's demise by a beating from Domenico Protelige, to what a newspaper described as, "Two Italians Fight Fierce Street Duel." As if watching gladiators fight to the death, "...a crowd of several hundred excited spectators [witnessed as], two men fought a bloody duel on Darien street, below Christian." An argument was the basis of the fight—a "Felica" [sic] Spatara asked Joseph Forestro to play cards with him. Forestro "became angry and struck Spatara, who drew a stiletto...and the two men began to slash at each other..." Only one person Thomas Sippola, tried to stop the fight, but the armed men "plunged their knives into his shoulder." The police then arrived and arrested Spatara and Forestro.[13]

Incidents such as this and the frequent Black Hand bombings in the neighborhood raise the question as to why these immigrant Italians and Italian Americans allowed this exploitation to perpetuate. Would these crimes have been committed by an educated middle class who operated their own businesses? And would an educated middle class, sole proprietor have allowed himself to be victimized or watch another be victimized? What intraethnic violence and serious crime existed apart from any gang activity was addressed by the Philadelphia Police, who noticed the consistently high numbers of suspicious deaths in South Philadelphia's Little Italy. Local law enforcement's solution to this rather contained problem came from New York.

Shortly after the number of Black Hand bombings, kidnappings and extortions drastically rose to the point where national attention focused on these unsolvable, uncontrollable offenses, New York's Police Department established its "Italian Squad." The most notable member of this unit was Lieutenant Joseph Petrosino who attempted to investigate the Black Hand crimes as well as some of New York's wealthy Sicilian Mafiosi, to whom he attached to any intraethnic criminal activities. Shortly after arriving in Palermo, Sicily, to further his investigation, Petrosino was shot by Vito Cascio Ferro, a local Mafia chieftain. Again, worldwide attention turned to New York and its Italian crimes.

But, Philadelphia had no such notoriety in the same area. A Detective Palma may have been the first from an Italian background to be assigned to Philadelphia's "Murder Squad," but he was not to be alone for long—Detective Joseph Geonnotti joined him and apparently he enjoyed his job—he would remain in the squad for decades. By 1919, the sudden rise in Italian-on-Italian homicides brought Detectives Comdeco, Salvino, Rago, Pagliotti, then Riccardi and Piliero on to investigate the ethnic-related deaths in Little Italy. A Federal inspector Garbarino worked on the "white slavery" cases in Philadelphia in 1917. And Doctor Greco was working at Pennsylvania Hospital by 1916 while Doctors Caracciola and Perri were in other local hospitals and faced the frequent arrivals of Italians from stab wounds and deaths from the trauma and loss of blood caused by gun shot wounds.[14] These men were reminders that many obstacles encountered in Philadelphia by the foreign-born could be overcome.

If one attempted to review the Little Italy environment and if the locus presented elements to elicit negative behavior among its residents, there was little upon which to cite, except for the overcrowded row houses and boardinghouses with too many males with too little outside interests. Adding to this was a possible need for more types of recreation, other than playing cards. Certainly there were many distractions: Christian Street's 700 to 1000 blocks were vibrant with stores, pushcarts in front of the stores, smells of food, music and lots of people. By the beginning of the twentieth century, there were enough businesses along Christian Street to identify the ethnic character of the area.[15] Ferruccio Giannini, the first voice in the world to be put on a recorded disc had his Verdi Hall on the 700 block of Christian Street for entertainment in comedy or in musical instruments in concert. There were *societá, fratellanze,* the Order, Sons of Italy Lodge and other groups for socializing. How evenly the positives balanced with the negatives here cannot be determined at this late date. Photographs taken of Little Italy before 1910 show prideful businessmen, children at play in the streets and real efforts to succeed materially.

However, if one were to apply the Chicago School of Criminology's Theory to Philadelphia's Little Italy by showing this neighborhood's location in relation to Center City for discerning environmental influences on the residents, the distance indicates that neither the City Fathers nor the "movers or shakers" in politics had reason ever to enter a neighborhood more foreign than its residents. But mutual alienation brought by class biases between the blue collar, relative newcomers and the white "old money" professionals intensified resistence, and gave criminal activities in Little Italy an economic base. Other typically working class row house neighborhoods occupied by immigrants in Northern Liberties, Brewerytown, Spring Garden and Grays Ferry, equidistant to Center City as Little Italy, had only some nominal homicides and crime, and did not collectively produce the homicide rate from the Caucasians in these neighborhoods as high as with the Italians in South Philadelphia.

Where noted on the record, at least seven (7) homicide cases of twenty-seven (27) in 1917 were against defendants of Italian ancestry and these were dismissed while only four (4) acquittals of twenty-six (26) occurred in 1918. In the next decade, the status quo on Italian-on-Italian (non-gang) homicides remained the same with the same motives of anger, substance abuse, jealousy and arguments over money prevailing. Individuals of Italian ancestry who are more Americanized now in language, lifestyle and sometimes in nativity, were, nonetheless, still dominating over other Caucasian groups in Philadelphia in homicides. What was interesting about this Italian American group was in the parity or leniency in the mostly second degree murder cases. Most sentences averaged seven (7) years in the 5 to 10 range while many defendants received two or three years. That these sentences were not excessive was on par with the general inconsistency of bias on Italians in Philadelphia. By the 1920s there were more doctors, police and professionals of Italian ancestry in the city, but still the homicide rate among Italian Americans as victims by Italian American assailants was remarkable and without explanation.

Richard Varbero detected class divisions in Little Italy in the early decades of the twentieth century, a not so unique phenomenon, but one not often cited in usual immigration history.[16] Varbero also noted that South Philadelphia's Italians displayed rather vague interest in higher education unless it were for a higher paying job. The economic-education issue went further when Varbero found that by 1930 that Italian American children were employed at ages 14 to 16 more than six times than the eastern European Jews (who outnumbered the Italians in population) and two and one half times more than the Polish.[17]

With regard to political activity Stefano Luconi considered the Philadelphia Italian American case as one of latent mobilization with regards to interest in the voting process. Luconi's study of other Italian communities in the U.S. showed that Philadelphia, the third largest city "did not exactly match the Italian American experience in other major cities" because conformity to social and political stimuli in Philadelphia took place later, as he estimated, in the years from 1934 to 1940.[18] What is strange is that Italians were initially recruited to work in the U.S. through politics. As Caroline Golab wrote, "Local political bosses would organize Italian newcomers into political clubs, garnering their support in exchange for job contracts with city-affiliated activities."[19] The delayed conformity to social and political stimuli in South Philadelphia by these Italian Americans was rooted in what Roger Lane referred to in the early years of the immigrants as a "slow absorption into the urban industrial revolution."[20] Clearly, for the Italians and the next generation of Italian Americans, that "absorption" took a long time to adjust; and the lengthy, perceivably arduous path to assimilation was marred by intraethnic violence.

During the 1920s, no other white group in Philadelphia amassed more violent or suspicious deaths within its own than the Italians, even though the gangs of Italian ancestry added to this toll. Only the black-on-black homicides far exceeded this Caucasian group, according to the Philadelphia Police's homicide records. The year 1928 conspicuously points to the high number of Italian-on-Italian killings that were caused by "altercations" to the majority of "gangland-style" killings which had "fugitive" or "unsolved" written on the pages. After 1930, the intraethnic homicides among Italian Americans bore little semblance to the individual, time and place within the context of the newly arrived in Philadelphia. The many unique and peculiar Italian colonies throughout North and South Philadelphia set the city apart complexly from similar ethnic settlements in other metropolitan areas in the United States possibly because as in the case of the local Mafia Family's "problem," there was no large, strong, supportive and contained colony of immigrants from a single Italian or Sicilian town (or *paese*). To generalize about Philadelphia's Italians would then be unfair without a comprehensive review of the individual groups which comprised the entire Italian colony.

The alarming number of intraethnic homicides did place the Italians in the position of inquiry so as to distinguish them from other Caucasian groups of that time. Perhaps the homicide rate also suggested some endemic factors. If much of the blame on the increase in violent

URBAN ARCHIVES, TEMPLE UNIVERSITY

Photograph above depicts the shooting death of John "Racetrack Johnny" Paone on December 3, 1927 by James Flori. Somehow, Flori escaped conviction on this murder, only to be mentioned in the September 10, 1928 death of hold-up man, Emilio Scarano and then again, in the April 24, 1929 killing of businessman Pasquale Livoy which ended Flori's criminal career: he was found guilty of first degree murder with the death penalty after Livoy, dying, identified him as his killer.

crime among Italians could point to the immigrant's economic status in Philadelphia, Golab found the job market open, not closed to the immigrant from Italy. External forces in Philadelphia never yielded information such as "No Italian Need Apply Here," as with the Irish, lending any conflict with Italians much to the internal difficulties that often resulted more in violence than anything else. Within the work force in Philadelphia, there also were immigrants from the lower middle class, the impoverished, the totally illiterate and lettered, the city dweller and the rural-raised who freely became repatriated after a brief American experience, an option which did not exist for the Irish or Jews, but for the Italians led to behaviors in Philadelphia that probably were not acceptable in their homeland environment.

Thus, within the scope of the rather long period of immigrant settlement, assimilation and acculturation arose within the Italian individually, the conscious decision of what to relinquish as well as what to adapt. The Italian-on-Italian homicide in Philadelphia, as shameful it was on an emotional level, was a fact that rested timely on how the socialization process became effective for some versus the contentious hypotheticals that still leave volition and nativity or genetics as non-ethnic points of reference.

The temporal effect of the Italian-on-Italian homicides in the 1930s rang true especially in the infamous "Arsenic Murders," casting a long shadow upon Italian Americans in South Philadelphia. Few remembered that some defendants and victims were of other ethnicities and from outside of Pennsylvania.[21] Just as in the 1860s when the stiletto killings by Italians in Philadelphia set a standard for ethnic stereotyping and criminal labelling, the "Arsenic Murders" cemented a perception of Italian Americans, this time to include Italian American females as offenders and murderers, perpetuating intraethnic victimization long after the struggles of assimilation. Arguably, the "frustration always leads to aggression" theory of John Dollard may have applied to an earlier immigrant group who internalized emotions, then acted out violently to those in proximity.[22] But the "Arsenic Murders" still revealed the lack of respect and sense of expendability for the individual and the community, a "village mentality" that had placed Italy in public criticism for having the highest homicide rate in Europe from the late nineteenth through the early twentieth centuries.[23]

In another time and place other than Philadelphia, these Italian-on-Italian homicides may have never happened. Or as Philadelphia criminologist Marvin Wolfgang noted in his contemporary homicide findings in the city: when there was a decline in the Italian-born population, there was also a drop in Italian-on-Italian violent deaths. But even more important was the fact that all Philadelphians by mid-century felt safer than before.[24]

• • • • • • • • • •

Chapter 2
GANGSTERS—Italian Ones & Others

A male Italian immigrant arrived in the United States in the 1880s and 1890s usually because an employment broker went to his hometown or *paese*, looking for workers, promising jobs. It was a choice for any able-bodied male to decide. Some Italians liked Philadelphia and stayed while others moved on to other sites in the U.S., or they returned to Italy. The employment situation for those who settled in this city also offered some diversion and responsibility which otherwise would have established an Italian gangster closer to the earlier years of the immigration period.

United States immigration history has only glimpsed at the negative side of the newcomers' experiences, presuming that the hopes and dreams of the desparate and disparate were realized only in the land where economic mobility in theory knew no inequity. In Philadelphia, the Italian immigrant did not immediately become a gangster. In fact, there is some question as to whether the Italian adapted local gangster behavior, as in what it meant to "act" like an American, or whether this deviance was an outgrowth of the ecology. Socially, the regional origins of the Italian gangster may not have been important in the initial grouping of Italian gangsters, given the heterogeneity in the neighborhoods in Philadelphia. In this city, however, as in suburban Philadelphia and in New York, there was a greater advantage to the longevity of the Italian gangster type when he, without much resistance, victimized another Italian. The Italian immigrant who chose the gangster subculture was then able to evolve into the character which much of mainstream American society was able to socially integrate because in part, this gangster was formed of America's culture of violence.

This chapter functions significantly in this volume because Philadelphia's first La Cosa Nostra boss, John Avena emerged as one of the earliest gangsters-turned-Mafiosi. This criminal type was bound by the "gangster code" in Philadelphia never to betray another from the underworld, no matter what his race or ethnicity. Using Avena as an example, this "Italian American gangster type" began his criminal career more likely in a peer group in Philadelphia with others in their late teens or early twenties around 1910 or 1912. It was a time when young men bonded in friendship and common interests in material gain. There may not have been much violent crime among these young males who perhaps just hung around the street corners, or who may have been engaged in some stealing and fencing of goods as their Irish Catholic predecessors had done in the same places about sixty years previously. How and why gangs of Italians formed seemed rooted in the native ecological, economic and social elements in South Philadelphia rather than any ethnic cultural factor. Evidently, there were some similarities drawn between the Irish Catholic gangs who operated in what later became the "Little Italy" for the Italian mobsters. Historian David Johnson's typologies for these groups in the "working class districts" of Philadelphia in the 1840s to 1870s were classified as "street, corner, theft and violent gangs."[1] Johnson interpreted these gangs as outgrowths of the "social disorganization" and "complex motives" current in Philadelphia with the mass migrations of Irish Catholics fleeing from a ravaged Ireland. There was no simple explanation for the "social disorganization"— the violence was internal as well as external. But the same location for Irish Catholic gang activity in the lower class sections of South Philadelphia later produced the Italian (Catholic) mobsters who likewise victimized their own. Johnson's typologies of the mid-nineteenth century Philadelphia gangs were admittedly without "sharp distinctions";[2] gangsters of Italian ancestry in the early twentieth century could equally fall into any one of these categories. Roger Lane in *Murder in America* described some Irish Catholic gangs that "had centuries of experience back home...forming secret societies" with initiation rites for new members, and "conspiring to kill others"—they brought these to the U.S. as well.[3] While sounding similar to the western Sicilians' Mafia, these customs were nonetheless transferences to this country like the Mafia and they were found only in particular areas in the U.S., such as in the rural mining villages in Pennsylvania's anthracite regions.

What sets the Philadelphia Irish Catholic gangs apart from the later Italian gangs was their chronological development. Unlike the Irish who formed gangs throughout the city closer in time to their arrivals and settlement, in the first wave of southern Italians and Sicilians in the 1880s and 1890s, there was no evidence that they produced counterparts to the Irish Catholic gangs. There is also very little information to deduce whether these southern Italians and Sicilians in the early decades of the Great Migration developed any type of group or other associations dependent upon criminal activity for survival. It is only after 1900, and after many "rags to riches" stories in Little Italy when the antithesis to the humble immigrant worker, the Italian American gangster arose.

Profiling the gangster of Italian ancestry in these first years of the twentieth century generally correlates to gangsters of other ethnic groups. Single young adult males with little or no education, these men were without any close, interpersonal involvements with females other than a few occasional minutes with a prostitute. These men were from the lower economic class and usually from a weak cultural base in their ethnic group. They experienced adversities in early life, maybe psychological and physical trauma, and maybe one or both parents were physically apart and/or emotionally distant. Any level of the depressive state could be the norm.[4] But how attractive the underworld life was to these males born into mostly large Catholic families could be seen in how few siblings of these gangsters indeed became fellow gangsters: with the exception of the Lanzetti brothers, it was rare to find more than one male in a family involved in gangland activity.

The rise of Italian gangsters in Philadelphia dated to around the First World War. These men were not from western Sicily or acquainted with the Mafia Organization —they simply chose an unlawful path at this time in Philadelphia for various reasons. Some of the men who later became the first La Cosa Nostra members with John Avena had gotten their first arrests at this time, whether the offenses were misdemeanors or felonies. The Calabrians, John Scopoletti, Joseph Ida and Marco Reginelli, then the eastern Sicilians, John Avena and Joseph Bruno, *né* Dovi earned criminal records and gradually gravitated towards others like themselves who were "branded" by local law enforcement as non-conformists.[5]

The heavy black line delineates the southern or lower part of Italy to show that area and the island of Sicily, the birthplace sites of most of Philadelphia's Mafiosi, gangsters and LCN members from c. 1880 to 1930.

Perhaps it was by happenstance that some Italian men bonded together in the workplace or boardinghouse; some men acted alone in crime to victimize mainly because of need, as in robbery and theft; other times, assailants blamed intoxication as aiding in the aberrant acts of passion.[6] Understanding the immigrants' emotions in the extreme and how volatile the natures were of the Italian men who, according to crime historian Roger Lane, exceeded other Caucasian groups in the commission of homicides in Philadelphia in the 1890s[7] and decades after, still does not explain the group dynamics that coincided with the peak in Italian-on-Italian deaths during the World War I years. (Refer to chart on page 11.) To be sure, none of the gangs' energies were directed towards curtailing the intraethnic violence—they were frequently the causes. Nevertheless, what pressures to earn the anticipated riches that the U.S. was supposed to bring to the impatient Italian immigrant were for the criminal deviant often coupled with greater disappointments because the Italian gangster typically was unskilled and most often unlettered. Lacking these even for the underworld, the Italian gangster before Prohibition faced limitations in providing the basics for real independent survival. Moreover, in the Philadelphia case, there is little to go on to form an analysis of the Italian gangster's genesis in Philadelphia from whatever was his source of illegal income to his rise in criminality. There was no Italian gangster model from this period in Philadelphia from which to study as a prototype for either ethnically-based criminal activity or for a foreign-born gangster who evolved into sophisticated crime as a career. The latter LCN members who had arrests in the World War I years were as Avena with the "handkerchief scam," Joseph Ida as a "disorderly person" and the like.[8] No Italian gangster was arrested at this time for such offenses as large-scale robberies or anything remotely as complex.

As the years passed, acculturation in Philadelphia with some of these Italian gangsters in South Philadelphia never was effected in the same way as with others born in Italy or Sicily. Part of the reasoning behind the Italian gangster's tendency towards deviance in the war years may have been the realization that few newcomers would indeed share in the nation's wealth because of their ethnicity, insurmountable economic status and lack of personal growth. A majority of Italians in Philadelphia continued to return overseas up to the 1920s,[9] but it did not seem to apply to the Italians who found criminal activity in the city relatively easy because there was little trouble from local law enforcement who only documented crime within the Italian colony as it was reported to the police. The social stresses encountered in this period in the city's Italian communities might have been more external than internal with the class divisions especially in South Philadelphia more evident to area residents. There was a mix of economic prosperity with some business owners of Italian origins living above their stores as with some service professionals, all near the ghetto-like tenements on South Seventh Street between Bainbridge and Catharine Streets.[10] While some citizens were reminders of success, there were the malcontents nearby who always blamed their misfortunes on a lack of good luck, or on others taking away something which they only deserved. Though not to account for deviant or criminal behavior, the persistent dissatisfaction among many of Philadelphia's Italians up until the 1920s was one reason for the repatriation.[11] Yet while the "have nots" may have been frustrated by the economic disparities in the Italian colony, this alone was not the basis for the Italian gangs. The elementary component to create, as well as to maintain an Italian gang of long-term duration was elusive until after the war years when planning criminal activities for profit using violence defined Italian American gangsters as members of organized crime.

Interpretation of some law enforcement data[12] from the years 1917 to 1920 indicated that some rudimentary Italian American gangs were active throughout Philadelphia and many might have been hired killers. For example, several Philadelphia homicide reports specifically noted, "altercation between several [Italian] men," or "attacked by 5 Italians," or "attacked by 4 Italians," or "a number of Italians...one of them took a Revolver...and Shot..."[13] The "gangster code" used by the Irish Catholic, Protestant and Jewish gangsters of this time also was adapted by the Italians in this pre-Prohibition era,[14] demonstrating interactions and exchanges among the different ethnic groups in Philadelphia's underworld. The extant information had nothing to suggest whether the police pursued the murderers or let gangdom take care of its own. The gangster-police relationship in the city seemingly did not exist as it had with the Mafiosi and their alliance with law enforcement. Many Mafiosi were living and working in Little Italy at this time, yet they did not have any arrest records.[15] The Mafiosi-police relationship in fact, led many to believe that there was no Sicilian American Mafia in Philadelphia then. Sources such as the Pennsylvania Crime Commission reasoned that no Mafia in the city existed at this time without investigating that Sabella and the others were called members of the "Protection Society." Book 1 contended that there had been this type of social control within the densely populated Little Italy, a kind of association comparable to that in New York City. Italian gangsters had no interest in preserving order in the community or in the paid protection rackets except as extortionists, hence the absence of cohesion between gangsters and police. Taken further with the Mafiosi-police relationship, former Secret Service Chief William Flynn quoted one of New York's Mafiosi before 1919 on how far the ethnic group managed their own affairs: "...if you pay the police or detectives they will leave you in peace. In this land, money counts, so that if you kill anyone and have money you will get out of it."[16]

Much of the development of the Italian gangster depended on the degree of antagonism from law enforcement in Philadelphia. This was one of the bases of differences between the Italian gangster and Mafioso since both deviant types began to occupy the same areas. Distinctions between the gangster and Mafioso were always somewhat vague however, because each deviant type involved itself in the dynamics of power and victimization, with varying roles. Whereas the Mafia was stratified in western Sicily to include the *alti mafiosi* who were the professionals and politicians, the *bassi mafiosi* or lower caste Mafiosi were often confused with the *latitanti*, the common gangsters or criminals engaged in street and violent crime. Documentation on Italian American gangsters believed to be Mafiosi appeared first in the *New York Times* in 1888. Flynn, then Gentile, then Bonanno wrote on the existence of Mafiosi with American law enforcement in a relationship before 1920 with no similar reports to verify ties between gangsters and police.[17] How different the characters of Italian gangsters and Sicilian American Mafiosi were at this time before Prohibition becomes more significant where the social and economic aspects of their lives were concerned. The Mafiosi held themselves out respectfully as law-abiding and their neighbors knew to go to these men if any extortionists harassed them. The Mafiosi were also typically called "family men" who were responsible for their wives, children, homes, businesses, went to Little Italy's Roman Catholic churches regularly and supported them same.[18] Apart from these Mafiosi were the corner loungers, the men seen loitering on the ends of streets all day long, talking, looking, passing time. They usually were waiting for something to happen or for someone to ask them to do something for a price. The common thug and thief belonged to this group of males ineligible for married life or fatherhood. They were type-cast as followers, sometimes addicts to some substance, sometimes drunks, always looking for dependency, unable to initiate substantial criminal activity or to organize long-term criminally-incurred income. Nonetheless, this type of individual may have found himself some employment by a Sicilian American Mafioso who would not sully his hands or image with street crime and violence, which often was the route taken when an adversary threatened business.

There was no information on any Italian American gangster engaged in any legitimate business as a front or for actual income before 1920. Questioning the level of competency for owning and running a legally recognized business, the Italian gangster in Philadelphia did not seem to possess the raw talent capable for such entrepreneurialship. To Mafiosi, the responsibilities came almost naturally, and their time spent in their businesses was in relation to maximizing their earnings and social status.The Italian American gangster, on the other hand, idled time away, leaving occasions to make some money to others, or to opportunity, or to caprice. His mobility was limited and contingent upon his available funds, leaving him too frequently without the stability of residence and work associated with the itinerant thief.

Proof of Sicilian American Mafiosi's legitimate businesses were cited in Humbert S. Nelli's *The Business of Crime: Italians and Syndicate Crime in the United States* where he stated that an estimate of New Orleans' Sicilians owned seventy (70%) percent of the "Italian-owned businesses" by the 1890s, a figure marking the self-starters from those at the will of others. Nick Gentile recounted in *Vita di Capomafia* that many Sicilian American Mafiosi-run businesses existed in the first decade of the twentieth century in New York, Pittsburgh, Pueblo (Colorado), Kansas City, Chicago, Boston, San Francisco and in parts of Canada. Francis A.J. Ianni referenced apparent oral histories he had taken of individuals in suburban Philadelphia who had told of the "leading Sicilian American businessmen in Norristown" in connection with "organized crime" in his past experiences. However, Ianni's information, while true, did not identify these Mafiosi and show that men such as "Zu Ninu" were indeed listed in the county's business directories as proprietors or owners of their own businesses, owned real estate and had, before 1900, assumed remarkable economic mobility without violence.[19] This period of the Sicilian American Mafiosi's settlement, in fact, has gone without notice because it does not fit into any law enforcement construct or criminological theory placing the Mafiosi in a uniformly criminal model.

The immigration history concerning Italian American crime does change by the first decade of the twentieth century with the second generation of newcomers. While the group from the 1880s had been asked to come to work and had succumbed to a more humbling experience in acculturation, the second group was different and more violent. Economics and power plays seemed to have been concurrent issues within most of the larger urban Italian immigrant colonies throughout the eastern part of the United States. From 1902 to about 1912, *The New York Times* printed stories about the Black Hand extortion trend as an intraethnic development. It was a predatory crime wave that soon spread beyond the urban locations to include Pennsylvania's mining towns and farms in New York.[20] This immigrant group who had arrived at that time had not brought any organized criminal gang from Italy or Sicily but had, rather, formed "gangs" of men here to victimize others of the Italian ethnos. Gentile wrote that regionally-based groups of Neapolitans or Calabrians would instigate violence against the Sicilians, which brought forth many Mafiosi in counterattacks.[21] Gentile mentioned no economic motive to the actions; there were no leaders or administrative body to direct the seemingly spontaneous bouts of exploitation that ran parallel to the Black Hand crimes nationally. Evidently, no individual and no group of Italian American gangsters were able to hold some type of superior position anywhere in the United States at this time.

In Philadelphia, the intraethnic violence did not include regionally-bound gangs as described by Gentile because the city's neighborhoods were too heterogeneous. Here, no solid group of citizens transferred from a single Italian or Sicilian *paese* or village to live together in close proximity. It was different elsewhere: in suburban Philadelphia, in Norristown's "East End," for example, entire blocks were occupied with western Sicilians. For an urban comparison, on the 100 block of Mulberry Street in lower Manhattan, New York City, it was as thoroughly Neapolitan as around the corner on the 100 block of Elizabeth Street where the Norristown Sicilians' *paesani* were cramped together. Philadelphia's Italians and Sicilians always had been scattered throughout the city, leaving them to learn how to live with other racial and ethnic groups who were their neighbors. The Italian American gangster in Philadelphia in the early twentieth century then, had grown accustomed to others in the lower income areas and accepted some behaviors and habits from interactions.[22] The Italian American also learned that what he had in common with those already in Philadelphia's underworld was that his social status brought cultural, economic and religious biases forcing him to make choices that very few of his ethnic group chose.

The paid-protection activities which the Sicilian American Mafiosi were supposed to have had exclusively in Little Italy, South Philadelphia were one of many relative points of intersecting interests between Italian American gangsters and the former. Mafiosi may have "bought muscle" from the gangsters during the Black Hand years and after, during the World War I period. Mafiosi had the financial resources which Italian American gangsters needed; the gangsters then became whatever the Mafiosi wanted them to be, and the reciprocal relationship began. It goes without saying that an element of trust had to exist between the few Italian American gangsters who would become involved with Philadelphia's Mafiosi because there were many Italian gangsters with whom the Mafiosi were incompatible. The underworld rumor mill constantly turned out gossip to color the reputations of its members, some just "hangers-on" or "go-fors," some who could plan more effectively in crime. News of heists, arrests, court appearances, whether someone spoke to a beat cop or whether someone walked into a police station or magistrate's office was communicated faster among gangsters than telephone calls. The Italian American gangsters who finally made press by the early 1920s were the ones with the "reps" verified in criminal records made while still young: Anthony "Musky" Zanghi, Leo Lanzetti and John Scopoletti.They became more newsworthy than other gangsters in Little Italy because of their broad range of criminal activities.

And, because they were not Mafiosi.

Before 1920, some names and places in Little Italy were noted in the police's criminal records to confirm that Italian American gangsters were actively participating in serious violent crime. Names such as Calia, Celia and Petruazelli, along with the ubiquitous "Bruno" figured prominently in the early years of the Italian American gangster in Philadelphia. Christian Street, between Seventh and Tenth Streets, also had the most killings among the commerce and traffic in Little Italy. There was the tragic death of Louis Reda[sic] of "gun shot wounds of the neck, left hip and palm of left hand" that occurred just off Eighth and Christian. The police noted that "Reda" was shot by an "unknown" assailant for an unknown reason. Philadelphia detectives concerned themselves with another individual at the crime scene: "Frank Picolo[sic] Res. 1626

S. 15th Street was shot in the breast taken to Pennsylvania Hospital later recovered and given hearing at Central Station and discharged." Another murder on Christian Street in 1918 was victim Vincent Petruazzelli[sic] whose death was avenged in the same place by Sicilian American Mafioso Gaetano Bruno the next year.[23] These and many other violent incidents by either the Italian American gangsters or Sicilian American Mafiosi before 1920 established the tradition of crime in Little Italy that would continue and would lead to the confusion of who was a gangster of note to the news media. Such may have been the case of John Scopoletti who was an Italian American gangster who became a reliable associate to the Mafiosi, then later an LCN member. Born in Calabria in about 1890, some of Scopoletti's early criminal arrests included his involvement with a group comprised of mostly fellow Calabrians who were violent. In April of 1917, he and six others were apprehended, then released by the Philadelphia police, in a murder at a hotel at Ninth and Fitzwater Streets, probably La Tosca. A few years later, Scopoletti was operating a "Gambling House" at 816 East Passyunk Avenue when some detectives happened upon a hold-up in progress by a group of Italian American gangsters who supposedly were competitors of Scopoletti's. There, one of the detectives, forty-six year old Joseph McGinn was shot point blank in the back of the head after Christopher Morano told all of the policemen to put their hands up on the wall. Though not identified as a "gang" in 1920, the group included others of Italian ancestry who furthered their criminal careers: Salvatore Battaglia and Michael Falcone, who later was attached to the Lanzetti brothers' gang.[24]

If there is any question about the fates of these post-World War I Italian American gangsters in view of the heinous killings of authority figures, there seemed to have been no equality in justice. There was no legal explanation as to why some gangsters of Italian ancestry received no unduly harsh penalties, even in capital murder cases against police officers. "Musky" Zanghi got away with the killing of Officer Joseph Swiercynski, but Willie Juliano went to the electric chair for taking another policeman's life. Was it indifference or corruption of the criminal justice system in Philadelphia by these foreign-born gangsters? It may have been a little of both given that the pre-Prohibition era was a time in which law enforcement still had not reached the level of professionalism desired. Philadelphia's police were not much different than other metropolitan forces mixing local politics with criminal behavior. As crime historian David Johnson found, "Until the 1920s urban politics had been notorious for being so totally opposite to...the middle class values which stressed efficiency, honesty, and economy as the basis of sound government..."[25] Johnson's view was in tandem with Walter Miller's theory on gangs of the lower class environment, but his statement also contended how significant foreign-born gangsters had become in the urban underworlds, in relation to the monied Protestant American elite who still were the elected officials.

• • • • • • • • • •

Political influence in law enforcement delayed some of the police's progress in organizing a record of criminal activities in cities as well as in establishing policies for curtailing criminal behavior. In Philadelphia, some criminal information provides clues as to how detectives showed some interest in serious violent crime, as in the homicides. But there were also some details inadvertently not given during the rise of intraethnic deaths among Italian Americans and Italian American gangsters' activities. There were, for example, many "gangs" or groups of Italian American males who operated in both North and in South Philadelphia, but no data to connect the groups who used similar motives to kill other Italians. There also were reports of "Black Hand-type" of killings in North and South Philadelphia well after this criminal trend had been on a decline, in 1921 and two deaths in 1926.[26] These homicides represented a regressive tendency in Philadelphia's underworld, not uncommon among the Italian American gangsters, but a type of implication that set the Italian American gangster in Philadelphia as behind his contemporaries in the criminal subculture.

In other areas of criminal or non-law abiding behavior however, Philadelphia's history abounds with more interesting cases: in numerous homicide reports, many deaths occurred inside some "saloons" which were still open past the enactment of the Volstead Act in 1920. Philadelphia police and detectives consistently recorded the violent deaths, many incurred while the assailant was under the influence of alcohol, but never the alcohol violations. Year after year, killings happened in named establishments, with bartenders present and serving alcohol despite what the contrasting newspaper accounts printed on the bold efforts of Smedley Butler to enforce the laws on the sale and consumption of illegal liquor.[27] The newspaper reporters also did not clearly define the bootleggers from the gangsters generally—a loss to historiography. Readers of these timely accounts would see that Max "Boo Boo" Hoff was sometimes called a gangster, sometimes called a boxing promoter, sometimes called a businessman and sometimes called, "King of the Bootleggers" in South Philadelphia, placing him with the likes of the major criminals in the city. It is doubtful that this individual began as a "suspicious" or "disorderly" person to become the owner of an industrial alcohol factory employing perhaps scores of workers. It was more plausible when the newspapers called some Italian American gangsters "rumrunners" because they were more likely to have been the simple delivery men for the distillers, again the subordinates, not the ones who took charge. The dearth of qualified information on this era has indeed led many to take the newsmen's words at face value and to form such conclusions about the Italian American gangsters and Mafiosi without much else to correlate with the other interacting gangsters and local law enforcement. There was, instead, simple deference as in the Pennsylvania Crime Commission reports generalizing on what may have been happening in Philadelphia as in other cities in the United States before 1920 and Prohibition. The attempt to hide defects in law enforcement's administration of crime fighting were no less challenged by the recorders of history who had no interest in exploring the rise of the gangsters, their development and how former "corner loungers," "idlers" or petty thieves became skilled so quickly to organize the manufacture and distribution of an illegal product.

• • • • • • • • • •

The emergence of the gangster-turned-bootlegger in Little Italy was surprisingly slow, given that many knew how to produce the clear liquor. Gangsters may not have been immediately interested in alcohol—perhaps they did not know what to do with it. It is difficult to estimate when Italian American gangsters began to bootleg the unlawful brew in Philadelphia during Prohibition, because the police's alcohol violation records are incomplete and not a good indicator overall of the extent of bootlegging in Little Italy. Gangsters such as the Lanzetti brothers and others were involved in narcotics sales in the early years of Prohibition; later, the Lanzettis sold bottles and corks, not liquor.[28] It was not until the mid-1920s that some "gangs" or groups tried to develop particular monopolies and defined some parts of the city for their operations. The apparent bloodshed at this time which caused the annual homicides to rise significantly came more from gambling-related motives, not gangsters with the alcohol. Thus it took several years for the Italian American gangsters to learn to become businessmen and to undergo several developments simultaneously in their rise from their former criminally-passive selves into gangsters who were forced to be friendly with payoffs, as well as to be organized in the illegal liquor industry. Such stresses gave way to the unsolved homicides in Little Italy by the Italian American gangsters in the summer of 1925 with the horrendous deaths of Leo Lanzetti, Joseph Bruno, "Dopey Pete" Murio and in the autumn, the violent end of Anthony Votano—with most of these murders involving Salvatore Sabella's Mafiosi.[29]

By the mid-1920s, the Italian American gangster in Philadelphia was newsworthy enough to have a following who liked to read about high crime in Little Italy. Thus, "Dopey Pete's" death was recorded as was the public execution in the electric chair at Eastern State Penitentiary of "Musky" Zanghi's "most deadly enemy...who had sworn to shoot him on sight," Willie Juliano. A friend of the Lanzettis, Juliano also owned the automobile or "death car" used in the killing of narcotics dealer Joseph (LoCascio) Bruno in August of 1925.[30] No photographs were taken by the newspapers of the dead lying on the ground and the Philadelphia Police were not interested in displaying any show of crime fighting to further the public's trust at the cost of gangland's foibles, even with the non-native born of the local underworld. It was perhaps during this time when the Italian American gangsters' movements in and out of various gangs, Jewish and other non-Italian ones, plus the local Mafia that confused many of the city's underworld's relationships among each other. While it was true that the Philadelphia-South Jersey Mafiosi discriminated against certain Italian gangsters, there was no impediment to prevent an Italian American gangster from associating with Mafiosi as well as with an enemy of the Mafiosi. As disconcerting as this may have been for the Sicilian Mafiosi, the gangsters, not the former, were usually the ones with the highest fatalities in the underworld.

It had been noted that Salvatore Sabella's Family extended to include South Jersey, allowing members an expanded area for mobilizing their activities. The same was not found with the Italian American gangsters—few left their geographical area of victimization, which for most was their neighborhood. In the 1920s, most gangsters of Italian ancestry still perpetuated this desire to extort, steal, con, lie and even kill their own neighbors, also of the same ethnicity—a plus for identifying the assailants for the police, but heart-wrenching for relatives living nearby the victims. Many crimes in the "comfort zone" of the Italian American gangster in Little Italy went unreported as expected, and the inaction of the neighbors intensified the role of the local "bad man" to be empowered, feared, and wealthy, from the hard-earned savings of his meek, fearful neighbors. This behavioral model would ensure future criminals of the same success in even the most insidious of predatory offenses as gambling.

As limited in mobility as the Italian American gangsters were in their neighborhoods in Little Italy in which they identified, from the street corners where they would "hang" with others, just the opposite was true of the Sicilian American Mafiosi who could not be as "territorial" in the City of Philadelphia as in their Sicilian towns. Here in Philadelphia, the Mafiosi were rarely still in one place without quickly moving about. Having wives, children and businesses, the Mafiosi under Salvatore Sabella could sometimes oversee the transportation of out-of-state liquor in the long hauls, or be asked to assist Friends outside of Pennsylvania. The Mafiosi's organizational structure however, defined their real purpose and transformed their character from the legitimate store proprietors and "family men" to the polished bootlegger who sometimes associated with the Italian American gangsters because he "wanted to make a little on the side." Sabella and the other Friends, Macaluso, the Pollina, Restucci and Maggio brothers along with Catanese, Catania and Riccobene, Fusci, Girgenti and Galante labored daily and legally;[31] minimum contact with Italian American gangsters seemed more to their liking. Though in time the illegal alcohol became more important as a source of income, it also became clear that local law enforcement acted more contrary to the law so as to minimize the meaning of the law and criminality in the gangster. Gradually, the Italian American gangster's character became more acceptable to the Mafiosi in the Philadelphia-South Jersey Family.

The gangster in Philadelphia rose to prominence during certain times and certain years in the 1920s. There were no steady lines of criminal activity—there were periods in which underworld killings waxed and waned throughout the years. Recklessness characterized the *modus operandi* of taking another's life whether the victim was a rival or an innocent bystander used as a warning to an opponent. During and after 1925, multiple shooters in moving vehicles were recorded in homicides in North and in South Philadelphia involving Italians and non-Italians in "drive-bys" witnessed by many onlookers.[32] By the 1920s underworld killings in the streets of Philadelphia became more commonplace and detectives began to write "gangland" on the pages of the homicide reports. Still, deaths from gambling were recorded more than deaths from bootlegging wars. There was a question of which underworld "gang" assumed superiority by the mid-1920s as well as what was the general state of gangdom in the city. The earliest bootlegging arrests did not come from the Italian American gangsters—those of Irish or British ancestry, along with those of the Jewish faith were among the first targeted for breaking the federal laws on alcohol.[33] In this respect, the Italian American gangster was behind, for years, the rest of the others in the Philadelphia underworld, a quality which still did not reflect that the Italian gangsters were by far the most violent of all Caucasian groups at that time.

While many gangsters met death, others sought out Salvatore Sabella's friendship because he was not overtly involved in the killings, yet remained as a silent power in the background. After the Zanghi-Cocozza murders especially, Sabella's "rep" as a no-nonsense individual with scores of alliances in New Jersey and in New York grew in Little Italy and spread. Italian American gangsters Leonard Nicoletti and Frank Piccolo accompanied James Flori in a killing presumably to make Sabella consider them favorably. One newspaper wrote that the trio tried to hold up a businessman at Seventh and Catharine Streets "to raise funds for the defense of Luigi Quaranta and other members...who faced murder charges..."[34] None of the men named by the police were charged with murder or any other offenses, lending more credibility to Sabella's work "behind-the-scenes."

The dynamics of killing in the late 1920s evolved into a more acceptable pattern for underworld gangsters and for the local Mafiosi who had nothing less than positive benefits from such acts in Philadelphia. How a contracted murder "hit" benefitted an Italian American gangster at this time was manifold in terms of how others beheld the presumed killer. The material gains were obvious, but the fear-respect response from within the community was the goal and had more lasting, profound effects. The killer got a "rep" from slaying another; more likely, the killer often had the neighborhood's blessings for taking down some former extortionists and thieves. Sometimes though, there would be someone killed while young whom many would believe was capable of redemption. In any event, the killer was a new man in his block of row houses and the word would spread quickly not to ever make him angry.

Fear and respect were synonymous in South Philadelphia's Little Italy—no one uttered the word, "honor" except the Mafiosi for whom the word truly had importance. "Honor," in fact, was never a word one heard in Little Italy because it had no connection with "fear" as the word "respect" did. And because fear was so profoundly a part of life and living in Little Italy at this time, the word "respect" was spoken more frequently. Hence, the contracted killer among the Italian American gangsters was one intended to advance within the underworld among his peers as well as in the community from which he left as a "straight." This Italian American criminal was also compelled to change in other ways as his newfound reputation and social status placed him above the corner loungers to be with those for whom a cold hearted killer was an asset. Although Prohibition brought about many levels of criminals, the underworld still valued as the elite those who ended lives.

What was happening to the Italian American gangster in Little Italy, however, was that things were going too fast in the criminal world for him generally. And without some experienced gangsters to aide him, the Italian American mobster was lost. Using the illegally-procured profits made during Prohibition, the gangster could do pay-offs; otherwise, law enforcement's indifference to the large lower class community meant that, in addition to whatever political ties to the magistrates and ward leaders guaranteed, many men would not be listed on the homicide reports.

One of the more dismal truths about Prohibition and gangsters in Philadelphia was the feeling of helplessness among so many. Those who left villages in Italy and Sicily sensed similar attitudes of worthlessness from authorities in Philadelphia who enforced the laws for some, but not all. The need for liquor and the flow of cash from gangsters to those in the criminal justice system left the average worker in the city with little social equity. Parity among peers now included the thugs in the underworld who made an obvious impact on the rise of crime in the city. One cannot separate the history of Philadelphia during Prohibition from the history of the city's law enforcement and administration at the same time because politics and money underscored the directions taken by those who succumbed to the wishes of the foreign-born gangsters who challenged American culture and what it was to be an American. Despite that the gangster of the lower class had values at odds with those who officially ran the City of Philadelphia, conflicts were slow in rising to significant ends. A failed 1928 Grand Jury inquest found that the indicted, these wealthy bootleggers, most of whom were of the Jewish faith, had been "burglars, bandits, dope peddlers and gunmen," who became millionaires at the cost of corrupting government officials.[35] But, Philadelphia's criminal justice system was already imperfect, if not immature in its development apart from politics at the ward level.

The Italian American gangster lived and learned in this environment made ready for him by other gangsters from other ethnic groups. The Italian American gangster may have not appeared to be as impressive and sophisticated as the Irish and Jewish gangsters who had considerably more influence on the city's justice system, but this criminal type picked up behaviors and skills from them as well as from Sabella's Friends whom many noticed had not been indicted in 1928 as the Lanzettis.

The Jewish gangsters however, brought other responses from Philadelphia's lawyers and judges who had acknowledged their progress in the underworld for quite some time in the city. The Jewish Mob was stratified with its echelon and grunts who worked in an organized manner for their common goals in bootlegging primarily. Many of these gangsters had ties to New York City's Jewish gangs and formed a network with them in narcotics before Prohibition began.[36] Jewish mobsters, most of whom had been foreign-born, often lived near the Italians and Sicilians in lower income housing in North and South Philadelphia's immigrant ghettoes. They were mainly from the area called, "Russia" which included the Ukraine and parts of Poland, Rumania, Lithuania and other countries now distinctly and separately recognized. Caroline Golab in "The Immigrant and the City" estimated that there were more than 120,000 eastern European Jews in Philadelphia "who outnumbered the Italians by two to one" in 1920.[37] Sam Bass Warner's data placed the "Russian-born" also in districts where principally blacks and the German, Irish and British-born lived. Warner's information—that the "Russian-born" accounted to about 81,000 to the 68,000 Italians by 1930[38] should have no bearing on any corresponding number of underworld figures: the total of gangsters was undeterminable. Apart from class distinctions that were common in all immigrant groups at this time,[39] it became apparent that the eastern European Jews may have had a different cultural effect on gangland activities in Philadelphia than the Italians or Sicilians.

Jewish organized crime had been considered by the Pennsylvania Crime Commission as an "ethnic successor" to the nineteenth century Irish, in a flawed chronological alignment.[40] If one presumed that gangsters entered the underworld by choice, and not by any organic bent, gangsters as judged from the generic whole at the beginning of the twentieth century already showed tendencies and variations on a socio-economic base, with distinctions in class defined by occupation and education. Golab's study produced information that eastern European Jewish immigrants in Philadelphia were more likely to have been found in skilled employment while the Italians were hired "primarily as general laborers in unskilled occupations," ranging from the usual outdoor construction work to street cleaning and garbage collection.[41] Her work featured the major difference in immigrant employment—the basis for most immigration—to be whether one was subordinated or whether one subordinated another by one's education and/or skill. Though Golab never hinted which group of her study of Jews, Italians and Poles was more marginalized than the other, she did discuss the early exposure to Philadelphia politics that only the Italians had. Golab, like Varbero, Juliani and Luconi noted the financial obligations between employment agencies who procured Italian labor and the "local political bosses" an introduction which may have put the Italian American gangsters at an advantage to their Jewish counterparts.[42]

But was it indeed an advantage? The Jewish gangsters' activities ran from narcotics sales, prostitution (or white slavery), to alcohol violations and gambling, the same offenses in which Italian gangsters participated. By the late 1920s however, the Jewish mobsters became more publicized, particularly because the 1928 Grand Jury targeted this group, not the Italians, save for the Lanzettis. It was not because of homicides by Jewish gangsters: their number of killings may be unknown because of their associations with Italian gangsters who could have been the hired guns. There were Jewish gangsters known by name and reputation to be murderers for hire who never experienced the Philadelphia Police's queries. In fact, Police Lieutenant George Richardson testified in 1951 that Samuel "Cappie" Hoffman, Joseph Herman, Moe Newman and Max Segal killed for other Philadelphia Jewish gangsters in the 1920s and 1930s, but they were never convicted for any murders.[43] The question then is: Why were only Jewish gangsters named in the 1928 corruption scandal and not Sabella's Family? This may be one of those instances where social politics won over in the news media and clouded the truth about Philadelphia's underworld during Prohibition. What has confused many writers of the Philadelphia gangsters during Prohibition was the newsworthiness of some in the underworld versus those, such as Sabella, who managed to evade the newsman's pad. Many newspapers could have inflated the Jewish Mob's importance in the city. As one of the few documented sources on contemporary history during Prohibition, the newspapers did, nonetheless, serve as instruments in competition. There were five major English-speaking newspapers in Philadelphia in the 1920s, each vying for readers well before legal claims to defamatory statements were in vogue. The 1928 Grand Jury investigation, brought on by the deaths of Hugh McLoon and Dan O'Leary, had, overwhelmingly, named Jewish gangsters, not those of Irish or other ethnicities. Court records from this inquest dwelled upon the eastern European Jewish gangsters leading some to conclude that if any Mafia was present and active in Philadelphia from 1920 to 1950, then these Mafiosi were passive, less competent and entirely powerless in comparison to the Jewish gangsters in 1928, then again in the 1937 to 1939 corruption investigation where the Jewish gangsters were prominent.[44] Yet, the blood evidence was there to include Italian American gangsters, if the Grand Jury had only seen fit to name the "unsolved" murders of Leo Lanzetti, Joseph Bruno, Anthony Denni, Anthony Votaro, George Catania, Carmelo Favata, Samuel Rugnetta and Antonio Cassella which more than likely may have had the local Mafiosi's involvement.[45] The Italian American gangsters were violent and known to the police, yet they were not singled out for bribing or corrupting any official for the most serious criminal offenses.

Ethnic bias may seem like the knee-jerk response to why the Jewish gangsters in Philadelphia were significantly arrested and indicted more than any other ethnic group, more than even the group with the consistent high rate of intraethnic homicides, the Italians. One attorney gave a belated explanation: before Prohibition and during the years when Philadelphia was supposed to have been "dry," Judge Harry S. McDevitt was, said criminal defense lawyer William A. Gray, "a very decided influence over the police force." An attorney in Philadelphia since 1897, Gray told the Kefauver Commission that McDevitt, from the 1920s to his death in 1950, "...was in the forefront of almost everything, whether it was baseball, whether it was fights, whether it was a community project, whether it was the ward policemen..." Gray recalled instances when he represented Jewish gangsters Harry "Nig Rosen" Stromberg, "Cappie" Hoffman and Willie Weisberg in cases arising from charges placed by police officials whom Gray intimated were "controlled" by McDevitt.[46] Some instances of McDevitt's judicial power spoke volumes of his influence upon Philadelphia's criminal justice system. In an uncontested show of abuse of power in 1925 for example, McDevitt broke some ground when he requested a " speedy indictment" for forty-five year old bootlegger Benjamin Skuller (also known as, Goldstein). Then in a stroke of his pen, McDevitt held Skuller in "the largest security ever demanded of a defendant in a liquor case here."[47] The judge's peculiar wrath against Philadelphia's Jewish mobsters flagrantly appeared to be more harsh than against the Italian gangsters, and for a longer period. Attorney Gray was quoted to say that McDevitt "had the reputation of being very close to Richardson,"[48] the Assistant Superintendent who had been part of the "Little Mob" of detectives set out to combat the Italian American gangsters. Along with Captain James Ryan and James H. "Shooey" Malone, Richardson tracked Philadelphia's gang-

URBAN ARCHIVES, TEMPLE UNIVERSITY
Pius Lanzetti, c. 1924

sters from the 1920s through the 1950s to check would-be tragedies before the whole neighborhood underwent distress. McDevitt's power was tested in one particular incident in 1926 when Pius Lanzetti shot at Richardson and Detective Slavin. Sentenced from fourteen to twenty-eight years in prison, McDevitt shortened Pius' term to just six years; then the judge paroled Pius before Pius' next arrest in June of 1931.[49] No Jewish gangster got the same, or nearly similar breaks.

The newspaper publicity on John Avena's and Martin Feldstein's deaths in August of 1936 lent some credibility to the Italian American gangster-Jewish American gangster gambling alliance without allowing the La Cosa Nostra to be identified as an individual "Italian-type" of criminal gang. Ethnicities did not seem to matter to law enforcement in grouping or defining underworld gangs, because all seemed to be operating essentially the same, using the same *modus operandi* to which homicide detectives would simply write "unsolved" on the gangster's death sheet. To law enforcement, it was the gangster, *per se*, the criminal type found in every racial and ethnic group that defined what the police sought to remove from society. The New Jersey Gangster Act was put into effect by the 1930s and gave law enforcement guidelines for identifying this social deviant:

> Any person, not engaged in any lawful occupation, known to be a member of any gang consisting of two or more persons, who has been convicted at least three times of being a disorderly person, or who has been convicted of any crime, in this or any other state, is declared to be a gangster.

With lawful employment cited as a criterion in the gangster profile, some Mafiosi in Little Italy began to wear aprons over their custom-made suits while they discussed their affairs. Other Italian American gangsters refused to distract local law enforcement and caught the ire of the "Little Mob" of Richardson, Ryan and Malone. Of particular interest were the known killers at large in the neighborhood, the usual suspects, the Lanzettis or "Musky" or his close friend, Anthony "Stinger" Cugino.

That Salvatore Sabella knew or was acquainted with some Italian American gangsters was speculative in view that by 1927 he did "open the books" to initiate new members who had been this criminal type and who were not from western Sicily. The gangster of Italian or Sicilian birth at that time noticed no cultural differences among underworld groups. This criminal type lacked specific knowledge about the Sicilian Mafia as well. But the reality for Sabella was that he had to induct "new blood," figuratively, and with his attention turned towards the war in New York, he had little time to scrutinize what many members had already resigned themselves to do to recommend new initiates for a family that already was in decline. Therefore, many gangsters who were associated with Sabella's new members in the 1920s were often men who later had violent deaths as a result of disrespecting or doublecrossing the Mafiosi of whom they only understood to be fellow gangsters.

One name that had been mentioned frequently as on the fringe of the Philadelphia-South Jersey Mafia Family's activities as this time was that of Christopher Leonetti. This gangster moved among others in the underworld of Italian American criminals during Prohibition. Leonetti made news in a 1926 shooting at 916 South Twelfth Street involving fugitive Clare McCabe and "Two Gun Joe" Corrado in the robbery of a certain "bootlegger."[50] What was odd was Leonetti's admission to shooting his fellow gangsters in "self-defense" when later information revealed that Philadelphia detectives were protecting John Avena, the alleged "bootlegger" by killing McCabe and Corrado.[51] In 1929, Leonetti's brother-in-law, another South Philadelphia bootlegger named Dominick "Tom Williams" Guglielmo was wounded by unknown gunmen, again at 916 South Twelfth. Police had heard that Guglielmo "had an argument with a well-known gangster" without disclosing who it was.[52] Thirteen months later, Guglielmo at age thirty-one, while sitting in the kitchen of his home was shot full of bullets by his two brothers-in-law, Christopher and Harry Leonetti. Harry was on the lam for about seven months before police arrested him and closed their homicide case.[53] Christopher never got arrested for his involvement in these incidents, suggesting that perhaps the local Mafiosi helped him again and again.

Other Italian American gangsters managed to be found legally elusive to convictions warranting capital punishment in the 1920s. Danny Day, born Deodato DelGiorno was sentenced to die as a codefendant in the murder of Sammy Jacobs in 1929. He was set free as was one of his accomplices, Anthony "Pickles" Piccarelli.[54] They had interactions with Sabella's Family members, perhaps tangentially. They were as other Italian American gangsters who "made their bones" during Prohibition and were sometimes considered as recommendations later in the LCN, after Sabella stepped down and when the composition of the Family became more integrated with a purely criminal type.

In the 1920s there had been a mention in the news, however true or false, that some Italian American gangsters did business with the local Chinese tongs, another organized crime group with an interstate network, structure and armed members. The Hig Sing tong members, with their headquarters at 932 Race Street in Philadelphia's Chinatown were in a national dispute with the local On Leong tongs during Prohibition. Not much was known about the internal, distinct characteristics of each faction, but both were involved in gambling, probably narcotics, but certainly bootlegging. One newspaper called the product at issue, "high-powered Chinese rice hooch," a 140% proof alcohol made in the Chinese stills in Philadelphia. Tong wars between Chinese gangsters and bootleggers in the major U.S. cities climaxed in such bloodshed as to necessitate a peace by about 1926, but fighting began again in 1929. A very brief statement about the local tong battles was made by an individual whom the press called, "a posted Chinese politician" here: "That's what all the row is about. The Chinese refuse to pay tribute to the Italians."[55] With Salvatore Sabella in charge of the Philadelphia- South Jersey Mafia, it was not likely that he would have associated with the Chinese because at the time he was too consumed with the Castellammarese War in New York, his interests and Family, his wife and children, presumably in that order by the old Mafia code. Wishing to keep their gangland affairs quiet, the "Chinese politician" said this on the record, knowing how often the "Italian gangsters" were publicized and the image projected from the Lanzettis and other Italian American gangsters in the city.

The "Chinese politician" though, did strike a chord of importance on what had arisen in the national underworld by 1929—that gangs and gangsters of various ethnicities were communicating and that crime was their vehicle for this type of socialization. It was a national trend, not particular to Philadelphia or to the East Coast when the convention in Atlantic City brought in the supposed most prominent mobsters. More probable was the fact that Prohibition affected most urban centers in the U.S. where immigrants on the fringe, corruption, lax law enforcement and huge amounts of illegally-procured cash contributed to an eruption in what had been an underworld of otherwise unimportant standing. Given the state of the national economy at this time and the weak platform upon which the Volstead Act stood, the gangster took advantage to become a "good guy" over the law enforcers with occasional donations to those put out by the Depression.

But within the underworld, the administration had to face its own growth during conflicts. In Philadelphia, homicides often revealed the interethnic violence which broke any cultural barriers. Coinciding with the "unsolved" deaths of Italian American gangsters and Sicilian American Mafiosi were the Jewish gangsters' own purge that had begun in the fall of 1929 and continued to the end of 1931 with such tragedies as in the death of North Philadelphia's Harry Herman. With the alias of "Irving Stein," Herman, at age twenty-six, was shot in the chest and abdomen from men travelling by in an automobile. His death was followed by that of forty-five year old Jacob

Levin, who died of "gun shot wounds of abdomen," Max Schwartz, a twenty-four year old who was shot "in the buttock" and the well-publicized deaths of mobsters Samuel Grossman, aged twenty-eight and a twenty-two year old Albert Skale, both who died of "gun shot wounds of face and head" by unknowns.[56]

Still, the number of Jewish gangsters did not surpass, or come close to the Italian American gangsters' murder toll in Philadelphia.

Nevertheless, for how violent all of these gangsters were in the 1920s, the character of the American-culture bore through the deaths and the emotional aftermath through lighthearted prose as Philadelphia's newsmen grew more familiar with the gangsters about whom they wrote. One *Bulletin* reporter said that Pius Lanzetti once paid him a visit to comment that even the bad press was much appreciated by him and his brothers.[57] The news media in Philadelphia used the gangsters' nicknames not exactly to clarify who they were in the underworld as much as to get the reader more comfortable with some very frightening human beings. The killers and killed—"Musky," "Scabby," "Shorty," "Dopey," "Fats," "Doc" and "Pickles" had nicknames that could be found in any gang in the city.[58] John Avena was "Big Nose," a name also used with Willie Weisberg. If the nicknames were used in derision, the ethnic label was diminished in the process, if not irrelevant. Thus, the foreign-born gangster by the late 1920s in Philadelphia faded into one who was accepted as an "American gangster" in a multi-ethnic underworld subculture. If any variable of criminal activity was used to measure an immigrant's assimilation into U.S. society, for the Italian-born gangster in Philadelphia, he certainly arrived as an American when he began to dabble in crime with the underworld.

• • • • • • • • •

The next chapter discusses how this Italian American gangster becomes accepted as an American Mafioso, or more specifically, a member of La Cosa Nostra in the United States. Both criminal types had been distinguishable in the 1920s throughout the nation. But towards the end of Prohibition and with the Castellammarese Wars continuing, more of the Italian American gangsters were given allowance to participate in Sicilian American Mafia affairs, although this meant killing whoever was the enemy at the time.

It seemed that the Italian American gangster, or individually as the Italian American criminal, was definable at an earlier date when the entire ethnic group had criminality attached to its cultural character, as others discussed. Initially, the written information in Philadelphia that bound "crime" with Italians from all regions, not just southern Italy and Sicily, began in the nineteenth century. Abroad, after the unification of Italy by about 1870, resentment arose from the political developments in the new republic, pitting the various regions and islands against each other. The documentation published then caused more dissent amidst the diverse social, economic and cultural conditions that imposed upon efforts in favor of extending the new Italy's boundaries and bolstering a national military and naval force. Of note especially were two volumes on Sicily's political and sociological issues which were immediately printed, translated and disseminated overseas. The authors, Leopoldo Franchetti and Sidney Sonnino wrote a scholarly work in 1875 that eventually became fodder for critics of Sicily's medieval, arrested lifestyle and culture. The authors also identified the Mafia in western Sicily's political and industrial milieux.[59] There were no obvious links yet to connect the immigrant Sicilians in Louisiana, most of whom were from western Sicily, to the Mafia. But Franchetti and Sonnino established a source for reference for Americans to trace New Orleans' and New York City's early Sicilian immigrants with criminal activity. Further compounding any negative observations of Sicily was anthropologist-criminologist Cesare Lombroso's theory that southern Italians, especially western Sicilians, were "atavists."[60] While the controversy concerning rule over the seemingly unruly and deviant grew over the years in Italy, ten men of Sicilian ancestry and one of mainland Italian birth were lynched in New Orleans because popular opinion held that they had killed the city's police chief. The incident brought world-wide attention. Anyone with an Italian passport in the U.S. was looked upon suspiciously. The Populist movement and more anti-foreigner thought fed into the xenophobia of the time. Lynching expert Walter White called the 1891 lynching of the ten Sicilians and one Italian a part of the "Nordic propaganda" of the 1890s, when politics and the press in the U.S. expressed their fears of the newcomers from eastern and southern Europe as the intellectually and culturally deficient.[61] Another scholar found that nationally just slightly less than one-half of American newspapers had approved of the lynchings of the unconvicted men.[62] Succeeding the 1891 incident in which views of "Dagoes" were more negative than positive on a national scale, the Black Hand crimes began to be publicized in countless reports and through the 1909 murder in Sicily of New York Lieutenant Joseph Petrosino. The widespread crime wave of Black Hand violence validated Americans' claims that Italians, including Sicilians, were inherently drawn to criminal, or just unlawful, activities.[63] Did it matter to Americans whether violence by an Italian American gangster or violence by a Sicilian American Mafiosi was distinguishable? It also did not seem important that the group victimized its own as long as the Italians did not move from within their own.

By Prohibition, Italian American males may have been regarded with the potential of social deviance because of at least thirty years of publicized accounts of Italian-on-Italian crime spanning generations to include now Italian Americans in crime. The "Americans" therefore had no need, nor an interest in, to know if the distinctive provinces and regions of Italy produced criminal variants or socially unadaptable individuals who chose a subcultural lifestyle which others before, who were non-Italians, had likewise chosen. When the alleged criminal was arrested and gave "Italy" as the country of nativity, the stereotype was reaffirmed. Thus, this popular attitude towards the Italian American criminal and gangster began; and then it was furthered, not by historians, but by early criminologists and law enforcement-related writers who already held the longstanding popular beliefs.

• • • • • • • • • •

Chapter 3
Italian Gangsters and Sicilian Mafiosi

There used to be more pronounced qualitative differences among the Sicilian American Mafia, the Black Hand and the many Italian gangster groups which appeared around the World War I period throughout the United States, including Philadelphia. Regional ancestry initially may have played only a small part in the primary grouping of members in the criminal gangs, with the exception of the Mafiosi who had a certain familial, genetic and cultural cohesion. This lent a particular ideological approach to crime that allowed Mafiosi to be more mainstreamed than the common Italian gangster who started out on a street corner. In Philadelphia, as in other areas in the United States with mainland Italian colonies, the young adult Italian male gangsters often portrayed elements of lower socio-economic class values, abjuring authority and society's norms, including a work ethic, belief in the family unit, and upholding education and formal religion. The pattern for the Italian gangster was not unlike that of gang-

Men "hanging" outside of Our Lady of Good Counsel Roman Catholic Church on the 800 block of Christian Street, c. 1933.

sters in other ethnic groups in the U.S. from what Walter Miller described as based in a lower status milieu. The Italian gangster, like his Irish and Anglo predecessors, defined his goals and behavior from his environment, which was psychologically confining as well as limiting to his mobility.[1] These Italian gangsters arose later than their predecessors, during World War I, towards the end of the migration period, and they generally remained in Philadelphia's Little Italy their entire lives, usually without wives, children and stable homes.

Sicilian American Mafiosi, on the other hand, continued the practice as in the middle class in western Sicily of becoming betrothed to marry while teenagers, with the fiancées selected by the parents, and assuming the responsibilities of an adult before becoming an adult. These Sicilians of western Sicily impressed the traditional roles of husband, father, provider and protector upon the young Mafiosi which gave them a much larger set of values and a future-oriented outlook congruent with both mainstream society and the perpetuity of the Mafia Tradition. These may have been the underlying factors determining all relative behaviors and reactions to divide Mafiosi from Italian gangsters. However, the common bond for all Italian or Sicilian social deviants in the U.S., as in Philadelphia, was American money. Consequently, the pursuit of capitalism was the reason why the Black Hand became synonymous with the Mafia and vice versa, enabling all "Italian crime" to connote a prominent element within the Italian ethnos borne in all of their socio-economic classes.

The written information on the Mafia, the earliest form of "Italian crime," arose first in Sicily then in the United States at a time when newspapers were the primary means of shaping perceptions of the new groups of ethnics entering the nation in the early 1870s. *The New York Times* first mentioned the Mafia in 1877 as present in Sicily—this article may have come on the heels of the publication of Franchetti's and Sonnini's *La Sicilia nel 1876*. Then, in 1888, the *Times* wrote on the possibility of the Mafia operating in New York City. The national presses noted the "Mafia" in New Orleans in conjunction with the mysterious death of Police Chief David Hennessey in 1890 by alleged "Mafia" members, then again in the lynchings of the accused in 1891, bringing more attention to anyone born in Italy or Sicily. Some early twentieth century articles in the *Times* specified that indeed there were "Mafia" incidents in the city. But by 1909, the *Times* Index listed, "Mafia. See Black Hand and cross-references," combining both entities, despite that under, "Black Hand" in the 1902 to at least the 1912 Index, no "Mafia" association mirrored the former. Detective Charles Corrao of Lieutenant Joseph Petrosino's Squad, who was of Sicilian ancestry, said that the Black

Hand name, "was invented by a Brooklyn police reporter some 9-10 years ago," in about 1900.[2] Indeed, crime historian Roger Lane wrote in *Murder in America* that the Irish Catholic Molly Maguires sent coal mine owners and supervisors "threatening notes illustrated with "nooses and pistols" in the 1870s.[3] These were similar to the Black Handers' letters with the knives, stilettoes or blood, or just the inked hand prints.

Initial perceptions aside, there were rather more aspects to the Italians' and Sicilians' use of the "Black Hand" other than that as a vehicle for simple extortions. Within the Italian and Sicilian colonies in New York, there were multiple instances to review whether the "Black Hand" was Mafia or just another "copy cat-type" of *modus operandi* used by Italian gangsters, as was referenced in Book 1.[4] Of the forty-eight (48) "Black Hand" designated stories for 1907 in *The New York Times*, there were many cases where those of Sicilian ancestry who were business owners were also victims. On the surface, this fact would seem plausible except that the "victims" owned a number of stores on Elizabeth Street in lower Manhattan where many documented cases of the Mafia's presence noted the Corleonese, Sciaccatani and other western Sicilians residing and/or having businesses there.[5] Mafioso Nick Gentile wrote much about this street and its Mafiosi who had businesses at the same time as these "Black Hand" crimes, but no one was a "victim."[6] Thomas Pitkin in *The Black Hand: A Chapter in Ethnic Crime* mentioned western Sicilians who were more likely to have been Mafiosi *and* involved in "Black Hand" activities, such as Ignazio Saitta and Giuseppe Morello and their relatives; but Pitkin also commented on his sources for this information and how the many "Black Hand"-typed crimes left the police without much to form models or hard paradigms.[7] For example, there was the case of Sciaccatano Calogero Billera, an undertaker on Elizabeth Street who was involved, "through the medium of the Black Hand scheme" by two fellow Sicilians from Brooklyn. The *Times* reporter did not write a follow-up story to see if the victim, Billera, gave the men the requested $1,000.00, but the reporter did write that Billera told Petrosino's Squad about the attempted extortion and handed over the extortion letters by the two men who obviously were not Mafiosi.[8] Though the case was an example of how numerous and successful the "Black Hand" crimes had become within the Italian and Sicilian colonies in New York by 1908, a year when the *Times* printed over sixty-one (61) reputed "Black Hand" crimes news clips, by 1909 many Sicilians in New York were reported to have insured themselves and their properties.[9] In the suburban Philadelphia Sciaccatani colony, some New York *paesani* ventured down and tried to use "Black Hand" extortion letters and threats while the western Sicilians, taking a lead from their relatives on Elizabeth Street, not only began to insure themselves and their properties but also insured their unknowing friends. Outside of Philadelphia, at least one large barn owned by a Sciaccatano was burned by a New York "Black Hander" in about 1909, but the extortionist never got any money and the owners collected on their losses.[10] Just how "outsiders" to the Italian and Sicilian immigrant ghettoes interpreted the "Black Hand" crimes in New York may be read in how so many *Times* and other newspapers rode on the superficial news rather than the many facts underlying this economically-based criminal trend. No writer was found to have documented how some Mafiosi throughout the U.S. in the early twentieth century during the "Black Hand" wave diverted victimization into redeemed insurance policies which they then used to expand their American businesses.[11] Pitkin's research still fell short of separating the Sicilian-born Mafiosi from the mainland Italian gangsters in "Black Hand" crimes and in so doing brought "Italian crime" to be more generalized and widespread.

The New York Times story that was perhaps the most confusing on separating Italian gangsters from Sicilian Mafiosi appeared in June of 1908 on the arrival in New York City of Sicilian Mafioso Raffaele Palizzolo. Originally from Cáccamo, then Palermo, Sicily, *The New York Times* called Palizzolo, "The King of the Mafia." He was fêted by a slew of Sicilian American lawyers and other Sicilian Americans with "Dr." prefacing their names, men whom Pitkin described as "Black Handers" coming "from the professional classes" from the western Sicilian provinces.[12] Sicilian Americans had raised over 75,000 lire for Palizzolo's legal defense against the Italian government's murder case against him. He was retried and found not guilty. Lieutenant Petrosino's detectives observed that Palizzolo had "very fine letters of introduction, is a man of good family, speaks well, is very well educated and wears an Italian Order of Merit jewel on his watch chain." By first appearances, he was a cultured gentleman who could cite the Roman poets in Latin. Palizzolo also defended the Mafia, but defamed the Black Hand which was why he said he came to New York, "...to purge this community of its Italian dynamitards."[13] A former member of the Italian Chamber of Deputies, Palizzolo was nonetheless the type of Sicilian Mafioso whom Mack Smith and Clark had written about as part of the corrupt, Mafia-influenced Italian Parliament in the 1890s to early twentieth century.[14] He came to New York, the major city in the U.S. where the true spirit of American capitalism was at its best, "to rest," or "to advise" Sicilians and Italians to obey the laws and place themselves under the protection of the authorities,[15] without regards to how high the crime and homicide rates were in his native Sicily. Nick Gentile, who was in the U.S. at this time and who knew when any prominent Mafioso was coming, made no mention of Palizzolo—he only spoke of this time as when regional groups were involved in conflicts relatively apart from the intraethnic "Black Hand" crimes.

Philadelphia's need for social control in Little Italy before 1910 was evident in the rising homicide rates, but there was no information on local Mafiosi participating in "Black Hand"-type of crimes. Some oral histories gave first hand accounts of "the Sicilians" who were called and paid to protect stores in Little Italy and there was a group of Sicilians whom the police distinguished well from the generic Italian gangsters in the early twentieth century.[16] Yet, there was no documentation to confirm that "the Sicilians" were organized against the local Black Handers, especially in the frequent bombings. On the contrary, in Book 1, Salvatore Sabella's first arrest in 1923, while he was *rapprisentanti*, tied the Philadelphia Mafiosi with insurance fraud by way of the Black Hand bombing *modus operandi*, adding more confusion to the Black Hand tales of victimization. [17]

Though Italian crime came to include the Sicilian American Mafia's crimes, Black Hand bombings and extortions, and other Italian-on-Italian violations, most publications failed to divide the groups criminologically because the intraethnic crimes included offenders from the "professional classes," and/or the "propertied people," victims of the lower class who had no social standing and many literate, educated criminals who wrote the extortion letters. There were, though, some variables that clearly separated the Italian gangster from the Sicilian Mafiosi: in the art of killing and in sending a message through death. Mafia killings usually distinguished the assailant from the Black Handers in the U.S. because they were well intended and symbolic, suggestive of the stagnant medieval-like culture in western Sicily. *The New York Times* called one Sicilian in New York a "Black Hander" erroneously, but the criminal record of Pellegrino Mulé from "the Province of Girgenti [Agrigento]" said otherwise: he had "chopped off" the head of his third victim of death, a man surnamed Pumilia. Then

Mulé "nailed [it] to a post near the village of Calibollata [Caltabellotta] and...[the head] remained for a long time on the post with a placard warning others of a similar fate..."[18] Mafia deaths were more direct, with the victim seeing his killer, unlike the Black Hander who would kill while one's back was turned, or in an explosion. By underworld standards, the Black Hander was cowardly as a killer, or, as Mafioso/LCN member Harry Riccobene said, "they were sneak killers," specializing in threats and harassment, prolonging their type of criminal teasing with repeated threats to the victims in person which visually rewarded the Black Hander. While the Sicilian Mafioso regarded crime only within the context of furthering his business interests or as a matter of preserving his *omertà* (manliness), the Mafioso felt no personal need to bother or to victimize others in his community as did the Italian gangster. To avenge and to balance justice was more within the mentality of the Mafioso.[19]

Returning to the Philadelphia case of Italian gangsters and Sicilian Mafiosi, it was clear that when Salvatore Sabella headed the local Mafia Family during World War I and Prohibition, that some of his members associated with some of the city's gangsters especially in the mid- to late 1920s when he "opened the books" and brought in the new members of eastern Sicilian ancestry. Where Sabella was reluctant to interact with anyone not of western Sicilian descent, there were cross-cultural criminal activities in which his Family members became engaged with many non-Sicilians mainly because of the local proximity to the Sicilians' row house dwellings. Sabella's Friends here propelled the Family forward to parallel other Mafia Families in the U.S. where western Sicilians with the Mafia Tradition were in decline, especially given any involvement in the Castellammarese Wars from 1927 to 1931. Corresponding more to a social rather than solely a criminal aspect in immigration history, there was within Sabella's Sicilian American Mafia Family an evolutionary process at work with the foreign-born criminal assimilating to U.S. society faster than the non-criminal Italians in Philadelphia. However, the Philadelphia case of the Mafia and LCN brought other social peculiarities which would be evident in the local La Cosa Nostra members of the 1930s through to the present. Particular to the Italian colony in South Philadelphia were some socialization issues noted by several scholars consistent with the overall interpretation of what an American was. Golab's data on the city's Italian immigrant workers in the early twentieth century revealed indications that a latent development in Americanization was evident in this group where essentially the issue of establishing social stability was difficult amidst such a large unskilled, undereducated labor force. Unlike the eastern European Jews and Polish, of whom she compared the Italians, Golab wrote that only the Italians had a place to return to if expectations were not met in the U.S., a reason for the behavior noted in the Italian-on-Italian crime data. Luconi's studies of the same group's participation in suffrage and elections showed that interest in these areas was not evident until the early 1930s, a period in which intraethnic homicides also had finally declined. Varbero's chapter on "Philadelphia's South Italians" evaluated the ethnos in relevance to how it somewhat finalized towards settlement and assimilation by way of accepting education and the formal religious regulations of the Archdiocese of Philadelphia by the late 1930s.[20] These studies presented a clearer picture of the environment in which Philadelphia's Italian gangsters lived in and thrived among their own, rendering a rather isolated character study of the Italian gangster in a colony as no other in the U.S.

As an independent social unit, Philadelphia's Italian gangsters of the 1920s were representative of the national trend. Mafiosi by this time allowed many of Italian ancestry who were thieves, robbers, narcotics dealers, white slavery runners and con artists to become involved in transporting their liquor opening themselves to socialization. It was at this stage during Sabella's tenure that the Philadelphia-South Jersey Family saw its first opportunity to degrade or as Gentile termed it, "degenerate" into a modified Mafia. To the younger generation of Sicilian American Mafiosi during Prohibition, the Italian gangster type fascinated them because they showed the brashness that all underworld criminals respected. The Italian gangster was a "stand-up guy," like the Mafiosi, though less discreet of course, but his reckless attitude was much admired.[21] Enrico "Harry" Riccobene, born into the Mafia Tradition through generations in his family, as a teenager was friendly with his peers in the Lanzetti gang and others who began as truants, corner loungers and "go-fors" for older Italian gangsters. John Avena, from eastern Sicily where the Mafia never existed, was brought into Sabella's Family after forming associations with eastern European Jews and mainland Italians from Calabria and Avellino. When he became the first boss of the American Mafia in Philadelphia, Avena facilitated Italian gangsters' entry into the new organization as he had been, filling in the voids with mostly gamblers and bookmakers of Calabrian origins. These individuals would establish the new traditions in Philadelphia's LCN Family regarding who would be a member, what the criteria for membership would be, and how these men would be able to relate, if they did relate at all, to the higher LCN powers in the five Families of New York.

In one respect, this new criminal type, the gangster-LCN member, accounted for the shortage of western Sicilians or any Mafioso who no longer wanted active part in the new American Mafia. Older, more emotionally

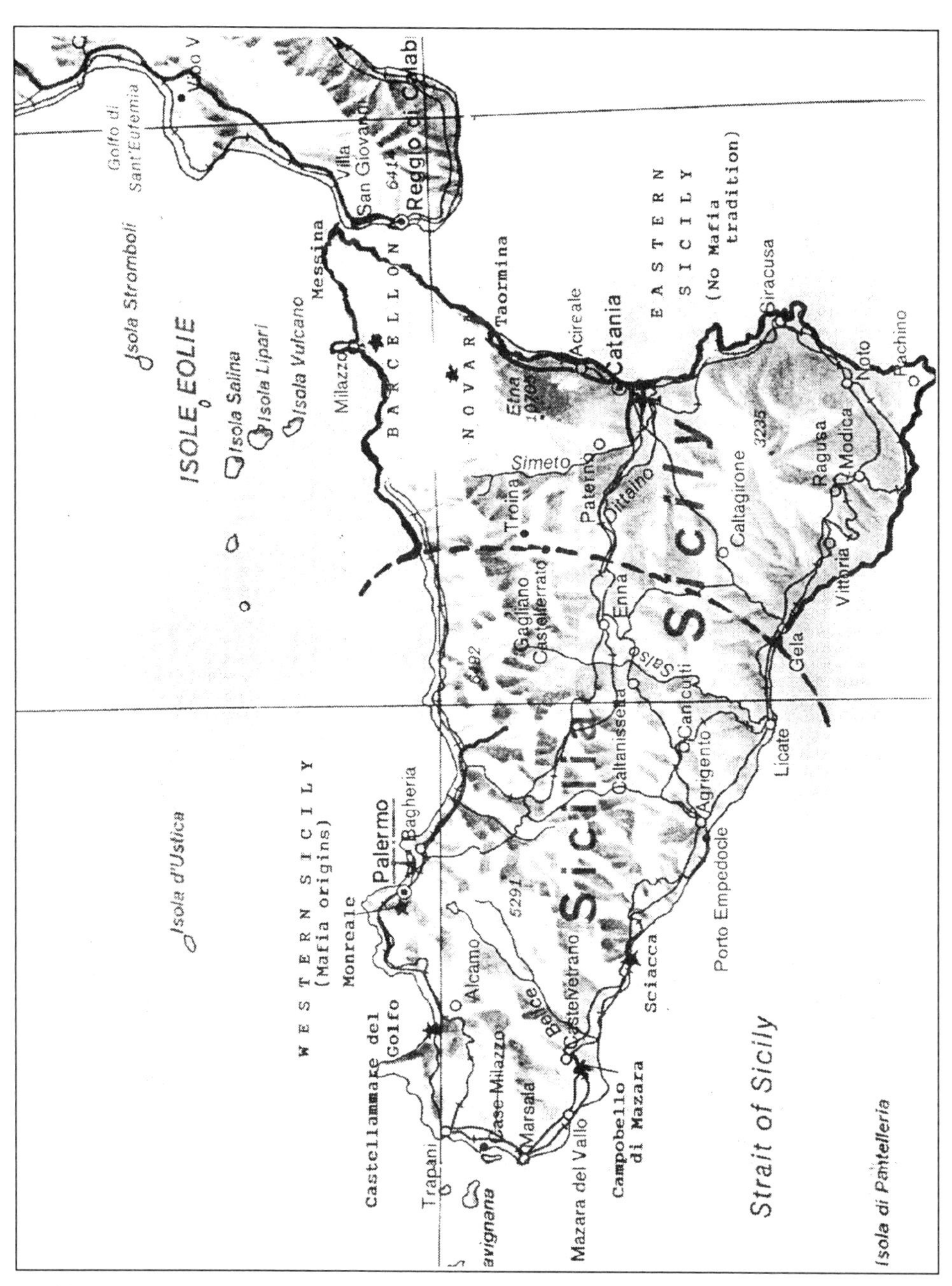

Sicily divided to show Mafia origins in western side and the non-Mafia eastern side. Note also Novara, the birthplace of LCN boss John Avena and Barcellona, where Avena's successor, Joseph Bruno, was born.

mature white males from southern Italy or Sicily who were primed in various criminal activities from their youth during World War I were the likely candidates as LCN members. They were accustomed to not having steady, skilled employment. They may have been married and sometimes had part-time legal employment, but these new initiates had "reps" and most of their income still came from illegal means because most had their starts as "suspicious persons," "loiterers," "disorderly persons" and then graduated to bootlegging and/or narcotics selling. Gambling was next in line to illegal employment in the 1930s, so few of these Italian gangsters-turned-LCN members ever had a reason to work a legitimate job as the Sicilian American Mafiosi did consistently and competitively. These differences were at times divisive bases for the silent schism that began in Sabella's Family just before the Castellammarese Wars and became more decided under Avena when the rift grew wider between the western Sicilians from the Mafia Tradition and the mainland Italians, the former gangsters, who not only remained socially segregated from most of mainstream society, but who also experienced the hierarchal superiority of those who did not reap the most in income for the Family.[22]

The memorable year in crime history, 1931 marked the genesis of the American Mafia, later called, "La Cosa Nostra" by law enforcement after Joseph Valachi testified in 1963 to what he believed the Organization was referred to by the Sicilian-speaking Mafiosi. Valachi had not understood that the word, "Mafia" was never said by real Mafiosi—Gentile always called it, *l'onorata società.*[23] It was a secret matter, not for every man in western Sicily. The "Men of Honor" deferred to using the ubiquitous word, *cosa* that means "thing, matter, a substitute for another word," to define to what no one but the Friends were supposed to belong. In the U.S., the Sicilian American Mafiosi effected an unintended evolution in a tradition that really had no purpose in this nation. From the beginning of 1927 to the fall of 1931, Sicilian American Mafiosi with those from the Italian peninsula formed coalitions with hopes of nothing less than more money in their pockets, and maybe more power.[24] If there was any major contribution in U.S. immigration history by these foreign-born it was how they implemented American capitalism during Prohibition as no U.S.-born individual did. The myths of the Castellammarese Wars simplified the "Greasers" and "Moustache Petes"[25] to vulgar, antiquated characters when it has been proven, at the least in the Philadelphia case, that Salvatore Sabella, the local Family's boss, was but forty years old when he declined further representation in the new Organization, the American Mafia or "La Cosa Nostra." While Gentile stressed that the wars involved primarily the "sciaccatani" and their allies, the "corleonesi" against the "castellammaresi," Gentile also perceived that the foreign integrity in the Sicilian American Mafia was doomed to end as abruptly as each casualty was buried.[26] Thus when Salvatore Maranzano, Sabella's *paesano* from Castellammare del Golfo, called for a meeting to "reorganize" the Mafia in the U.S. and collected over $100,000.00, attention was diverted to an individual who was said to have been hungry for power, not to the individual(s) who plotted his-death shortly after and stole his money.[27]

American capitalism had broader meaning to all underworld types during Prohibition. Earnings from illegal alcohol elevated the gangster to a higher level of criminality while the Sicilian American Mafioso became resigned to greater integration into mainstream society. In many cases, the Mafioso father was left to either recommend his son to the new Organization that promised some financial stability or to divert his child to a lifestyle that American fathers promoted. Nationally, an overwhelming number of Mafiosi fathers opted for the latter. In Philadelphia, there would be, of course, at least one case worth noting, that of Harry Riccobene. In the nearly ten years of interviews, Mr. Riccobene never admitted that his father had any influence in his initiation into the Philadelphia-South Jersey Family. Riccobene said that he "became a man" at a formal ceremony after someone "recommended" him. He spoke with pride on the fact that he was but 16 years old, going on 17 when he was brought in with men much older than he, one of whom may have been John Avena. Riccobene said that no gun or knife was placed at a table by Sabella, the oaths to the Mafia were recited in the Sicilian language as the rest of the meeting, and the elder Mafiosi used a piece of paper, not a holy card, to burn in his hands. This ceremony was unlike that done by Avena years later with the spectre of blood and violence implied with the firearm and blade present over which the vows were taken.[28] This modified version of the traditional Sicilian Mafia initiation ceremony took on an exciting, violent tone, more in deference to the type of initiates inducted into the La Cosa Nostra. Among Avena's new crew was a young man who was not quite as the other newcomers to the foreign-based Organization. This man, in his early twenties, had been a bootlegger as a teenager, running illegal alcohol and stills while managing his father's grocery store. He had to leave South Philadelphia High School to help his father in their business, and, in effect, he became a second provider for his family. How unlike these other men, those Italian gangsters who became his associates before the beginning of his time in the LCN was this individual who changed his surname from Annaloro to Bruno upon "becoming a man." But Angelo Bruno did, in fact, take a tripartite oath to a Family which under Avena quietly acknowledged this rift because it was now a Family composed partly of foreign-born Sicilian American Mafiosi and partly of Italian-born gangsters. And Angelo Bruno was a part of both.

Angelo Bruno could not be said to have been a model for the early La Cosa Nostra Family in Philadelphia, but he was a wilful participant in their gangland activities, which placed him more with the gambler-bookmaker group that dominated Avena's Family. This was a far cry from Bruno's background. His father, Michael Annaloro was the typical honest, humble, hardworking immigrant from Villalba, Province of Caltanissetta, Sicily who came to the U.S. alone to set up a home for his family's arrival. In 1911, Michael Annaloro greeted his wife, Vincenza and two young children, Giuseppina and one year old Angelo in New York and then led them to their home in the Queen Village neighborhood in South Philadelphia.[29] Two other children were born into the family that was, by everyone's opinion, neither poor nor well-to-do, but fostered education for their children and wholesome American beliefs.

Angelo Bruno's potential in life was witnessed in his early adulthood, borne by the security of a close family, education in the arts, and ability to listen and to learn. Though related to Mafiosi in his birthplace of Villalba,[30] no information confirmed that his father was a Mafioso or a bootlegger or that Michael Annaloro knew Salvatore Sabella. It was evident in the Italian American community, as in other ethnic groups, that most Americans had opposing views regarding temperance and may have held the opinion that illegal alcohol was inconsequential to violating the law. Certainly the monetary benefits of bootlegging or making a little liquor to augment the household income was encouraged by local law enforcement's unwillingness to arrest. This may have been the timely reason why an individual such as Angelo Bruno dealt with alcohol, unlike his contemporary Harry Riccobene who chose, instead, to sell narcotics during Prohibition.[31] Bruno and Riccobene, both born in 1910 in Mafia towns in Sicily, both migrating to the U.S. with their parents as preschoolers and both who experi-

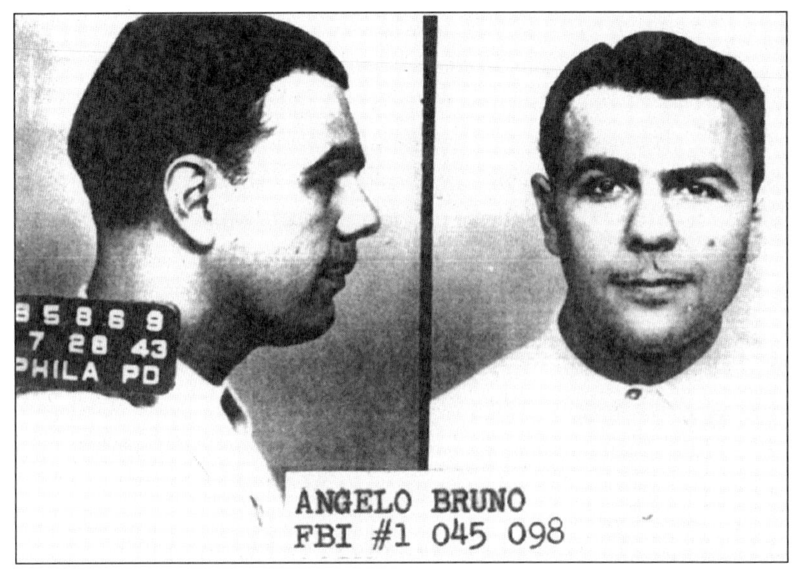

Philadelphia Police photographed a thirty-three year old moustached Angelo Bruno for operating an illegal lottery. Bruno's slight grin said it all—the matter was discharged.

enced Prohibition and the local Family's transition from a wholly Sicilian American entity to an American-influenced organization possessed diametrically opposed characteristics which negated the gangster stereotype for Bruno and the Mafioso stereotype for Riccobene. They were in a group with conflicting ideologies at a time when Italian gangsters were becoming reasonably respectable. Some gangsters were said to have helped those hurt by the Depression while other gangsters from the early years of Prohibition decided later to settle down with a wife and start a family. In effect, some of these gangsters almost became the "family men," but they used illegally procured income to support their families, representing more to the confounding interpretation of American social values in an already foreign cultural and underworld cultural mix of identities.

Reviewing Bruno's and Riccobene's first "pinches" (arrests) suggests the types of niches each carved for himself in determining their fates in Philadelphia's Mafia and

La Cosa Nostra. At the age of 18, Bruno was cited in a clumsy automobile accident, knocking down a police call box. Shortly after, he was caught "rumrunning" and then freed. Neither arrest resulted in a visit to a jail cell. In stark contrast to this, the young Mafioso with the Mafioso father in Sabella's Family, Harry Riccobene, was arrested in 1927 for feigning a hold-up with a firearm and sentenced to six months in jail. He took the sentence without dispute—senior Mafia members would have deftly compromised with authorities and used remuneration to close their pact. Mafiosi considered jail or prison shameful, but Riccobene chose to go away.[32] A few years later, Riccobene again was arrested, this time for narcotics, and he voluntarily went to jail for an offense that even the Lanzettis knew how to get discharged. That Bruno was not yet a member of the local Family and still evaded the considerations of jail indicated much about his background. As criminologist Walter Miller would have applied his theory about why Riccobene allowed himself to be jailed, "the lower class culture's close conceptual connection...[is] made between 'authority' and 'nurturance.'[therefore] To be restrictively or firmly controlled is to be cared for."[33] Riccobene admitted that in his childhood he was "spoiled" by his sickly mother who died while he was in early adolescence. Both of his parents doted on their only child who was born with the physical deformity in his spine that stunted his growth. But Riccobene's father, who was a stone mason and contractor, never took his son on as an apprentice in his trade or ensured his son a skill or profession in life as other Mafiosi fathers. Riccobene the son was never raised to accept what society would have wanted in a responsible citizen, the job or some work, the wife, the children, the home. He escaped the work ethic, legitimate employment, family, avoidance of narcotics and prostitution and other things which would have classified him more in line with the older Sicilian Mafiosi.[34] Moreover, living in

Little Italy, Riccobene never was known to have the "negotiator" or "take charge" role common to Mafiosi, to resolve dilemmas, help the needy or to mitigate social strifes. His defiance to these rather routine, if not natural roles of the Mafioso however, was somewhat forgiven for his position as more of a *basso mafioso* or "lower Mafioso," the type that the *alti mafiosi* needed as triggermen with the wits of the common street gangster. Riccobene could be trusted to keep his ear to the ground for any underworld activities and schemes.Though standing barely five feet tall, he was feared nonetheless, and known among the other Mafiosi and LCN members affectionately as "Little Harry."[35]

What Riccobene had in common with Bruno was in business, any income-generating kind of business that would ingratiate themselves with the local Family. Higher earnings meant higher prestige, no matter how one looked. Unlike Riccobene, however, Bruno had his parents, siblings, new wife and son to support, giving him another incentive to work on ways to increase his income. Bruno and Riccobene learned at different times in their lives how to bring in money though, which should speak volumes as to how their lives often ran in opposite directions except in matters of money. While Riccobene was "thieving," he said, "in grade school with the Lanzettis," experimenting with various drugs as an elementary[36] school drop-out, Bruno was learning music at the Campbell-Lyons School that produced the child prodigies who later became jazz greats, Joseph Venuti and Salvatore Massaro (Eddie Lang). Bruno was encouraged to further his musical career but had to decline to support his family. Yet his early experiences in his father's store no doubt polished his skills in diplomacy, courtesy, bartering and dealing. Bruno would have known the many Mafiosi in Little Italy who had grocery stores and would have watched these gentlemen with the impeccable hygiene and manners who knew how to handle matters as no one else. Having assumed the "take charge" role his father gave him at the store, Bruno was unintentionally being groomed for the type of individual that Mafiosi wanted to be part of their Family. Bruno could initiate as well as administrate. Older Mafiosi noted his friendly style—he was a "people person," helping customers in his store, bringing individuals together, getting along with others from other ethnic and racial groups.[37]

Riccobene always said that men were "recommended" not asked, not chosen to be members of the Mafia. Many Mafiosi have to "watch you and how you handled yourself," he said of those times. It greatly benefitted if your father, or uncle or grandfather was already in the Mafia, he said,[38] a quality that continues today in western Sicily, said Mafioso Antonino Calderone. However, one must have the same character traits as one's Mafiosi relatives. By 1931, that Sicilian tradition was gone in Philadelphia as all over the U.S., meaning that Angelo Bruno was not subjected to the same criteria as Riccobene had been years before.[39]

Bruno's aggressive business acumen impressed Avena and the others, but his image with a firearm had never been noted at this early phase in his LCN membership. That he was "recommended" suggested that he qualified on a number of levels, but not even in rumor were there any hints that the young Bruno "made his bones" through violence. Riccobene always affirmed the dual duties expected of LCN members, i.e., to earn and to kill, but what Bruno did to prove his loyalty to the Family to "even scores" or to eliminate enemies in his gambling and bookmaking was undocumented at that time.

As each gangster or Mafioso in Philadelphia had his own integrity to identify his relationship with another, it could not be said that the young Italian gangster in Philadelphia in the 1930s was of the same criminal type as his predecessors. The norms of Philadelphia's ethnic communities had changed, varying with how well each group became more accustomed to the general cultural environment. Unlike in other ethnic colonies such as in New York, Chicago and Boston, in Philadelphia the gangsters of Little Italy had ambiguous roles in their communities and often did not fully realize active participation in larger community affairs—these usually were left for the "associates" of the LCN members. One example may be found in the efforts of the Democratic Party in the 1930s and the absence of the LCN when John B. Kelly, the chair of the Democratic City Committee in 1934 endorsed Joseph Marinelli for the U.S. House of Representatives. Kelly had also gotten Michael Spatola as a running mate to get the Italian American vote in Philadelphia, to no avail. In 1932, Generoso Pope from New York City bought the Philadelphia Italian newspaper, *L'Opinione*, to push the Democratic Party on to local Italians for their vote, again without much success.[40] However, the Sicilian American Mafiosi supported the Republicans who carried on with the tradition of corruption, not to cause divisiveness in Little Italy, but for the sake of continuing their illegal businesses. Luconi found supporting data showing this attitude of: "Why should I work? The number writers are the real committeemen nowadays," in any crossing of gamblers-bookmakers and local politics.[41] Given the priorities of the Friends in Avena's, then in Joseph Bruno's Family through the 1930s, politics was not of interest to these men, only money. Neither Riccobene nor any active associate of the Family in the 1930s would agree that the elections had any interest in them—they only agreed on whoever was in office that could be bought got their vote![42] Besides, for the Italian Americans in South Philadelphia in the 1930s, employment and politics did not coincide. University of Pennsylvania professor Walter Licht substantiated that it was relatives who found work for their kin in the 1930s, not a *padrone* or employment agency who was tied to local politics as in the earlier decades of immigration.[43] While stories had been told of Antonio Palumbo and Frank DiBerardino's office and other job brokers who connected Italian newcomers of the 1880s and 1890s to the bureaucracy of local government, not even hearsay could tie Philadelphia's Sicilian American Mafiosi to the politics and politicians then.

At yet another level again, the Philadelphia case of gangsters and Mafiosi in the 1930s contrasts sharply with developments in Chicago and in New York with their criminal organizations. Ranking third in the U.S.'s most populous cities, Philadelphia's underworld was spared the national news coverage of its fatalities at the end of Prohibition that characterized Chicago's Al Capone, Dion O'Banion and Jack Guzik, the "so-called brains of the Capone Organization."[44] They were not only well publicized, but they brought Chicago's underworld to prominence despite mob wars and struggles for power. So knowledgeable about the New York mobsters were readers of that city's newspapers, that at one point during the Castellammarese Wars, the press printed pleas to the Sicilian Mafiosi to try not to involve innocent bystanders in their publicized battles.[45] Although the Mafia boss, Giuseppe (Joseph) Masseria and his underboss, Peter "Clutch Hand" Morello received considerably more press than their opponent, the "Alien Smuggler," Salvatore Maranzano, New York's underworld received a higher place in the headlines when District Attorney Thomas Dewey rebuffed the gangsters' compromises and pay-offs and used them for his own public crusade as a "crime fighter."[46] Again, what happened in Chicago and in New York never happened in Philadelphia.

Aside from the Philadelphia Jewish gangsters and their formidable ties to their New York contemporaries, no Italian or Sicilian Mafioso or LCN member in Philadelphia experienced the same media attention as other underworld types locally early in the 1930s as the Lanzetti brothers except "Philadelphia's Public Enemy No. 1—'Kill Crazy' Anthony Cugino."[47] Known to the "Little Mob" detectives and Philadelphia's gangland as "Tony Stinger," Cugino was from Sixth and Fitzwater Streets in Little Italy and reputedly killed at least ten, including his close friend, Anthony "Musky" Zanghi. The Philadelphia Police first arrested Cugino at the age of twelve for theft, and thereafter, "his name became a regular entry on police blotters." His associations included the Lanzetti brothers, but unlike them, Cugino's "rep" as a "cop beater" began while as a teenager. As an adult, he progressed in crime to kill Philadelphia Patrolman Charles Stockberger in 1932, then New York Detective James J. Garvey in 1934. Cugino was quoted to have said: "I don't give a damn if I die, but before I do there's just one thing I want—to knock off those heels, Malone, Ryan and Richardson," the Philadelphia Police's "Little Mob."[48] Such impudence was rare in Philadelphia in the 1930s, especially between the Italian gangsters or Mafia members with local law enforcement. A bitter man hardened by a long prison term outside of Pennsylvania, it was apparent that Cugino only slightly fit the true gangster typology. He had some temporary alliances based on some common criminal goals, but overall, Cugino's sociability with other underworld types seemed tenuous. When finally apprehended in New York by the "Little Mob" in 1935, Cugino was locked in a cell and was said to have "hanged himself." Gangland rumor claimed that Stinger was never "yellow"—that Detective Jimmy Ryan allegedly administered the justice. Cugino's body was then returned to Philadelphia and placed in an unmarked grave.[49]

Anthony Cugino was an extreme offender of the most dangerous criminal kind and atypical of the underworld of Philadelphia in the 1930s that did not usually include the murder of women. Review of the police's homicide records noted in the early 1930s an absence of the usual violent gangland deaths that had been remarkable years before, then reoccurring by about 1933 with more frequency. The police rarely wrote of any motives to the killings, many of which took place within the narrow section of Little Italy between Bainbridge and Washington Avenue, Sixth to Twelfth Streets, by the usual "unknown or unknown persons" often appearing near the "unsolved" in the margins. Among the few deaths in that area in 1936 to have made the newspaper headlines were of John Avena and Martin Feldstein in August, then in December, the revenge killing of Pius Lanzetti.[50] Joseph Bruno, who became the boss of the Philadelphia-South Jersey LCN Family "unanimously" upon Avena's tragic death asserted his members' positions over local Italian gangsters reputedly through many killings here, recalled his soldier, Riccobene.[51] It was also the manner in which an underworld member made a type of preemptive strike to anyone who had any question of his authority. For Joseph Bruno living in New Brunswick, New Jersey, he had to exert a longer arm of strength to those who may have doubted the power of the Philadelphia-South Jersey LCN Family. The Avena killing was not only a raw murder and shock to the local Family, but it portrayed the Family as weak and vulnerable to the common gangster, an affront worse than the death of Avena himself. Bruno and the others knew they had to "save face" in the underworld, avenge Avena's death not only as a Friend, but to rectify their status as above the Lanzettis and others who considered the local LCN as just another gang.

John Avena had taken the LCN into the direction of gambling, a rather late and dated criminal activity that was associated more with American gangsters and "...nineteenth century organized gangs...[who were] involved in extortion, labor racketeering, bullying at the polls and sometimes liquor sales."[52] Sicilian Mafiosi traditionally had no links to games of chance or any form of gambling in western Sicily. The timing of gambling's ascendance as the primary source for the new American Mafia (LCN) after the repeal of Prohibition in 1933 then provided a firmer ground for more Italian gangsters to contribute their skills and knowledge to the Organization formerly composed of Mafiosi bootleggers. With Avena, Italian gangsters gained somewhat higher status in the LCN, although as members they still were expected to continue their responsibilities and to make them grow in order to keep their positions within the Family. These Italian gangsters-gamblers-LCN members of the 1930s drove late model cars in their stylish suits and did not understand why Mafiosi were understated in their dress and lifestyles and chose to live quietly outside of Little Italy. The conservative Mafiosi also wanted nothing to do with gambling, favoring the stability of their factories and stores as the Mafiosi in northeastern Pennsylvania and in New York. Outside of Philadelphia in Montgomery County, the Sicilian American Mafiosi who had migrated as young men in the 1880s and 1890s were now too old to become involved in any novel activity; they also had not recommended their sons to the Mafia Tradition. Just one Mafioso who arrived first in New York then came to suburban Philadelphia was alone in his generation, but he was not responsible for bringing gambling to Montgomery County—Italian gangsters from Philadelphia with ties to Avena's and Bruno's LCN Family established the numbers and horse betting games throughout the industrial towns among the factory workers in Chester, Delaware, Bucks and Montgomery County surrounding Philadelphia. "Tribute" was given to these Italian gangsters who would mention the name of the underboss, (someone like Marco Reginelli) or prominent captain, and the money came forth from individuals who only knew these men by reputation.[53]

URBAN ARCHIVES, TEMPLE UNIVERSITY
Willie Lanzetti, c. 1935.

As far as the criminal typology was concerned, the Italian gangster-LCN member of the 1930s and 1940s was not much different than the 1990 model in Philadelphia. The character prototype in film, newspapers and popular books that described a timeless underworld figure of the 1930s who was of Italian ancestry and who was somewhat caught doing the same thing in the same place later continued, relatively unchanged, well into the 1970s, confirming this absence of any progress within the criminal subcultural environment in Philadelphia. With few exceptions in the city who had some ties to New York's Mafiosi, Philadelphia's Italian gangsters experienced the same provinciality in the 1930s on, because there were no *paesano* colonies in Philadelphia to keep links to New York consistent and on par with criminal developments.

American history related with crime history in a strange but fitting way in the post-Depression/ New Deal Era by glorifying the gangster, yet in Philadelphia there were some that were no one's suckers. As Judge Curtis Bok stated for the record when he oversaw the 1937 to 1939 Grand Jury corruption inquiry: "...There are three kinds of fools who talk about organized crime—first, those who say it doesn't exist. Second, those who think the little fellows in the rackets are unimportant. Third, the biggest fools of all are those who say that gambling and prostitution are as old as the race, so why get excited?"[54] Judge Bok appeared as a solitary figure when he denounced organized crime in 1937 as a "greater menace to American institutions than Communism, anarchism...Fascism and Nazism rolled together."[55] If Philadelphians wanted assurance, or perhaps an affirmation of the law, the events in the late 1930s proved that the city's gangsters, especially those of Italian ancestry, had quite a long future in the rackets. The Grand Jury of 1937–1939 was a total disappointment. A repeat of the sensational 1928 Special Grand Jury, the nearly two year inquest ended with the police department again undergoing the usual demotions and promotions. At the same time, a mob war from about 1937 to 1940 took down many gangsters, another Lanzetti (Willie) and more "unsolved" homicides.[56] Willie's death was by Sicilian American Mafiosi—they killed him with a single bullet behind his ear, then his head was wrapped in towels to absorb the blood. Willie's body was found on an estate in Montgomery County, sewn in two burlap bags, far away from his neighborhood.[57] It was a murder which proved that the Sicilian American Mafiosi's influence still lingered despite the overwhelming presence of Italian American gangsters.

On the national level, the relationship between Italian gangsters and the aging Sicilian American Mafiosi had found common ground in keeping the Organization well financed from whatever sources each group used to make money. The LCN proved to mutate well through each transgression brought on by the Government or by the locals. Philadelphia's underworld, on the whole, did better in the 1930s and 1940s than Chicago and New York who had publicized defeats of their leading organized crime members such as Capone, Luciano, Genovese and the Jewish mobsters whose arrests remained consistent since the early 1930s.

Historian Humbert S. Nelli cited one source that proclaimed a "decline" in organized crime at this time, but he apparently did not notice the absence of any publicity on Philadelphia's underworld, as did FBI Director J. Edgar Hoover—he declared that no criminal syndicate existed anymore in the U.S.![58] Philadelphia's Italian gangsters and the gangster-LCN members mobilized themselves more in this war period, appearing more at horseraces, at the fights, baseball games and nightclubs with the musicians, dancers and celebrities. Some of the city's moneyed clientele were often seen with the gangsters. "Such nice guys," the unknowing would say, not realizing that the gangsters got the "suckers" to put their hard-earned wages on numbers and bets with high odds. Everyone was fair game to be taken.

It was at this point in time when all Italian gangsters, including the LCN members, lost the ethnic labelling and were truly Americanized at a level where their part in immigration history was at an end. They had realized acculturation, despite what sociologist Donald Cressey had proposed in the 1950s as a sort of ethnic bonding among those of Italian ancestry.[59] History shows that the Italians, Sicilians and Jews had an almost inextricable connection that was decades-old in Philadelphia as elsewhere in the major cities. In Philadelphia, the Italian gangster was Italian American and no longer excludable from many social circles because he had been empowered by his illegal earnings and a system that provided an affirmation to his illicit acts.

The Italian gangster and LCN member who grew to be a synonymous entity externally by the late 1930s represented the silent power in what Sam Bass Warner called, the "segregated city" in Philadelphia. Indeed, there still is no simple explanation as to why the City of Philadelphia's criminal justice system and law enforcement were silently emasculated by the Italian gangsters who abused these offices. As Warner keenly noted, Philadelphia's "public problems" resulted from "the unwillingness and inability of Philadelphia's citizens...to conceive of democratic regulation of their private economic affairs [that] prevented the political conflicts from defining the problems of the city in a way suitable for public action."[60] Warner said much in this passage and his words held much significance in that he tied in the conflicts of foreign cultural ideologies with local economics and politics. Without blunt reference, Warner suggested that Philadelphia's immigration history emphatically changed the politics of local government, beginning with the Irish Catholics in the 1840s. The Philadelphia Police Department was established in response to the constant violence in that period (1850), as was the House of Industry (1846) to curb lawlessness among the hungry, poor and homeless. Expanding on Warner's suggestions and his observations on the social chaos and "disorders" which immigration caused, there seemed to be more answers found in the predictable violence associated with both the Irish and Italians and Sicilians coupled with their employment-political "connections" to the city. These ties apparently led to more tolerance for the members of these ethnic groups. In contrast, the same employment-political factors put the more independent, progressive Jews in an inferior position to city officials. However, unlike the Irish and Jews, it took the Italian gangsters longer in Philadelphia to benefit from any legitimacy without the accompanying threats of violence. In this respect Warner correctly contended that the historical issue in Philadelphia's immigration history in the twentieth century was the confusion with having an honest political system within a democracy.[61] Miller would argue that the lower class culture which in Philadelphia was composed of a majority of foreign-born, could not manage the ideals of the democracy independently. This was precisely why the "authority-nurturance" concept played so well among some Italian Americans in Philadelphia and why the Italian gangster's might magnetized Little Italy neighbors.[62]

The Italian gangster and Sicilian Mafioso in maturity became better defined in criminal typology in the 1940s, after a few spent nearly thirty years living obliquely or obscurely in society. Without naming names, Philadelphia's Italian gangsters who became LCN members experienced little growth criminally and seemed content as gamblers-bookmakers in their designated blocks in South Philadelphia. They were mostly neighborhood-bound and the row house dwellers depended on them for safety as well as to place a number, with the LCN member maintaining a type of social control over his area through violence. There was then, no need for him to leave. Locals in the community worked for him and the cycle continued to keep the numbers playing. This was a routine, reliable, sure practice that kept everyone content. For the Sicilian American Mafioso who rejected gambling, the ambitious, progressive, serious industrialist profile fit him more than his gangster-LCN Friend. The Philadelphia Mafioso in the 1940s found greater fulfillment in business with New Jersey and New York contemporaries, using at times the competition-at-any-cost sentiment to buy into another company through whatever means at his disposal, then redeem himself and his position by charitable contributions to needy causes. These men educated their children well and did not, presumably, expect them to associate with the same characters that the Mafiosi fathers had in the old neighborhoods.[63] In short, the Sicilian Mafiosi sought and made a legacy, while the Italian gangster never believed that one ever existed.

• • • • • • • • • •

Chapter 4
GAMBLING

"The Lanzettis took a liking to me when I was a kid [in the 1930s]...I watched and I learned...I was six years old when I began working in gambling. I was a street kid and watching the older men shooting dice—that's how I learned math. I'd see women in the street and I'd walk up the street and tell people to put a penny on a number and they'd make $4.00. Jobs were scarce then. The number wasn't fixed." By the 1930s, this gentleman said, "The mob said to put it [numbers] on race tracks. The street number then came from the tracks" not the Treasury number. He continued: "It was cutthroat in them days and people stopped others from betting with certain gamblers. I met John Avena. The old mob guys liked me. I got paid very well because I was a hustler. If you hustled the game, you made more. After every third roll, I'd collect $1.00 from each shooter. 'made $15.00 an hour then cutting the game."

This early gambler is still a La Cosa Nostra member though a "sleeper"—one undisturbed by law enforcement.

"I'm still respected," he said in a humbling tone so like the men who were "made" because they were indeed men of character: "I was made at the age of sixteen when guys older couldn't. I was an independent bookmaker...whosever territory I was in, I gave them a piece of what I made. I was respected." He used terms that the first mob gamblers said in the 1930s like, "hustle the game," "switcher" and recounted what was started then that continues today, with or without the LCN. Working in the illegal gambling rackets were good profits. In the 1930s during the Depression, there were individuals taking numbers and bets all over Philadelphia's streets, railroads, factories, "Mom & Pop" grocery stores and even in the elementary schools. It was not really an "Italian gangster thing" to do or a West Indies-based custom that went from the Caribbean northward. Gambling attracted those in Philadelphia who played the Irish sweepstakes while the On Leong group in Chinatown kept their gaming as an "honored occupation"[1] apart from the whites and blacks. Ordinarily cast as a product or service of organized crime in the twentieth century, bookmaking and other forms of gambling arose in a subculture with Philadelphia's newest arrivals from the South and southern and eastern Europe who associated this vice with the process of Americanization which included violence. Hence, numbers and bookmaking began within the context of concepts too often involved in making money at all cost. There were false hopes—the word, "hope" is a constant with gambling—hopes and fleeting thrills mixed in with what the immigrant construed to be the realization of what this country would render to its residents. That life was cheap among the lower classes also had its significance.

And organized crime groups would seize upon the most desperate of those forming roots in the city, beginning with the victimization of their own.

• • • • • • • • • •

That gambling as an activity is multi-ethnic, multiracial and millennia years old,[2] adds to its longevity in the human element. But in the United States, gambling generally became more adaptable over the decades to suit temperaments and lifestyles. Crime historian David R. Johnson said that "most gambling was informal and extremely decentralized in the eighteenth and early nineteenth century" in the U.S. In Philadelphia, Johnson added, as in other major cities, gambling had its variations and varied clientele.[3] Horse races, cards, tables and wheels became the vehicles for power and the "symbiotic relationship between politics and vice"[4] took effect with gambling before 1900. Published reports on the accepted view of gambling in Philadelphia in the late nineteenth century had local politicians as gamblers, controlling a great deal of Center City's commerce through the "first-class" gambling houses. Restaurants, hotels, saloons and transportation were only a few of the ancillary businesses that benefitted greatly from gamblers' monies. Eventually, as Roger Lane pointed out, "There was often little distinction between clubs and speakeasies, gambling 'parlors' and bawdy houses, one of the things they all shared was the need to pay off police and politicians in one coin or another in order to stay in business."[5]

But with the rise in population from southern and eastern Europe, then a little later with American blacks moving northward, gambling as a vice took on an anti-social connotation. The Populists, members of the temperance movement and fundamentalist religious groups were eager to conclude that gambling among the new arrivals in the city tested American values such as the Protestant work ethic[6] as well as family stability. Gambling, they opined, should therefore remain illegal so as to regulate the unlawful behavior of those trying to become American.

Towards the beginning of the twentieth century, gambling underwent a transformation in Philadelphia and was divided from its more elitist group of gamblers with political ties to a subgroup with less social clout and considerably more violence which they attached to gambling. Lane wrote of the African American gamblers who migrated north to settle in the city in the pre-World War I years as those who "played with, or preyed on, their fellows,"[7] spurring an intraracial predatory element that led to more violent crime. The Philadelphia Police's Homicide Unit reported on a predominance of blacks involved in deaths from a variety of gambling offenses such as specifically craps, cards, "skin," "selling policy" and owning a gambling house.[8]

The chart below compares the group with the highest number of gambling-related homicides, the blacks, with the group with the second highest number of deaths in the total demographics in Philadelphia, those of Italian ancestry. This chart illustrates the violent consequences of gambling during this fifteen and one-half year period.

DEATHS INFLUENCED BY GAMBLING*

Total homicides from May, 1914 to December, 1930:	61
Black-on-black	35
Italian-on-Italian	15
Police killed by blacks	3
Police killed by Italians	1
Uncertain race/ethnicity	6
Acquittals	1

* Identified by notations made by detectives in determining motives.

Source: Philadelphia Police Homicide Records, Volumes 3 to 9.

Such variables as economic class were easier to verify than a newcomer's rate of assimilation and his perception of gambling which cannot be determined at this time. All of the deaths occurred in lower income neighborhoods. Asbury wrote in 1927 that immigrant enclaves throughout the U.S. during the latter half of the migration period (1900-1920) used gambling as a type of "pastime," while criminologist Walter Miller saw a fitting relationship between gambling as a ruse for misleading those in the lower class.[9] Factually, it appeared that Philadelphia's newest residents at the margins of its society were the working poor who threw dice, played cards or bet with hopes of being financially independent. And they were the assailants as well as the victims of the homicides attributed to gambling.[10] Challenging the nativist attitudes, gambling became one of the instruments that those from the European peasant classes used to assert a different exercise of power, and in so doing transformed a game that had been a sport and form of entertainment in the city into a highly emotional activity that could possibly end in a killing.

None of the deaths from gambling happened in Center City or among the middle or upper class in their neighborhoods. During Prohibition (1920-1933) there were some striking variables about the blacks and Italian Americans that the homicide records noted. Though detectives recounted most motives in this era of bootlegging and gang wars, there were no notes to indicate if victims or assailants were part of the "most violence-prone" group, the bachelor subculture in Philadelphia,[11] or of any gang organized for gambling activities. The breakdown of gambling during Prohibition showed it to be as violent as dealing with liquor.

Compared to the 1914–1919 years, the latter period showed more stability among the Italians whose death rate was kept high by other motives. However, the homicide detectives caught some interesting data on the rise of black gambling-related deaths in relation to all deaths described.

GAMBLING-RELATED HOMICIDES DURING PROHIBITION

YEAR	NUMBER OF DEATHS
1920	2
1921	1
1922	1
1923	6
1924	8
1925	8
1926	4
1927	3
1928	2
1929	1
1930	3
1931–1933 (no motives noted)	
TOTAL	39

TYPES OF GAMBLING NAMED IN HOMICIDES	
Craps	23
Cards	9
Skin	1
Selling Policy	1
Gambling House	1
"Games"	1
Poker	1
"Gambling"	2

METHODS OF KILLING	
Firearm	29
Knife	5
Blunt Instrument	5

Source: Philadelphia Police Homicide Records, Volumes 5 to 9.

Philadelphians of Italian ancestry shared some characteristics with the migratory blacks in the pre-World War I era as to how gambling became the underlying reason for the rise in violence. Most of the causes stemmed from a combination of educational and economic factors in the changes in gambling from a form of entertainment for one class to an indicator of fate and whether work, the bane of the lower class, would be relieved by profits from gambling. Escaping daily labor was for some in the city a dream which activities such as gambling provided temporary hope. Tying work with educational capacities at this time in the immigration period brought seemingly sensitive attitudes from the city's social institutions, however many concepts appeared to advance ethnic and racial stereotyping. Richard Varbero had found, for example, that Philadelphia's educational system, as late as the 1920s, had "modified school programs" and introduced more "vocational training to immigrant and Negro children...to be ori-

GAMBLING-RELATED HOMICIDES DURING THE FIVE YEAR PERIOD PRECEDING PROHIBITION

YEAR	NO. OF GAMBLING-RELATED DEATHS	ETHNO-RACIAL DESCRIPTION
1914 (incomplete) . . .	2	Italian-on-Italian
1915	1	Italian-on-Italian
1916	4	(2) Italian-on-Italian
		(1) Italian-on-white
		(1) Italian-on-unknown
1917	3	all black-on-black
1918	6	(4) Italian-on-Italian
		(2) black-on-black
1919	5	all black-on-black
TOTAL	21	
TYPES OF GAMBLING IN THE HOMICIDES:		
Craps	10	black-on-black
Craps	3	white-on-white (non-Italian)
Craps	1	Italian-on-non-Italian
Cards	6	Italian-on-Italian
Morra	1	Italian-on-Italian
CAUSES OF DEATHS IN GAMBLING-RELATED HOMICIDES:		
Gun shot wounds . . .	16	
Stabbings	4	
Fractured skull	1	

Source: Philadelphia Police Homicide Records, Volumes 3 to 5.

ented to their working class backgrounds." Further research in this era found that "economic necessity overrode educational aspirations" and "...the Italian laboring class subordinated unrealistic aspirations to immediate economic gain," thus pulling together the elements needed to justify gambling for profit.[12] Sam Bass Warner added that just after this period, by about 1930, the social interactions in the neighborhoods placed more stress on the "working class elements of friendship and loyalties of the gang, the street, and the saloon, all...necessities to help bolster the families and individuals...against the successive crises of poverty"[13] which maintained the static nature of these areas begun well before the Migration Period in the late nineteenth century.

Miller's criminological theory reasoned correctly that the lower class mentality focussed "on the search for excitement or 'thrill'...the widespread use of gambling of all kinds—playing the numbers, betting on horse races, dice, cards...complementing the notion that 'only suckers work' is the idea that once things start going your way...all good things will come to you."[14] Consequently, according to Miller's theory, the typical gambler in Philadelphia after World War I and during Prohibition continued to give way to frustration, then aggression and anger at how unlucky he was for those few seconds to lose what cost hours, if not days, of sweat.

As his money is taken, the gambler takes his weapon and slays the winner...or perceived cheater.

• • • • • • • • • •

The most obvious feature of gambling in Philadelphia at this time was that no other Caucasian group in the city came close statistically to those of Italian ancestry with the gambling-related homicides. As noted, Italian-on-Italian killings in this era of the rise of the Italian American gangster were done rather quickly without much premeditation, thus rendering the second degree verdict, a sentence running from four to eight years in either Eastern State Penitentiary or the County Prison, Moyamensing.[15] Each victim apparently had unsure access to money and placed a high emotional value on their play, weighing as well upon dreams, omens, good luck charms and the supernatural, just as the blacks. Homicide assailants of Italian ancestry usually were inexperienced killers and not part of any proto-organized crime group. But these gamblers knew that they always had to be armed more often with a firearm than less with a knife to protect their few possessions from loss. The "false hope" element in gambling attracted a developing underworld who saw in the lower class row house dwellers the means to draw their hard-earned money through the emotionally manipulative lure of gambling. The former sport, or game of the wealthy or chance for loftier good luck soon became perverted into a predatory commodity which gangsters like Pius Lanzetti used to sharpen their skills in victimization.

It was a picture of the underworld by late Prohibition of gangsters flashing cash from bootlegging, not reluctant to play the high stakes or to lose—their killings were not gambling-related yet! Local law enforcement and the news media figured that the numbers racket in Philadelphia became organized in the early 1930s.[16] These sources may have been on target because Salvatore Sabella's Family was not involved in gambling, only in loan sharking, paid protection and alcohol manufacturing and sales, according to soldier Riccobene. Though Sabella stepped down as boss in the summer of 1931, there was no evidence to suggest that John Avena brought gambling into the Family as long as Prohibition was in effect. Traditional Sicilian American Mafiosi had known about the Italian lottery on the island of Sicily—it was a game similar to the numbers betting but with two digits. Yet the American bookmaking was not well supported by the western Sicilians who may have recognized the potential for taking advantage of individuals with a weakness for risk taking. Early numbers and bookmaking, said Riccobene, was not too lucrative either: usually, gamblers placed one cent on each three digit number.

Avena's past experiences with bets in boxing, to gambling houses with gangsters enabled him to connect with the fledgling numbers and bookmaking industry. But his involvement in this new type of racket also disconnected him from the traditionalists known to be in the "Protective

Society" who saw gambling as anomalous to their ideology. In time, during Avena's tenure, gambling became more of a divisive tool to separate those for, versus those against, the illegal business which pushed Avena to gradually advance in the rackets. He then began recruiting more associates to be on the pro-gambling side to outnumber the gambling antagonists. Evidence of an evolving gambling industry was seen in the arrests of future LCN members who proved their mettle in bookmaking and in numbers in 1933 and 1934 such as Marco Reginelli and Alfred J. Iezzi.[17]

Playing the "small bets" during John Avena's years as the local LCN boss continued to about the mid-1930s.[18] The typical row house dweller played on the three-digit number by selecting any three numbers at random from zero to nine. He or she could repeat the numbers but the bet was placed on one fixed trio set. Another bet could be on another set. Sometimes bookmakers were said to try different games with the numbers with the "bleeder" or "switcher" number, which was placing a bet on the first two or last two numbers of the three digit betting number. One of Riccobene's longtime associates, who proved himself well enough in the late 1930s and early 1940s to be recommended for LCN membership, at that time said that the LCN's gambling territory was much more narrow then, giving Avena less area, but more competition. This gentleman said that the three digit number used to be based on the U.S. Treasury Department's figures in the late 1920s. Soon, the three digit number was obtained through the horse races which were controlled by gangsters. "The races could be fixed and they were, to draw its winners," he said. Each digit in the "street number" came from the tracks at the first, second and third race, or, the third, fourth and fifth race, "which bookies on the East Coast use." The LCN member said that to place a bet, bookmakers wrote your number on a slip and they then put all of the slips in before

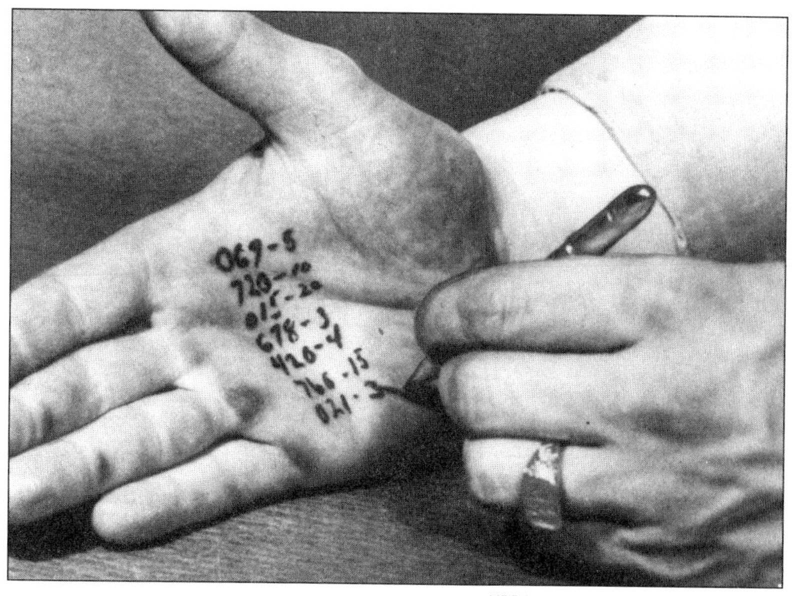

URBAN ARCHIVES, TEMPLE UNIVERSITY

Hand of bookmaker taking plays, 1938.

the first race. As the horses finish, the winner's numbers would reflect the "street number" and who "hit", i.e., won.

Gambling as an organization with gangsters matured in the 1930s with a hierarchal formation. At the lowest end of the organization were the runners who took the pieces of paper with the three digit numbers to the bookmaker. Children and the elderly were often the least suspicious participants at this level, but the bookies kept them compensated and encouraged them to compel others to place bets, promising the runners more money for more gambling clientele. These gambling operators still were not without threat of or real violence as in the deaths of twenty-two year old Joseph Marazzo whose eighteen year old brother died at "The Bloody Angle" as he the next day of gun shot wounds because of their gambling activity.[19] One of the youngest runners to have his story told was twelve year old John Dembra who worked for Pickles Piccarelli. "It was the first day I ever had a job," Dembra told police who found four numbers slips in the boy's pocket. He could not understand the wrong of "just holding papers for a man" who would give him money to buy sneaks.[20] Gambling was made to seem innocuous, even a blessing during a time when employment was difficult and doubtful. But the force behind the victimization could not be reckoned at a time when so many were in need.

By the mid-1930s, all ethnicities and racial groups throughout the Philadelphia area were involved in gambling, interacting in the common interest of numbers and betting as a source of income. Evidently, some females also saw this opportunity to make some cash independently with attention drawn more to males as the principals in the crimes. The Lanzetti brothers employed women and often had girls hide numbers slips on their persons where law enforcement would not notice.[21] Agnes Stein, called the "Queen of the numbers racket" by the *Bulletin* was so prosperous in her business that she retained the same legal counsel, Arthur S. Werblun, as her male counterparts, Mickey Duffy and Pius Lanzetti.[22] And then there were females such as "Mrs. Minnie Smith, 30, colored, Marshall st. near Fairmount av., [who] was held in $1,500 for court after police testified she threw some numbers slips out of a window when they raided her house yesterday."[23] The universal appeal of gambling then spread to outside of the city's limits where the interest in the numbers and gamblers was far less threatened by any law enforcement body.

The research on gambling in the suburban counties of Philadelphia produced information on two main traditions. In one, nominal sums of the gambling proceeds were sent to Philadelphia's LCN or to an associate with the Jewish Mob. This occurred in the industrialized towns of Chester, Media, Norristown and Bristol. Some individuals recalled that Marco Reginelli's name was spoken to gamblers in Bristol and in Norristown as the end of the money drop in the numbers rackets until the late 1940s or early 1950s. There were some independent bookmakers in these mainly blue-collar worker towns, but it was understood that anyone of position in the gambling there was a "representative" of a much higher ranking underworld figure from Philadelphia. These representatives' duties included ensuring payouts, overseeing the banks, collections, debts and forwarding the gambling proceeds to the Philadelphia gangsters. In many of the suburban towns, blacks freely moved among white gamblers. In all areas, there were no divisions or impediments to gambling based on one's race or ethnicity.[24]

Many confidential informants also verified that by the late 1930s, gambling throughout the Philadelphia-South Jersey area developed to such a degree as to accommodate all socio-economic classes by combining enhancers like alcohol, music and sexuality to tantalize players in the exquisitely appointed gambling houses. These houses were common in suburban Philadelphia and saw to the gambler's every need, leading to complementary vices in prostitution and narcotics. The gambling established by the underworld then became as a drug, numbing the gambler's mind, destroying his ability to reason and leaving the bettor to believe as Nick the Greek: "The best thing in the world is to gamble and the next best thing is to gamble and lose."[25]

Gamblers, bettors and whoever was involved with the vice of numbers and bookmaking in the 1930s became intoxicated with the activity that now evolved into a culture borne of underworld perversion. The same principles used to corrupt Philadelphia's criminal justice system during Prohibition eventually found their way via gambling profits at a time when few recognized how betting could break up families. As early as 1925 in one Little Italy homicide, a seventeen year old bride was acquitted of killing her

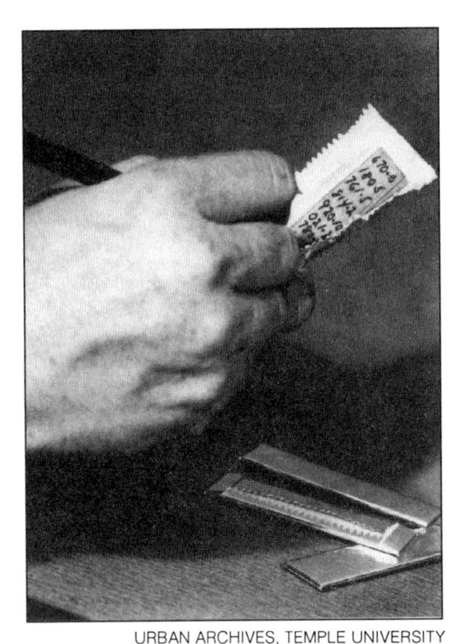

URBAN ARCHIVES, TEMPLE UNIVERSITY
Another bookmaker taking plays on chewing gum wrappers, 1938.

husband because he had stolen all of her savings "to try to win back his own money which he had lost during night of gambling."[26] Another motive to kill at Swanson and Christian Streets not far from Little Italy involved a police officer placing a black male under arrest "for selling policy." Apprehended, the man then "seized the officer's baton, beating him and knocking him down with it when... [the officer] fired his revolver...striking him in the chest."[27] Such was the pall cast over betting and numbers.

What has made the Philadelphia case in organized crime so impressive in respect to gambling is that it serves as a model in the distortion of organized crime history. As with the illegal alcohol during Prohibition, gambling had a tradition in the city which predated the institution of the local police department, seemingly compelling the enforcers of the law to impose on a type of lifestyle that was what Philadelphians would call, "grandfathered." That gambling was a part of city life, no one would question; but how gambling developed into more of a lifestyle for the lower class and immigrant groups identified this activity more as a socially destabilizing factor in relevance to the family, the neighborhood, the controllers of social behavior and the judiciary in the city. The compromising of all of these units, the corruption from gambling proceeds, and the results of same at this time in the 1930s would have made the social history of Philadelphia certainly more intriguing within the context of the decline of the old Founding Families and the influences on the city's various established offices by eastern and southern Europeans and blacks—that is, if more, much more, had been written on these individuals' activities in the vices. Moreover, the documented accounts on urban life and living do not yield how the newcomers to Philadelphia perceived gambling, prostitution and alcohol as offenses. Dissenting from lawful behavior, many non-native Americans may have felt that capricious arrests lacked the true seriousness of a crime and hence, very little shame was felt in the commission of the vices. However, the gap between economic classes, and between the foreigners and natives, widened because gambling, was usually blamed on the former group.

Numbers racketeers used various tactics to fix betting and to ensure that the banks were not emptied. But nothing discouraged gamblers from picking numbers in Philadelphia. The Philadelphia-Camden gambling network in the mid-1930s, in fact, included many rogue gangsters acting in smaller factions or as part of the Lanzetti, Jewish, Avena's LCN or other multi-ethnic mobs. The emergence of several high-ranking, well-known underworld names appear at this time though their exploits pale by Lanzetti standards. Harry (or Hyman) "Nig Rosen" Stromberg, and Marco Reginelli attained greater "reps" courtesy of the news media especially when Camden police arrested them and their associates as part of a political design. The Rosen-Reginelli faction did work well with Avena. "The Jewish Mob worked 'hand-in-glove' with the Italians and Sicilians," said LCN member Riccobene. The Jews, he said, often asked Mafiosi "to act as go-betweens, negotiators" in certain affairs. Riccobene expanded on this. He said that the Jews also had a hierarchal structure in their "Mob,"

Camden Police photograph taken just after Pius Lanzetti's murder in January of 1937 shows (from left to right) Pasquale Massi, Harry "Nig Rosen" Stromberg, Raymond J. Boyne and the powerful Marco Reginelli, standing at 5'3" tall.

and "Nig Rosen" was the boss in New Jersey and in Pennsylvania. "The 'high class' Jewish mobsters, like Moe Annenberg and the 'low class' Jewish mobsters in South Philly rarely socialized," said Riccobene of the stratifications in this particular ethnic organized crime group. "The Jewish Mob did everything in a business manner." They also had their own numbers racket separate from the LCN's. One bookmaker explained that rarely did anyone bet on the "Jewish line" if one did not have a clearance from someone in the Jewish Mob to do so. There were separate telephone lines to place bets on horses or on numbers begun in the 1930s for the Jewish Mob, demarcating the handling, not the ethnicities, of the gambling networks. Some in the underworld might acknowledge that the separate gambling lines with Jews apart from the Gentiles suggested a higher order of organization with the Jews and their way of keeping the integrity of their gambling separate from the non-

Jews. The Jewish Mob was credited with diversification in gambling—to sports, then to more betting by telephone to the "lines" in New York or to Las Vegas later.[28]

• • • • • • • • • •

Gambling became more criminalized in Philadelphia during the 1930s as a matter of economics and politics in a city where both were tied to power. What was underlying the mass arrests and prosecutions of so many Jewish and Italian American gangsters was possibly a struggle within Philadelphia's government, which involved its criminal justice system with law enforcement. During Prohibition, the 1928 Grand Jury probe into corruption identified a sufficient number of gangsters and police officers who were also involved in gambling, with evidence to prove payoffs and bribes. Firings and resignations thinned the ranks within the police department, yet despite all of the developments, nothing within the underworld essentially changed, as did the collusion with those who were a part of the criminal justice system here. The 1928 investigation revealed "large establishments" in Center City "fitted up with elaborate gambling devices, including roulette wheels, bird cages and dice. Liquor was served free of charge and food provided for the patrons"[29] not too differently than in the century before with the politician-gamblers. Additionally, the Grand Jury found, "All of these places...operated over a period of many years without molestation by police authorities...In the police districts in which these establishments were maintained police officials were affluent and other police officials known to be friendly with the overlords of the gambling syndicate were found to be in possession of enormous sums of money."[30] Why it took another Grand Jury eight years to convene in Philadelphia later, this time on gambling and corruption charges, begs the question to "why?"

As in the 1928 probe, Jewish gangsters far outnumbered the Italians in the 1937–1939 Grand Jury investigation on corruption. Again, as in 1928, the lower ranking police officers took most of the brunt from those in higher levels who may have been the worst offenders in compromising the arrests. Politics protected those in the hierarchy's more important positions, shielding the strong relationship that many judges had with the underworld figures. In 1935, local elections revealed that "Nig Rosen" was "working for and voting for the Democratic ticket in this city," with the "night club operators and bookmakers to elect the Democratic" candidate, John B. Kelly, father of actress, then princess, Grace Kelly.[31] When the Republicans maintained their seats, the expected campaign against Rosen and his fellow gangsters apparently was executed. What is incongruent to this newspaper article, which had others following it similarly, is that Philadelphia's underworld had been solidly Republican and continued to be Republican at least with the Italian American gangsters. It may have been characteristic for the Sicilian American Mafiosi to have kept close relationships with the Republican machine in the city, but during John Avena's years as boss (1931–1936), there were irregularities that point more to his inconsistent ties to the local criminal justice system that were weakened with his ascendance as boss of the new Organization and the passive participation of Sabella and the other Mafiosi traditionalists who were non-gamblers. It made sense then, when Marco Reginelli, "making his bones" with "Nig Rosen" and other gambler-gangsters in the mid-1930s, was convicted and sentenced under the Disorderly Persons Act to six months in jail by none other than John Avena's boyhood friend and *paesano,* Judge Samuel P. Orlando.[32]

Gambling brought out the weaknesses of the LCN in the 1930s, but it also gave the organization some strength. Numbers and bookmaking, along with other timely factors dated Salvatore Sabella's Family and made its relative position seem impotent to the rise of the Italian American gangsters who welched upon lowly row house dwellers in the only work they would ever know in counting slips and money. The gangsters were not the only ones working in abuse, however. One LCN member said that when he started in the late 1930s, "cops were a bunch of thieves, crooks. If you wanted to run a game, they [police] wanted to get paid $5.00 an hour...The lieutenant, the captain, all wanted a piece, then they'd get guys from other districts. They would make more than the gamblers! You had to pay them off and they let the games go on a long time to get more money." The worse problem was that in the 1930s, through to the 1940s, few in the LCN knew who was in charge, knew who the other Friends were or knew what the Organization was about. As this LCN member who worked with Riccobene said, "if a made guy wanted to retire, he could. Any made guy could do whatever he wanted—no one tied him down to do criminal stuff" including gambling. It was a time when the "independent bookmaker" could call his own, without a boss or anyone to report to regularly as other LCN members who were involved in the high-end of gambling. Of course, there was the occasional "shakedown" by another gangster, but generally, the disorganization established in the 1930s in the LCN set a traditional basis for present activities. From this decade, the suburban counties' gambling networks stood shakily with the city's gangsters who sometimes said that monies paid out were going to "Marco Reginelli," the name that was supposed to elicit fear. While some LCN-associated gambling sites were founded, others were never successfully controlled in the suburbs by the Philadelphia- South Jersey LCN.[33] "They tried, but they could never fully come in and take us over in Montgomery County," said one bookie of the Philadelphia LCN, implying that the violence-prone gamblers of the city never frightened the numbers writers and bettors in this suburban community. Inconsistent racketeering was only one of the terms used to describe the gambling network which John Avena attempted to introduce into the American Mafia or La Cosa Nostra, the new Organization which he, as boss of the Philadelphia-South Jersey Family was supposed to do, at least on par with the Jewish Mob. While it did take decades to organize a gambling enterprise, what Avena and other gangster-gamblers did in the 1930s could not be coordinated well until, some said, Angelo Bruno "combined everything together" much later.[34] In the interim, gambling remained a fixture for the Philadelphia-South Jersey LCN's image of power and violence from sheer abuse.

• • • • • • • • • •

Chapter 5
JOHN AVENA

Thirty year old John Avena closed his eyes in thought—it was October 7, 1922 and he was en route in a long ride to the state prison in Boston, Massachusetts. Someone in Philadelphia knew he was on parole and that he could not legally carry a firearm. The police then arrested him and sent the felon who called himself, "John DiNatali" back to Boston. The prison's examiner noted in his impressions that the five feet nine inch, hazel eyed John Avena, alias "John DiNatali": "His speech and manner are very suggestive of Hebrew blood. The result of his activities in business and sporting circles would indicate the possession of considerable business ability. Claims he has never been arrested for theft, but once (the crime for which he was sentenced to Massachusetts State Prison) and apparently has centered his aims and interest in the field of sports, more particularly of prize fighting, and is probably to be classed as more of a sport than anything else."[1]

John Avena was to be Philadelphia's first boss of the American Mafia, or La Cosa Nostra, nine years later.[2]

Avena's second prison term in Massachusetts required him to recall his life to officials who studied possible causes and effects of criminal behavior in the still relatively budding science of criminology. Avena's story was a credible one, but it lent little to any hypothetical of why individuals commit offenses. The "Ethnic Succession Theory" which subjected the economic needs of immigrants to the commission of crimes for material gain did not apply to Avena's case. He told a different story of his life to the investigators, one that was incorporated within other information.

Avena said that he was born on "April 7, 1893"[3] in Novara di Sicilia, in the province of Messina on the island of Sicily. The village had steadily held a population of about 3,000 for at least two hundred years like others in the mountain-tops in the shadow of the volcano, Mount Etna. Avena's parents were literate, worked in their own business and owned real estate. He was the family's third son with a sister who likewise figured in the typically "honest, hard-working citizens" mold. Born as Giovanni D'Aveni, he began school by age six and continued in formal education as he trained to be a bread baker. By 1909, the teenaged D'Aveni boarded a ship bound for Philadelphia to join his brother Gaetano there.

Novara di Sicilia was more remote in 1909 than today, though not in a physical sense. Two perilous winding secondary roads still are the only means to enter the God-forsaken town which almost is equidistant (twenty to thirty miles) from either the Tyrrenean or Ionian Sea. The largest city, Messina is about forty miles away by air, but would have been about sixty miles by rough land travel because one must use the outlying coastal roads from the mountain village. To leave such a place, one would have had to be desperate or have a deep desire for adventure. Neither would have been satisfied in Messina.

The modern history of Messina generally referred to it as a commercial port of major significance in the Mediterranean. Its trade and harbors welcomed sea merchants markedly since the 1200s when Sicily's king, Frederick II left Palermo's court and focussed on eastern Sicily's development which presented more advantages to the ruler. Merchant ships from the Middle East relied on Messina's natural harbor. Access north from Messina to Naples, then to Genoa brought more foreign products to the European market. Moreover, Frederick's civic problems with the small number of Muslim groups in eastern Sicily were resolved with either the destruction of their towns, or displacement and death to the people. Frederick had faced the Muslims with disdain and tried to drive them out of western Sicily where they were the majority[4] but they were tolerated better there and made more useful by the "Latins"—the Normans, Provençals, Genoese and Pisans who had already intermarried with them. As Sicily's tendency to progress was constantly in conflict with any regressive elements in its native population, growth in all areas was slow, but even more sure was that there was a definitive cultural division on the island from the thirteenth century, on.

Two volumes on the political and social issues present in Sicily written by Leopoldo Franchetti and Sidney Sonnino in 1875 set forth a formal, dated version of the cultural split between the western and eastern halves of the island.[5] Mack Smith described eastern Sicily's attitude towards its heritage in commerce in the early twentieth century as "forward-looking…[which] helped to create conditions where it was harder for criminals to win economic and political power."[6] Messina was across the strait from the "toe" of Italy, Calabria; its citizens were aware of its location in relation to the ebb and flow of merchant ships and realized the importance of such a safe harbor. "Ceaseless energy," was how one American described Messina's harbor in 1905, while he wrote that the city had a "combination of agreeable qualities" that made it, "cosmopolite."[7] Mack Smith also wrote that in the beginning of the twentieth century, "the differences between western and eastern Sicily were without doubt growing wider," with more industry coming to the eastern half, and Palermo in the west losing "its political hegemony over the rest of Sicily." This was viewed as a positive, particularly then.

Eastern Sicily's history and people were evaluated also at this time to correlate information for the growing group of political and social scientists who wanted to examine this secret society called the Mafia. Cesare Lombroso (1836–1909) the anthropologist-criminologist from mainland Italy applied his work on prison inmates to eastern Sicilians and western Sicilians, noting that the influence of the Greeks in the former group allowed them to be less prone to criminality than the Muslims' and Normans' descendants in the western half.[8] Antonio Cutrera, Palermo's police chief published his work in 1900 on criminal gangs and major crime in Sicily and established that violence in the western section of Sicily far exceeded that of the east. In fact, in contained villages, such as in Novara di Sicilia in eastern Sicily, crime was rare. Though this mountain town may have been the polar opposite of Palermo in 1909, and perhaps too backward in many lifestyle aspects, it nonetheless had no Mafia there at any time. More recent literature by Pino Arlacchi cited Sicilian Mafioso Antonino Calderone confirming a large void in Mafia interest in eastern Sicily that was only temporarily filled after 1925, well after John Avena left.[9]

The Messina of 1909 was, however, not such a promising place for a teenager yearning for a life. A series of earthquakes in 1908 destroyed most of the city and surrounding area, leaving whoever survived without much to reclaim. Those from the mountains would have had problems finding skilled work anywhere in Messina. Gaetano D'Aveni was already in Philadelphia where a few from Novara had gone, along with other eastern Sicilians from Gesso, Milazzo, San Pietro and especially from Spadafora where they set up their pushcarts or owned businesses in the vicinity of Ninth and Christian Streets in Philadelphia's Little Italy.[10] Young Giovanni, or Gianni, came then to Philadelphia by 1909 and held the generic occupation of "laborer," working in the city[11] at odd jobs or on the farmland in South Jersey.[12] It was in Cumberland County that Gianni found comfort with the Orlando family whom he had known in Sicily. Samuel, né Salvatore Orlando, boyhood friend of John, and his family lived near Bridgeton, New Jersey and was employed by Seabrook Farms where he got John a job. According to the man who became "John Avena" later, he returned shortly thereafter to Philadelphia to be with his brother in his bakery/grocery store on South Sixth Street, near Carpenter where western Sicilians in this neighborhood outnumbered the eastern European Jews and other ethnic Jewish and non-Italian groups.[13]

Philadelphia in 1909 was the third largest metropolitan area in the United States, following New York and Chicago. The city had two baseball teams, department stores to shop and lots of automobiles or "machines," sights unseen in Novara di Sicilia. Center City Philadelphia thrived on the wealth of many who benefitted during the Gilded Age with the railroads, steel, coal and the many factories in which immigrants labored. D'Aveni was still "Giovanni," or the americanized, "John" despite that Little Italy in Philadelphia depended greatly on employment outside of the community which would expose the newcomer to the cumulative, instead of the gradual stresses of a new

URBAN ARCHIVES, TEMPLE UNIVERSITY
Philadelphia's Little Italy environment, shown here on Christian Street in 1906, presented young immigrants, such as John Avena, with choices rather than limitations.

environment and lifestyle. The newly arrived had been leaving Italy and Sicily in volume for about thirty years before D'Aveni's landing, and they had settled in numbers large enough for quite a few national churches to be founded by 1910.[14] But, the "Italian section" of Philadelphia was identifiable from other neighborhoods by 1909, and it suggested that language, products and folkways distinguished it from the "Irishtown" it had been about fifty years before. Though not entirely a solidly ethnic community, Little Italy in 1909 was where Philadelphians acknowledged that quaint things like "duels, and "secret societies" and "bombings" occasionally happened as nowhere else in the city. Not much was ever written to criticize this neighborhood. One *Bulletin* reporter wrote in 1910 of an annual procession to St. Michael the Archangel that drew "hundreds of Italians in the city" together to celebrate Mass at St. Mary Magdalen de Pazzi Church. Begun in the 1890s by immigrants from Campobasso, Italy, a brass band led the society's members. "The Italian colony is gaily decorated with flags, streamers and bunting...One large banner showed a likeness of St. Michael with a sword in the right hand and scales in the left. Below were the words, 'Who is more powerful than God?'"[15] A week later, another procession to the Blessed Virgin Mary was formed by the children of Our Lady of Good Counsel and St. Paul's Schools of the 800 and 900 block of Christian Street. *The Public Ledger's* writer depicted the Little Italy procession as "...beautiful to behold...2,000 youngsters...through the streets." Children dressed as angels, others carrying flowers, little girls in white, "crowned with blossoms of the Maytime." The reporter said of the adults, "...the Italians are a sympathetic people," and cited a recent case when neighbors helped a fellow parent when his child got hurt in a horse and buggy accident on Christian Street.[16] Yet Black Hand bombings and the high intraethnic homicide rate did nothing to color the residents of Little Italy as with the nineteenth century Irish.

Studying the environment to piece together the framework of a criminal type has a Little Italy in South Philadelphia by 1910 representing only about ten percent (10%) of the entire city's foreign-born population.[17] The 1906 published work, *La Colonia di Filadelfia* and the 1910 illustrated *Memorandum, Coloniale, Vita Coloniale degli Italiani*[18] detailed impressive prosperity with self-employment, business and property ownership, and the names of Italian-owned offices, corresponding to the listings in Gopsill's and Boyd's Business Directories. That the Octavia Hill Association chose certain areas within Little Italy to document the lack of domestic civility, noting offensive living conditions of some Italian immigrants only highlights some of the class differences that had been brought over and reestablished within the Italian and Sicilian groups.

Therefore, the Little Italy of 1909 where Gianni D'Aveni arrived was complex in its social composition and presented to the individuals there choices rather than limitations.

D'Aveni's family structure in Philadelphia involved his brother Gaetano who was four years his senior and a maternal uncle, Frank, who lived and worked in his grocery store across the street. D'Aveni's father had died when he was seven-years old; the oldest brother, Giuseppe stayed in Sicily with his mother and sister. *Paesani* from Novara in Philadelphia were exceedingly few, leaving D'Aveni to associate more with Sicilians from other towns, mainland Italians, the Jews from the western frontier of Russia and *'mericani*. During these early years in Philadelphia, D'Aveni admitted to his "introduction" to life in a big American city and maturing into a young man. He learned poker and gambled, getting arrested, pleading guilty and paying a fine.[19] Once the Philadelphia Police nabbed D'Aveni for a "handkerchief swindle,[20] a reference which placed him in the habits of the American lower class "street corner culture" that Miller used to describe a form of deviance: "Individuals continually practice duping and outwitting one another through recurrent card games and other forms of gambling, mutual exchanges of insults, and 'testing' for mutual 'conability.'"[21] Perhaps had D'Aveni stayed in Sicily, this arrest would have never happened because he was from a working class family. D'Aveni probably imitated his Philadelphia neighbors' behaviors so as to be construed as an "American." Nevertheless, he was an adult during every arrest. Comparatively, Salvatore Sabella, just one year older than D'Aveni, was living about six blocks away and was recorded as a "laborer," or a day worker to compilers of the city's business directories who likewise docketed other working Mafiosi in Little Italy.[22] There was nothing to hide—these Sicilians were responsible, legitimate working people interacting with others, and they had no criminal records.

Nonetheless, Gianni D'Aveni picked up more antisocial influences from those around him. He started smoking cigarettes in which he overindulged and said that he had his first sexual encounter with a woman by age sixteen.[23] Some neighbors from around the corner also got him into trouble. On Carpenter Street was another Sicilian named Rosario Conti. He too was a baker and had a friend, an experienced criminal named Giovanni Costa, who had spent a year at Eastern State Penitentiary for "receiving stolen goods," then two years at Holmesburg Prison for larceny.[24] Costa's previous record was outside of Philadelphia, in Cincinnati Ohio for "false pretenses." They would be a trio. They planned to rob from someplace outside of Pennsylvania.

Early in 1916, D'Aveni, Conti and Costa teamed up to go to Boston and there each took separate residences in the North End section of the city. The plan was to break into the safe at St. Mary's Roman Catholic Church. Located in the northernmost section of Boston where mainly Italian immigrants settled, this church supposedly remained with its traditional non-Italian congregation and had an archbishop in residence.[25] According to the Boston Police's account, a small boy said he overheard D'Aveni, Conti and Costa discuss how they were to enter and steal from St. Mary's. Watching the three men climb the eight foot high fence, the boy then ran to the police who quickly arrived at the church before the break-in. The surprise of the police apparently made D'Aveni draw and point his revolver towards one of the policemen. Once apprehended, the police found in a snow bank, "a press drill, three loaded revolvers, one stick of dynamite, three percussion caps, five fuses, one flashlight two jimmies, one screw driver and four drill bits,"[26] all evidence of intent to burglarize and to blow up.

MEN AND TOOLS IN ATTEMPT ON CHURCH

John Avena, alias "John DiNatale" | Giovanni Costa | Rosario Conti

Boston Police Department's photographs of suspects and burglary tools used to break into St. Mary's Roman Catholic Church in 1916. Avena and Conti were Philadelphians; Costa from Ohio.

The seriousness of this arrest made D'Aveni's prior offenses for gambling and the "handkerchief game" swindle seem trivial. He told Boston's police that his name was "John DiNatali," "to conceal knowledge of arrest from relatives,"[27] a line that he used before when he told Philadelphia Police that his name was "John Doren" or "John Arene."[28] He pleaded guilty to attempting to burglarize and enter, and having burglary tools.[29] At the age of twenty-four, John D'Aveni, alias "John DiNatali," "Doren" and "Arene," formally became a felon.

There was no evidence of any type of ethnic bias towards D'Aveni and the others in a town noted for its strong Yankee conservatism. The arrests and guilty pleas by all were indisputable and given relative sentences, which was to be four to seven years in D'Aveni's case. His was the shortest sentence, serving thirty-two months and appearing to prison officials more hopeful to lead a straight life than the dubious futures of repeat offenders Conti and Costa. Sicilian Mafioso Nick Gentile identified a Mafia Family in Boston during D'Aveni's imprisonment. In fact, the *rapprisentanti* of Boston, Gaspare Messina heartily welcomed Gentile and informed him that there was going to be an interstate conference with all of the Families in the United States in the late 1910s or early 1920s.[30] If D'Aveni knew Messina or other Friends in the city, he would have never gone to prison, but then, a Mafioso would never have thought of robbing a Catholic church. Boston's Mafiosi were never contacted because at that time D'Aveni was neither a Friend nor, at the least, an associate of any Sicilian American Mafia Family in the U.S. D'Aveni was evolving as a gangster, but his development as an underworld figure still had far to go. He had yet to decide whether he would repent and forego the temptations in crime, or to resume his life as a simple, but honest, law-abiding bread baker.

In late 1918, D'Aveni was returned to Philadelphia and became a partner with his brother Gaetano in the bakery and grocery store across the street from his uncle's. Gaetano became "Thomas" or just "Tom," D'Aveni became "Avena," and their store was registered as the "Avena Brothers" with John and Tom as owners and residents of 1027 South Sixth Street.[31] John may have experienced some benefits of increased income at this time because his interests in gambling and professional fighters lead him in directions still less socially acceptable, but no less profitable. John would go to learn about boxing and the business of promoting fighters for the ring. He went to boxing clubs and met the usual crowd of foreign-born or first generation eastern European Jews, blacks and some other locals of Irish and Italian ancestry who gravitated to the lore of the boxing arena and the excitement of waging on a winner. Avena did not have to travel far for this either. "In the 1890s the first venue in Philadelphia to run regular boxing shows... [without the liquor] was the Ariel Club on Christian Street, near Eighth," wrote boxing historian Chuck Hasson.[32] Shortly after the Ariel proved to be a success, John J. "Jack" McGuigan opened the Pennsylvania Hall, a boxing club also near Eighth and Christian Streets in the burgeoning Little Italy.[33] By 1893, McGuigan, then aged nineteen turned "an old market house" at the northeast corner of Eleventh and Catharine Streets into "the biggest boxing club in the east," the National Athletic Club. Hasson said that by the time that Avena became a promoter there, the National was one of, if not *the* foremost boxing club in the United States. Boxers fought almost daily in Philadelphia, then one of the most active cities promoting boxing as entertainment, and as a site where drinking and gambling carried on well without females.[34]

Hasson and others, notably Nat Fleischer of boxing history fame, wrote that by the time that John Avena became interested in the sport, "the Jewish boxers...began to replace the Irish as the dominant force in local boxing." Herman "Mugsy" Taylor, (1887–1980), long-time boxing promoter who was born and raised at Sixth and Catharine Streets, just three blocks north of Avena's home, got his first job with Jack McGuigan at the age of fourteen at the National Athletic Club. Taylor told Hasson that he started at a time when learning the fundamentals of the promoting game mixed with underworld activities.[35] Stephen Fox wrote that boxing was common in "urban immigrant districts...tied in with saloons, gambling, and corrupt politics," all of which made Philadelphia fertile ground to combine this sport with gangsters.[36] Hasson mentioned a Johnny Spatola from Little Italy as a "power" at the National from about 1915 to the early 1920s, a former

BOXING - BOXING

NATIONAL ATHLETIC CLUB

ELEVENTH AND CATHERINE STREETS

Saturday Eve., Dec. 7th, 1918

KNOW THE TRUTH

That Young Robideau is the best, the hardest hitting, the most pleasing, ever tearing in, always mixing, battling, giving the spectators a run for their money.

DON'T FAIL TO SEE HIM IN ACTION

BATTLING MACK
NEW YORK SHIPYARD
VS.
CHARLIE BEECHER
BRO. OF WILLIE

BATTLING MANTON
VS.
BILLIE GANNON

HUGHIE HUTCHINSON
KENSINGTON
VS.
FRANKIE EDWARDS

SEMI-FINAL

Presenting the great little Italian-French Featherweight

YOUNG ROBIDEAU

Who did what World's Champion Johnny Kilbane, K. O. Chaney failed to do. Robie, on Thanksgiving Day K. O. Eddie Morgan Champion featherweight of England in two rounds.

VS. JOHNNY HAYES

OF NEW YORK — The Featherweight Abe Attel is grooming for the Championship

THE FINAL BOUT

Johnny Mealy VS. Johnny Dundee

The Fighting Harp with two recent fresh decisions over Terry McGovern

That glorious and most interesting great little fighter who never backs up. The Scotch Wop

REFEREE: FRANK (POP) O'BRIEN

RESERVATIONS: 50c 75c $1.00 $1.50

Poster from National Athletic Club for December 7, 1918 bout.

boxer who used thugs and "strong arming" for certain gamblers at ringside. Undoubtedly, Avena knew these men. And other men were watching Avena as a boxing promoter.

But in 1920 John Avena may have had some contact with Sicilian American Mafiosi in Philadelphia. Sabella was the *rapprisentanti* of the group of "protectors" paid to stave off Black Handers and other extortionists with a payment of "25¢" per week—most businessowners would have known about these men.[37] Many western Sicilians who were also Mafiosi lived in Avena's immediate neighborhood, such as Mario Riccobene on the 600 block of Washington Avenue, Philip Pollina on the 1000 block of South Randolph, George Catanese two doors up from Avena and George Catania on the 500 block of Carpenter with others from Cáccamo and towns in western Sicily. [38] They had customs and traditions different from Avena, which may have seemed to him as attractive, but the Mafiosi in this neighborhood who were born and raised in the Mafia culture were also husbands, fathers and worked daily in their stores. This Sicilian American Mafia was not yet identifiable with underworld gangsters and certainly not legally defined as organized crime.

It would be Avena's choice on how he was going to proceed in his life and whether he would put the Boston matter in his past, or conform to the social majority in Little Italy who was not from a Mafia culture.

One such example of lifestyle choice was in Michele (Michael) Annaloro who was from the Mafia town of Villalba in central Sicily. Related to Mafiosi there, but apparently not initiated into the organization or retired, Annaloro chose not to associate with the Sabella Family. Instead, Annaloro and his wife and four children lived on a block in the Queen Village section of South Philadelphia where Yiddish was heard more than Sicilian or English. There was no evidence that Mike Annaloro exposed his son, Angelo to the foreign culture of his youth in Sicily by familiarizing the son directly with Mafiosi.[39] It was said that Angelo Bruno was recommended to Avena's LCN Family by another individual, possibly through the local food industry, but for sure, not by the father. If Mike Annaloro was indeed a Mafioso, he would have wanted to repudiate a cause that had no purpose in the United States and to encourage what Mafiosi other than Mario Riccobene were able to do with their children of same age.

What other activities that may have occupied John Avena's time in the early 1920s for him to carry a firearm are unknown. Avena said that he had another job, as a "theatre manager and proprietor" at 733 Christian Street next to a place once called "Verdi Hall." The latter was a failed attempt to create a local opera house. Avena's theatre was likely the one that Christoper Morley wrote about in *Travels in Philadelphia:*

> "No account of Christian Street [in Little Italy] would be complete without at least some mention of the theatres between Eighth and Seventh Street. The other afternoon I stopped in at one of them, expecting to see moving pictures...but instead I found two Italian comedians—a man and a woman—performing on an odd little stage to an audience which roared applause at every line...The manager [of this theatre] walked continually up and down the aisles, rebuking every sound and movement other than legitimate applause with a torrential hiss. Everytime a baby squalled—and there were many—the manager sibilated like a python. The audience took this quite for granted, so evidently it is customary."[40]

Despite the life surrounding Avena at this time, someone in the community knew enough about him to know about his parole and that he was not permitted to carry the revolver. Reported to the Philadelphia Police who notified Boston, local law enforcement gave additional information to the Massachusetts parole board which differed with that submitted by Avena's Philadelphia lawyer, a "Mr. Spatola." But what infuriated prison officials most in Massachusetts were the repeated efforts by "DiNatali" (Avena) "to use money in trying to obtain his parole" which placed "the Board to discourage the use of large sums of money in the corruption of parole."[41] Avena estimated his bank assets at "$10,000.00" a fairly good amount of money for a single man his age at that time. But the money could not positively impress prison and parole board officials because the information that the Philadelphia Police passed along was credible enough to have a bearing on their decisions.[42] After all, Avena in 1923 was still a bachelor (although he had a "sweetheart" named Grace) and at the age of thirty-one was without much family social interactions in his gambling, fight promoting and theatre proprietorship activities. He used three aliases in Philadelphia and more in Boston before 1918, and after 1918 added to the list the surnames of "Devine," "Daven," "Lavina," "Averns" and "Levana."[43]

To law enforcement, by all appearances, Avena was a gangster. But perhaps a better understanding of Avena's status in 1923 in either Boston or in Philadelphia can be appreciated when compared to Sabella's and Giuseppe "Joe" Girgenti's arrests in May of that year. Accidently caught too quickly in what seemed to be the claim for insurance money at the Maggio's store at the Ninth Street "Italian Market," Sabella and Girgenti were released immediately after the dynamite blew up the property.[44] Their prosecutions were never pursued. Nor did law enforcement press Mr. Maggio for further action—typical of the local Sicilian American Mafia's influence. The incident and participants were thereafter ignored despite considerable damage to the buildings which were later repaired.

Avena's return to prison in Boston because he was "ratted out" meant that he had not yet formed an association with Philadelphia's Mafiosi. Sometime after 1923, however, Avena was noticed by Sabella and his Friends, though it was not because of a common cultural background, related businesses or through marriage alliances. Whoever recommended Avena had been observing him for awhile, watching how he handled himself and matters at hand. It was unusual for Sabella and the others from western Sicily to recommend someone not from western Sicily, not from a Mafia family with other males who were Mafiosi and someone as old as Avena. But this would be the trend in the Philadelphia-South Jersey Family from this time, on. Harry Riccobene verified the qualifying process that was described by Sicilian Mafioso Antonino Calderone: "Men of honor become such in large part through heredity, but not in the same way as the aristocracy...In the Mafia it's more complicated. There's observation, a study of the best young men by the oldest ones...[who] watch the young ones, some of whom come to stand out from the others...when one of them distinguishes himself because he's clever, determined and ruthless, he is then cultivated, encouraged by adult men of honor who teach and guide him, and if he follows them they start to let him do a few things..."[45]

Sicilian males are initiated into the Mafia while as teenagers on the island; in the U.S., and especially in Philadelphia where qualifying males was of longer duration, "making" (i.e., initiating) men of Avena's age, with some even older, became the standard in a Family where substitution for tradition soon became the norm. Training a mature man such as John Avena in western Sicilian Mafia ethics was difficult. As New York Mafioso-LCN member

Joseph Bonanno had articulated in his *Autobiography*, using "Lucky" Luciano as an example of what later became a national trend in the LCN, if one never "lived the [Mafia] Tradition...[one] therefore never truly understood it instinctively."[46] Such was the challenge posed to Sabella and the other traditionalists.

By the mid-1920s, Avena had settled somewhat and married his sweetheart, a Sicilian girl who lived with her family and had a store. But Avena's choices in life in Philadelphia by this time could have been different and led him on the same path as his childhood friend from Novara, Samuel P. Orlando. He had gone on to college, then to law school, becoming a lawyer at the same time as Avena matured as a gangster. And in another time and another place other than Philadelphia Avena may not have been recommended to be a Friend in a Sicilian American Mafia Family. It may seem strange, but in many ways, Avena's association with Sabella and the other traditional Mafiosi actually may have given him some structure in the social path his parents intended for him. The Mafiosi gave Avena grounding and confidence. And the Mafiosi diverted Avena more from the gangsters who previously influenced him.

Some of Avena's early press concerned his whereabouts with common thugs. Police in Philadelphia had recalled that Avena was shot in the leg in 1925, a time when he already was involved in bootlegging. One newspaper article read that "It had been reported in the underworld that Avena was once shot by Sabella,"[47] an allegation which Avena and Sabella denied to police. Several seizures and raids by law enforcement for alcohol at Avena's store on South Twelfth Street were made,[48] apparently when he was not yet a member of Sabella's Family. Probably between this 1925 shooting incident and the July, 1926 shooting was when John Avena became a part of a very large and powerful group who would guard him and his illegal businesses and who would give to him a newfound reputation with local law enforcement. Indeed, the changes included no more aliases—he stuck to "John Avena."

Avena got attention indirectly with the violent deaths of Joe "Two Gun Joe" Corrado and Claire McCabe who were gangsters of the time—young, bad characters who lacked the legitimate employment, the wives and children, and all other indications that they were respectable citizens in the community. "Two Gun Joe" died of gun shot wounds at the age of twenty-five while he and McCabe held up a certain "bootlegger" in 1926. The papers wrote that Corrado "had a long record for highway robbery, dope-peddling and larceny of automobiles" while McCabe was "a fugitive from justice," being wanted for three hold-ups downtown in which he was assisted by Patrolman Abe Silverman."[49] Probably Avena was there at Twelfth and Montrose Streets because he had a "cigar store" there that was actually a front for his alcohol sales.[50] Police said that Christopher Leonetti, living at 916 South Twelfth Street, near Montrose, admitted to shooting at both Corrado and McCabe,[51] but he was never brought to trial.[52] Later press on Avena cited that it was "the most sensational shooting...in...a street battle...and two of the men who were said to have made an attempt upon his [Avena's] life were killed by detectives."[53] If this were true, and the police sought to rid the city of two violent gangsters while protecting Avena, this may have been a sign that Avena was finally, in 1926, a Friend in Sabella's Family.

But not everyone in the underworld recognized Avena's new advancement. The January, 1926 incident which law enforcement and the news media characterized as the "first attempt" on Avena's life was followed six months later in the same vicinity by another shooting in which Avena was wounded in the back, thigh and shoulder. Also in the shooting foray, a Mrs. Bianculli, who was carrying a quart of ice cream into her home, was struck in the neck. Nearby, patrolling police "gave chase" in their car, exchanging gunfire while "children and women were screaming...and everything was in confusion." Three to five gunmen "believed to have been foreigners disappeared in an old model touring car," wrote the news reporter.[54] Avena was carried off the street and laid in Howard Hospital in critical condition. His wife Grace was home, about to give birth to his first child, Salvatore. Avena recovered, only to be the target of yet another attempt on his life in early spring of 1927 while walking into a restaurant on Eighth Street near Christian. Many bullets raced past Avena with one round hitting him below the shoulder and another lodging in his spine. He recited to police the gangster code: "Never mind who did it, I'll get him when I get out." The press added that "Avena steadfastly refused to name anyone who might have been seeking revenge."[55] And again, the Philadelphia Police gave an official characterization of the incident to the media: "a bootleggers' feud." It was a conflict that involved Avena in about five shootings in less than two years.

These shootings never indicated that Avena was armed or defended himself at any time. To all gangsters, arming oneself and using a firearm were part of the lifestyle and underworld culture. Character-wise, Avena may have fit the gangster model, but there is very little information on what type of personality he had for so many to be so angry with him as to want to kill him. A gangster with rumors circling about him in Little Italy, Avena, though a member of the local Sicilian American Mafia, got what other Friends did not—a nasty, derisive nickname. In March of 1927, a *Bulletin* reporter first wrote that Avena was "also known to police as John Nazone and 'Big Nose Jim'."[56]

Months later, the newspapermen would write more about Avena in the story of the year, the double murders of Joey Zanghi and Vincent "Scabby" Cocozzo. According to the claims of "Musky" Zanghi in all of the local newspapers, Avena was standing with Sabella and Antonio Domenico Pollina at the intersection of Eighth and Christian Streets in South Philadelphia. "Avena gave me a Judas greeting," said Musky, whom Riccobene and other Mafiosi called, "an outlaw," and "a nobody." Then Avena was said to have patted Musky on the back and inquired about his health. "It struck me as funny they were making so much fuss over me," Zanghi said and added that "because it was a holiday, he left his 'rod' [gun] in his car." He walked over to Eighth Street near Christian where he saw Avena and Sabella. "I knew they were a couple of Scapelitti's [sic] men." The reporters noted what Zanghi said had happened next: "While the shotguns poured out their stream of lead Avena, Sabella and Domenico [Pollina] drew revolvers and from their position on the pavement poured out a cross-fire. Within a minute the firing had ceased, the three men on the pavement—Avena, Sabella and Domenico—had leaped on the running board of the blue automobile and the car had disappeared south on Eighth Street."[57] A short time later, police found the "bandit car" at Passyunk Avenue and Reed Street, in front of the cigar store where "six young men were playing cards." Detectives arrested all of the men who swore they were "playing cards all afternoon and knew nothing of the empty car" outside. Apprehended there after the killings as "material witnesses" were Mike Romeo, Giuseppe (Joseph) Caro and Joseph Rugnetta who would become LCN members under Avena. Leonard Galante, Sabella's brother-in-law and fellow Mafioso was also among the arrested. All were later discharged.[58] Hours later, when police went to find John Scopolitti at his home on the 2800 block of South Fifteenth Street, they found instead, Scopolitti's neighbor, John Avena, sitting on his doorstep. Avena would be the first defendant named as the first arrested for the murders.

Inside of Scopolitti's house, detectives found shotguns and handguns. Then the telephone rang. Detective Baldino lifted the receiver and "shoving a pistol against [Scopolitti's cousin's] side, the detective told him to answer into the mouthpiece 'yes' or 'no'...It was Scapellitti [sic] speaking. He asked if the coast was clear and gave a number to telephone if anything went wrong. The number was the grocery store of Philip Polono [sic]..."[59] Avena was brought to City Hall alone, to be met by the others a few minutes later. There, Zanghi pointed and said, "'That's Avena,'" the bootlegger, "known as 'Big Nose' in Little Italy." Musky then added that Avena "'shot at me and my brother.'" "Zanghi said that he had received his first warning after he sold La Tosca Cafe, 9th and Fitzwater streets to one of Avena's friends," wrote newspaper reporters.[60] The little gangster added enough information for the police to process Avena, his Friends Sabella, Pollina and Quaranta, and the Family's non-Sicilian associates, Dominic Festa and John Scopolitti.[61] All of the defendants stood atop a stage illuminated with bright lights to be photographed just like the other groups of Philadelphia gangsters who posed en masse before police and detectives. "'Avena,' said a detective, 'look this crowd over and see if you recognize the man that shot you.' Sabella, standing next to Avena, smiled." Avena said, "'The man who shot me is not here.'" "'Oh, stop lying,' shouted one captain, 'You're rubbing shoulders with the man that shot you.'" "Avena affected an air of surprise as he looked at Sabella. 'Him? Oh, no! That's a mistake,' and they both laughed."[62] The suspects were then taken away to be processed.

On June 16, 1927, Philadelphia detectives questioned to no avail Mafiosi Andrea Restucci and Avena's next-door neighbor and his son's godfather, "New York Mike" Macaluso. "Police believed that these men bought off Musky with a sum of between $25,000.00 to $50,000.00."

Macaluso told the police that days before, Restucci had taken Zanghi aside and spoke to him while he, Macaluso slept. Macaluso, a partner with Sabella in the Third Ward Republican Club at Eighth and Catharine Streets,[63] found himself then arrested with Restucci. The District Attorney's Office initially considered that the two Mafiosi might be "surprise" witnesses for the Commonwealth. They were quickly disqualified after leading the detectives to believe that they witnessed the double murders at Eighth and Christian. Possibly because Restucci spoke through a translator, possibly lost in their zeal, the District Attorney's Office dropped the two Mafiosi after their testimonies proved unsubstantiated.

One of Musky's friends, described as an "Apache dancer," named Pete Francesco failed to put Avena at the crime scene; Musky's cousin, Dominic LaFauci spoke otherwise.[64] He told District Attorney Charles Kelley that he saw Avena emerge from Scopolitti's car at Eighth and Christian, just fifteen minutes before the shooting. On Avena's side as an alibi witness was Mrs. Kate Ruggiero who had a grocery store near Avena's cigar-soft drink store, (or as he revealed, a "speakeasy") on South Twelfth Street. She testified that she saw Avena "sitting on a bread box outside her store the entire afternoon...leaving about 5:30 PM." Mrs. Ruggiero's father and husband gave supporting testimonies.[65] The next day, John Scopolitti told the Court that his neighbor, "New York Mike" had come over to his house a few doors away and that he drove him to Center City at the same time of the shootings, about three miles from their homes. Scopolitti reluctantly disclosed that he was a bootlegger, but would not name his supplier of the liquor. When Scopolitti's other neighbor on South Fifteenth Street, Avena, took the stand, he admitted that he was a bootlegger and to selling "a little liquor" in his soft drink store on South Twelfth Street. Avena continued responding to inquiries: he said that he bought his liquor from Scopolitti and on "Memorial Day [sic] Scopoletti [sic] came to his store and brought him five gallons of alcohol in his machine." Amidst the confusion and alibi stories, Assistant District Attorney Charles Kelley asked Avena the question upon which the double murders was based: "Isn't it a fact that you and the other defendants were out to get 'Musky' because he was shaking down bootleggers whom you and your crowd were protecting?" "No," answered Avena. "Didn't you once threaten 'Musky' if he didn't make his gang behave?" "Nothing of the kind," said Avena.[66] Avena never denied his prior conviction in Massachusetts, but to his intention to kill: "No."

A few days after these proceedings, Luigi Quaranta was found guilty, sentenced to Eastern State Penitentiary and the remaining defendants' trials were continued. Bail was set for the Friends and associates, showing the names of some prominent businessmen in Little Italy who posted thousands of dollars. Scopolitti had the highest bail: $20,000.00, which was supplied by funeral director Pasquale Ingenito and wine importer, Rocco DiNubile. Avena's bail, like Sabella's and Pollina's, was set at $10,000.00 and was posted by South Ninth Street "Italian Market" merchant, Joseph Giunta.[67] What happened to Avena's matter subsequently was not documented except that in one day, precisely on March 7, 1933, Avena, Pollina and Sabella were tried and found not guilty.[68] What remained more furtive than the Mafiosi's legal case however was what was transpiring in the District Attorney's Office in Philadelphia. Judge John Monaghan presided over Quaranta's trial and over a courtroom in disorder: Kelley was determined to find all of the defendants guilty, but instead he was rendered powerless to the deals made between defense counsel Henry Stevenson and the Assistant District Attorney's superiors. The local Mafia let part of the trial run its course, let Quaranta be tried and let him take a rap for the public executions. Then, the principal members of the Family told the Commonwealth offices what the outcome would be. In effect, the proceedings were suspended, kept in a legal limbo until Sabella, Avena and Pollina could sort out matters and deal separately with Musky.

John Avena's place within the Philadelphia Sicilian American Mafia at this time was to observe and to follow what Sabella and the senior Mafiosi members said. They would take care of him, his wife and baby Salvatore—Avena was not to worry. His counsel was Henry Stevenson, an attorney with political ties and political know-how to make deals in defenses more financially feasible than moral and legal—that was Stevenson's function, and his work was no less unusual than other defense attorneys who had wealthy underworld types as clients during Prohibition. John Avena was in a Family who cared for his well-being as an asset to an interstate network. He was valued because he vowed his life to the Organization.

The years between 1928 and 1931 were for Avena times in which he learned from Sabella and Pollina how their western Sicilian culture was indelibly inseparable from the Mafia Tradition. The son of John Avena, Attorney Salvatore J. Avena said, "My father's mentor was Sabella," but he added that Pollina used to tell him that he tried to teach John Avena the ways of the western Sicilian Mafiosi, too. In time, what Sabella, Pollina, Macaluso and the others did and said was affected by Avena. *Omertà*, which had defined the essence of the Mafia's exclusivity, became identified simply as an intangible, similarly to the "gangster's code of silence" which separated the gangsters from the "straights." Other Mafia rules wore well with Avena, such as appearing always as a gentleman, clean and mannerly, and having a chivalrous bent. Avena was said to have allegedly avenged a "wrong" by killing an individual who attempted another man's life, but misfired and blinded the man's wife.[69] Mafiosi imparted the "domestic" quality, which Joseph Bonanno had written was so important to their culture.[70] It was a stabilizing feature, to be seen as a husband and father, someone's son and brother. A paternal sentiment was cultivated to know to give, to show charity to the orphaned, elderly and infirmed. Senior Philadelphia Mafiosi also taught by example, by respecting their local Roman Catholic churches' needs when Protestant groups drew disheartened Italians and Sicilians to their soup lines in the 1930s. Some Mafiosi like the Pollina brothers let grocery tabs remain unpaid during hard times when those not involved in gambling and bootlegging tried not to let their dignity wane.[71]

Life in South Philadelphia was not easy in the late 1920s and early 1930s. To Avena, the adjustment to the American culture may have been compounded by the pressure to please his Mafia Family by trying to absorb the rigid customs of the western Sicilians, no small feat for the undisciplined and unstructured. Though Sabella and other Friends taught Avena that Rule I in the Sicilian Mafia was obedience to the Family, Avena had his own family now. He had married pretty Grace Minuto, a proper Sicilian girl who worked for her father. Avena's pride however, was his son, whom by Sicilian naming tradition, was baptized "Salvatore," after John's father. "New York Mike" Macaluso, the bootlegger and Friend who was Sabella's partner and who probably recommended Avena into the Family was baby Salvatore's godfather or *compare*, creating a bond between the Mafiosi. Macaluso lived next door to the Avena family on South Fifteenth Street, across from the park. By 1930, the Avena household was one of content in which a garage for the late model car, new appliances and trips to the Jersey shore to vacation were realized.

Emotionally, an individual who had so many encounters with near death empathized with those who held him dearest as his wife and son. John Avena's heart was heavy in his love for a wife who patiently stood by his arrests, imprisonments and attempts on his life. Avena also recognized a future for his son that did not include the Philadelphia underworld. "My father always wanted for me to be a lawyer," Salvatore J. Avena, Esquire said, and added that "my father used to buy me these 'big-little books'. I had lots of them because he liked me to read." One of the son's most vivid memories of his father was that "every Sunday morning I would awaken to read the comics by my bed. My father would pull the comics out of the newspapers for me because he knew how I liked to read them." Then there were the toys for little Salvatore—enough for a school of children! But John Avena also felt for others' children: "Everytime my father visited my uncle in Palmyra [New Jersey], he would give the poor Italian and black kids in the neighborhood candies. And that happened often." Silent charitable contributions. Giving to the needy. That side of John Avena had also been a member of the Order, Sons of Italy and secured his "First Papers" towards U.S. citizenship, something not really considered congruous to the gangster or corner lounger type.[72]

Philadelphia Police photograph of John Avena, c. 1930.

The 1927 Zanghi-Cocozzo murders were a turning point for John Avena in relation to his Sicilian American Mafia and to others in the local underworld. He had proven his loyalty to his *rapprisentanti*, Sabella, and to the senior Friends by drawing, aiming and shooting at both Joey

Zanghi and Scabby Cocozzo. Then he went home alone while Sabella, Pollina, Lou Quaranta and Scopolitti went to Philip Pollina's house to eat and drink to their accomplishments. Avena was found and arrested alone. Then in the line-up at City Hall, he was singled out and reminded that Sabella once shot at him. The instance when Avena was mentally as well as physically distant from Sabella and the others were times when Avena felt especially alienated from the others in the Family. Sabella and the western Sicilians advised Avena not to associate with the Jewish mobsters and were said to have been angered with the ties that Avena made with them. "Rather than compete and be adversarial, my father wanted to prevent violence with the Jews," said Avena's son. "My father and 'Nig Rosen' (Harry Stromberg) were extremely close as with Fogelman and Needleman. My father found the Jewish element acceptable." Of Martin Feldstein, Attorney Avena said that Feldstein's allegiance to Rosen complemented his friendship with the future LCN boss, Avena, as well as to others in the local Jewish mob. Other Mafiosi offered advice to Avena during Prohibition against the perils of drugs: "'Mr. Migs' [Dominico Pollina] told my father to stay away from the Lanzettis." But Avena's prowess as a bootlegger and businessman drew him towards everything that his Mafiosi members had warned him against. The Jews got him involved in gambling by the early 1930s while he was still earning substantially from illegal alcohol sales. And despite Avena's distaste for narcotics, dope peddlers and users, gangsters who were involved with the aforementioned, such as the Lanzettis, were difficult to avoid in Little Italy.

Leo Lanzetti was killed in 1925, before Avena was initiated into the Philadelphia-South Jersey Mafia and before the LCN had any interest in gambling. Rising to take his older brother's lead was the handsome but devious Pius

Lanzetti. This brother had a criminal record quite unlike his older brother who dabbled in narcotics and was frequently arrested as a "suspicious character," "disorderly person" or "corner lounging." One individual born in 1904, just about three years younger than Pius and close to all of the brothers said that the nemesis of the Lanzettis, the "Little Mob's" Captain James Ryan "was no damn good. He picked on everyone down town, him, Richardson and Harry Peltz [another detective]. He [Ryan] made corner arrests—no one could hang around!" Mrs. Lanzetti, this individual said, used to cry to the police and especially to Captain Ryan and say, "Why don't you stop bothering my family?" In his simple language, exasperating, the Lanzettis' friend said, "We couldn't stand on corners. We didn't do nothing wrong in them days. There were many crooked cops then, they'd ask us, 'Where's my bottle of whiskey?' and ride by on their motorcycles." Most gangsters and "guys at the corners" knew that Captain Jimmy Ryan would come up to Pius Lanzetti, slap him with the back of his hand on the face and then leave, and Pius would stand there silent as if nothing happened, "with the blood rushing to his face..."[73]

Pius Lanzetti's eighth arrest in three years was for "rape"—he pleaded guilty to "fornication and bastardry," paid a $25.00 fine and costs and went home. Three years later, just before the Zanghi-Cocozzo murders, Pius was charged with "aggravated assault and battery by shooting with intent to kill" then-detective George Richardson of the Philadelphia Police's "Little Mob" and Lieutenant Detective Michael Slavin who were chasing him. The police had guns drawn and ran after Pius up a flight of stairs, shooting at him. Pius shot back at Richardson, hitting him twice in the chest. Richardson lived. "He just couldn't get around for awhile," said one close to the incident.[74] Pius was given a new trial by Judge McDevitt in the shooting. Though not an unusual ordeal then, Pius was serving time in Eastern State Penitentiary and then other penal institutions, but not for long. Harry Riccobene remembered Pius Lanzetti as an "inquisitive person who would get others in trouble."

At the same time that Pius was honing his skills at manipulating the criminal justice system of Philadelphia, John Avena was cultivating ties with the Jewish mobsters and gangsters of mainland Italian ancestry, notably those from Calabria, like Marco Reginelli, Joe Rugnetta, John Scopoletti and Joe Ida. In the late 1920s, Avena's responsibilities also grew with the absence of Sabella who was "at war" in New York with his Castellammaresi *paesani*. These were years in which Avena's administrative business abilities were decidedly more important for the Philadelphia-South Jersey Family's illegal activities which included the liquor making, sales and distribution, the loan sharking and the paid protection rackets. With the *rapprisentanti* not in direct control, Avena seemed to have been more receptive to the non-Sicilian gangsters' unlawful schemes at making money, such as in the local lotteries and in the pool rooms where gambling was slowly enticing individuals of all races, ethnicities and ages. Avena not only was primed for the gambling rackets, but he had proven leadership in this vice from his early years before and between prison time, on the street corners to the boxing arenas. Organization also was in Avena's resumé from the time he was a teenaged bread baker to running a grocery store to managing the theatre and promoting boxers. Where the western Sicilian Mafiosi were confined in their conservatism, Avena ventured into the same new avenues that the city's underworld tred, at first as the neophyte, then as a competitor.

But perhaps the best lesson that Avena learned from Sabella and the others was the value of the network system within the Families. Though Avena was not known to have had business contacts with others from Novara di Sicilia, he did recognize the primacy of the Jews in certain rackets, the Calabrian gangsters and those like himself and Joseph Bruno from eastern Sicily who were taken in by the western Sicilian Mafiosi—for all of their intents and purposes, they became part of the Family in the medieval definition of the word. Avena's physical boundaries in his network were limited however, and far narrower than Sabella's and the other western Sicilians who had dependable *paesani* in colonies throughout the U.S. with Mafiosi Friends. Sabella did not pass on to Avena his *paesani* contacts, but Avena's local associates kept him equated with the gangsters, partly because he had a nickname, "Big Nose" which no one with due respect would have had.

When Sabella was away, Avena's gangster past was resurrected further. In contrast to the western Sicilian Mafiosi who made every endeavor to leave few traces of their existence on paper, Avena was mentioned in the press alongside of common, but notorious gangsters. And he was photographed, again by the Philadelphia Police, a clear violation in the Mafiosi's efforts to appear as law-abiding. For as much as Sabella wanted his Friends to remain mainstream, average and normal, or at the most, anonymous racketeers with the high pay-offs, Avena took few measures to prevent such incidents of arrest. Just who was in charge while Sabella was in New York is now unknown. What is known is that the Sicilian American Mafia hierarchy remained the same as did each member of the hierarchy in function within the Family. And the press knew nothing of this, or of Avena's rank.

While Sabella was in New York fighting or waiting "on the mattresses," an eighteen year old rumrunner and fledgling alcohol distiller got arrested for "reckless operation of an automobile, misuse of license tags and damage to 'city property.'" Angelo Annaloro, who would soon change his surname to "Bruno," accidently hit a "patrol box" (the "city property") on the corner of Passyunk Avenue and Federal Street. Patrol boxes were found usually at the ends of streets to use in emergencies to call the police. So the police came. What would be the first arrest for the Philadelphia-South Jersey boss in 1959 named Angelo Bruno was soon discharged.[76] But the arrest stayed and became a "rep" associated with the "bad guy" image instead of a bad driver, a young bad driver. The criminal label thus was fixed on Angelo Bruno.

John Avena's presence in Sabella's Family dismantled the status quo of an otherwise solidly western Sicilian clique. Avena's recommendation as a Friend was necessary, but it disrupted the conservative nature of the Family. If Avena was a renegade Mafioso in Sabella's Family, his immediate earnings and income potential compensated for any inability he had to adapt to the western Sicilians' ways. It also became increasingly clear to Sabella and the others that their foreign Tradition had no real compatibility with the U.S. culture and society. In an urban environment during years in which immigration was on the wane, ethnic bias was practically a non-issue and there were enough policemen and bankers of Italian ancestry to put the paid protection and loan sharking rackets out of business. In terms of the Family's purpose and function, what was obvious to Avena may have totally eluded Sabella that the Family's essence was lost by failure of its stagnant, medieval form. If Avena was a less than astute student of this Mafia, it was an advantage then that he, more than any other of Sabella's Friends, had the foresight, experience and spirit to progress or to evolve comparatively with other Sicilian American Mafia Families in the U.S. who eventually renounced some of their rules during the Castellammarese Wars (1927–1931). Likewise, Avena's background and role in the Philadelpbia-South Jersey

Family during Sabella's absence contributed to his qualifying for a higher place all within the U.S. Mafia overall.

Humbert S. Nelli in 1976 wrote a chapter entitled, "The Americanization of the Mobs," using as examples in his thesis the U.S.-born gangsters of Italian ancestry, and Italian-born/Sicilian-born gangsters who migrated to the U.S. either as children or adults. Nelli postulated that those gangsters who were more americanized because of longer exposure to the U.S. culture were most apt to have caused the conflicts experienced within all underworld groups during Prohibition.[77] Peter Lupsha in 1981 then took this concept to another level and explored the influence of American capitalism during Prohibition and found that nativity and ethnic disparity had little to do with what eventually have happened with major bootleggers everywhere in the U.S.[78] Nelli and Lupsha had hypothesized rather soundly in part, but neither recognized any Philadelphia Mafioso in their comparisons and what part that an "adapted" Sicilian American Mafioso such as John Avena had in what was an "evolution," not an "americanization" of the Sicilian American Mafia.

A born businessman arriving as a teenager from a section of Sicily with no Mafia culture, forming friendships in the U.S. with local gangsters and learning about the Mafia as an adult, Avena realized that money and power were forces aligning him with the other underworld elite who silently transformed most of urban America's criminal justice systems during a time in which Mafiosi with gangsters ruled by violence. That violence was the result of political and economic instability in environments where American and Sicilian Mafia Families were sustained in the late 1920s and early 1930s was one reason why the "Men of Honor" suddenly found themselves in categories as gangsters, or worse, as criminals who were social deviants and adversaries of the law. Clearly, economics changed internal as well as external sentiments about Mafiosi who associated with gangsters everywhere in the U.S., as in Sicily. Lyttelton wrote that the class structure within the Mafia had "upper mafiosi [*alti mafiosi*] in Sicily [who] did not object to Benito Mussolini's prefect, Cesare Mori's, arrests of 'lower mafiosi' [*bassi mafiosi*] in the 1920s." Duggan cited a communication to Mori advising "no need to proceed against the upper mafia as its components had a vested interest in collaborating with the police to maintain order on the island." Gentile had more personal experiences in the gangster-Mafioso definition fusion, recalling a statement that his relatives made about him in Sicily at the time of his arrest—he was considered "only as a gangster who dishonored them" not as a Mafioso of a higher standing.[79]

How closely the American Mafiosi identified with the Sicilian ones at this time depended upon class, as well as upon which particular Family had strong *paesani* origins abroad. In New York, there were bridges between the ranking Sicilians from traditional, centuries-old Mafia families in the island's western half such as senior Mafiosi Terranova, Saitta and Morello and others, and among the younger Mafiosi, Joseph Bonanno, Carlo Gambino and Joseph Profaci.[80] In Philadelphia, there was less contact with Sicily by Sabella and no contact with Sicily by John Avena, leaving this Family more vulnerable to modification along local lines. With the only connection to Sicily in his birth, John Avena stood a better chance than the others in Sabella's Family to push for further development criminally, and away from the foreign relationship.

With the Castellammarese Wars into its fourth year, there were gangsters of mainland Italian and Sicilian ancestries who paid no heed to the tradition that created the Mafia. Making money was the objective for the new crop of LCN members, while the diehard western Sicilians mulled on an abstract, honor, that was beyond the comprehension of the former "suspicious persons" and "loiterers." The Sicilian American Mafiosi's regime had gradually been surpassed by these new gangsters' displays of power in violently usurping others' businesses in liquor and killing indiscriminately on the orders of either Masseria or Marazano to whom honor was attached to wealth. Gentile correctly characterized the U.S. Mafia as a "disjointed state" at this time.[81] Before Maranzano's death on September 10, 1931, a Commission as well as new *rapprisentanti* in all of the U.S. Families were assigned to reorganize the fractured organization.[82] For the Philadelphia- South Jersey Family that meant that forty year old Sabella stepped down for thirty-nine year old John Avena to be the new *capo*, a decision which many bore with silent indignation.[83]

By the early 1930s, most Mafiosi were not classified as gangsters, at least not in the eastern half of Pennsylvania. A gangster was a gangster and Mafiosi were not yet downgraded. However it was then very difficult for John Avena to change popular opinion that had not accepted his new persona of Mafioso. Indeed, the muddied perception of a gangster as a Mafioso did not wear well with many within the Philadelphia-South Jersey Family at that time. To date, Avena's reputation, plus the schism between the western Sicilians and non-western Sicilians prevails in how LCN members spoke of the former boss. Riccobene offered an ambiguous, "he was strict, but lenient. Fair. A good boss"; to another LCN member, "...at times you had to be afraid of him...other times he was pleasant"; and to "He [Avena] was nothing but a gangster and everyone knew it!" from yet another Friend.[84]

Violence seemed to be key to understanding how the American Mafia or La Cosa Nostra (LCN) evolved from the Sicilian American Mafia. Written accounts in fact and in fiction reported on how the LCN was derived from nothing more than a gang of Sicilians "first" in New Orleans, Louisiana where ethnic bias against all Italians came early and deep.[85] So much of the Mafia's origins in this country parallel social issues of a given venue that it is often difficult to ascertain consistencies in the Families. For example, some Sicilian American Families experienced a fair amount of freedom in economic mobility before 1900, as in New Orleans and New York City, though none was recounted for Philadelphia.[86] And no violence was associated with these Sicilians' financial strides in New Orleans by Nelli and in his contemporary sources, or in *The New York Times* accounts of western Sicilian-owned businesses and professional offices in the city.[87] How the Sicilian American Mafia is then seen in retrospect is one that was essentially not of violence, was socially and economically progressive and was conforming to American norms quite in contrast to the gangster of lower class values. What happened during Prohibition in the nation's urban immigrant colonies seemed to have laid the groundwork for an LCN with the corruption of the criminal justice system through bribery, thus clouding the legal and moral tones of those in concert with the system.

It is debatable how many Mafia Families in the U.S. were in total agreement with the presumed "creators" of the LCN, "Lucky" Luciano and/or Salvatore Maranzano in 1931 when the traditionalists clung to the tried and true in their given locale. How evenly acceptable this "new" organization was to all of the Mafia Families in the U.S. became subjected to the individual Family especially to those Families in rural or suburban areas who were not accustomed to urban stresses and the "shell shock" of continued violence. Bonanno wrote that communicating events and the war's ends was through meetings held in May of 1931.[88] In the Philadelphia-South Jersey case, sources told of some rejections and hostility to the new type of organization, and that Avena as the new boss had his share of internal problems with his members.[89]

It was somewhat painstaking for Riccobene to respond unbiasedly about whether the Sicilian American Mafia's transition from Sabella to Avena was better. Riccobene after all, could not denounce or criticize the former organization that had found him a "Man of Honor" at the age of sixteen going on seventeen. Riccobene used weighty words to describe both Sabella and Avena as bosses good for their times and purposes. But Avena did not have the intended standoffish manner to him as Sabella—this boss may have been too aware that Riccobene was friendly with the Lanzettis, used to see the Lanzettis smoke opium and shoot morphine, associated with pimps and prostitutes and never once showed any inclination towards accepted respectability outside of the Family. Avena was more liberal to Riccobene, with attitudes less demanding than Sabella apparently because Avena's underworld connections often crossed with Riccobene's. But Avena, nonetheless, was indifferent to Riccobene's 1932 narcotics arrest and conviction.

When Avena became boss of the Philadelphia-South Jersey Family in mid-1931, it was near the beginning of an illegal gambling enterprise by Jewish and Italian gangsters. By 1933 with the repeal of Prohibition, gambling evened the losses and bootleggers became bookmakers. The LCN in Philadelphia also had apparent problems at this time, not with the new criminal activities introduced, but with the lack of energy and participation of former Sicilian American Mafiosi from Sabella's Family who were now a part of Avena's. Mafiosi who were in legal businesses continued as they were, but now Italian gangsters who became LCN members under Avena unabashly had illegal "businesses" without any fronts or other diversions used as covers for their crimes. Avena was in a position of overseeing a new type of Family where *fuoristieri* ("outsiders") from Calabria and Bari on the mainland, and from eastern Sicily were initiated to be Friends by taking oaths to the Family.[90] These oaths still involved the finger prick for blood and the burning of tissue paper carried over from the former organization, although Riccobene denied that the Sicilian Mafia used the knife and gun display. Riccobene stressed that involvement in a murder had not been a requirement for recommendation under Sabella, but under the LCN, the rules changed. He said something quixotic to highlight this: "Angelo Bruno [an initiate under Avena] never killed anyone intentionally" followed by, "Honor is what we cared about." LCN meetings and the "sit-downs" were now in the Italian language in deference to the new initiates who did not understand Sicilian. Other rules were laid out more or less as "dos" and "don'ts," said Riccobene, still bearing most of the western Sicilians' influences when it came to prostitution (a "don't"), to maintaining good contacts with law enforcement, politicians and judges (a "do"), to "ratting" (an emphatic "don't"). Riccobene estimated that it took about thirty years for the new rules to be fully incorporated within the Philadelphia-South Jersey Family, at no fault to Avena. However, within Avena's LCN Family, there was much room for potential conflict and it was apparent that those with one type of belief would simply be content as mere soldiers, relive their pasts in their memories and fulfill what they construed to be *mafiusu* as good husbands and good fathers.

By the time of his own initiation into Sabella's Family, John Avena assumed the "domestic" quality preferred by the traditionalists. His family was his wife and son, and he tried to make more time for them in the 1930s as the LCN Family firmed its gambling status through most of Philadelphia. Avena's son, Salvatore remembered that every New Year's Eve was their time together, "just the three of us." The LCN boss of the Philadelphia-South Jersey Family would turn down all invitations on that holiday and "we would go to the movies, just the three of us. Then my father would go out back behind our house where the garage was and set off fireworks." Taking a deep breath, Salvatore Avena stared blankly, visualizing his father lighting the fireworks and running away fast as they shot up into the sky. To an eight year old, his father made the pretty magic lights that special day, every year. It was a time he said he looked forward to, "just the three of us, Mom, Dad and me."

Gambling was mentioned as Avena's main cash source, if not his only type of income, unlike his Mafiosi contemporaries who diversified their financial interests. As intent as Avena was to further his "book," he reasoned that it was best to know others in the same field. These years were when Harry (or Hyman) Stromberg, better known as "Nig Rosen" and Marco Reginelli associated closely with Avena, going over to his home on South Fifteenth Street, and over drinks and eats, strategized. This was not good for Pius Lanzetti, who ran his numbers rackets in the same areas of Pennsylvania and New Jersey as they did and who did the same as Avena in forming quasi-coalitions in the numbers business. The competition however, was second to the personal enmity that Pius had for Avena. A friend of the Lanzettis and John Avena said that one day, two ne'er-do-wells as gangsters went to Avena and asked him for some money. Avena supposedly slapped one of them and in his deep voice, told them to get out. Disclosing the incident to Pius Lanzetti, the gangsters saw Pius take a $500.00 bill and tear it in half. "Here! You kill Avena and the other half is yours!" Betty Young, Pius' moll, later told Philadelphia Homicide Detective Samuel Ricciardi that she saw and heard Lanzetti give John "Fats" Focoso and Peter "Petey Wallace" Gallo the money to kill Avena.[91] With one-half of the $500.00, the two went out to look for their target.

How long Focoso and Gallo searched and stalked Avena is not known. In the summer of 1936, Avena's wife and son were down at the shore in New Jersey while he remained close to his bookies in South Philadelphia. Newspapers called John Avena "an alleged murderer," "Black Hander," "labor racketeer" (which could not be confirmed), "big shot in the numbers racket," and only rarely as a "mob boss" or "gang leader."[92] Prevailing opinions of Avena's character today are not much different than in the 1930s when he was not known as "Don" or "Mister," but "Big Nose" to South Philadelphia row house residents.[93] And when recalling what in the community he did, gangster-like activities come to the minds of locals, not that he was a member of the "Protective Society." His official occupation noted on his death certificate was that he was a "clerk."[94] Unlike Sabella, Avena was regarded more with the Philadelphia underworld of Zanghi, the Lanzettis and the rest of the gangsters with nicknames, not with the Mafia. Some quality about Avena brought verbal attacks in volume to the many attempts on his life which did not seem to abate while he rose in rank. Evidently, mixed feelings for John Avena were stronger in the 1930s beyond what LCN members expressed in 2001—"respect" and "honor" apparently had not been well absorbed into Avena's Family. Testing the credibility of the Sicilian American Mafia was challenged in Avena's Family, leaving many members caring less for character ideals than in who had the largest book.

The district magistrate at the Seventh and Carpenter Streets station, Vincent J. Girard in August of 1936 was getting "dozens of anonymous telephone calls" about Avena's two chief gambling places. They were located at Eleventh and Christian Streets and at Ninth and Christian, about one block north from one of the Lanzettis' banks at Ninth and Carpenter Streets. Someone was planning something behind Avena's back. And ironically, something was bothering Avena—some kind of rumor was going around about him, some strange talk. Avena went in to see Girard: "Sat in my office. He [Avena] complained about the remarks I'd been making about him. I questioned him about his numbers racketeering. He had the biggest numbers clearinghouse in South Philadelphia on Federal Street near Front. The cars are lined thickly there every day at payoff time." Girard continued: "'Big Nose' assured me then he was out of the racket. I knew he was lying and the police knew he was lying. They could have arrested him—like they arrest the Lanzetti brothers. Thousands of dollars changed hands every day at his gambling joints. Why he [Avena] even announced certain times of the day when the play would be for big stakes."

This kind of talk would incense Pius Lanzetti.

Magistrate Girard, one of the lone Democrats in a Republican bastion, was once arrested himself and put in a jail cell at the Seventh and Carpenter station for having a disagreement with Inspector John H. Driscoll on arresting local gangsters. "I am convinced they [Avena and his LCN members] could not have operated without police knowledge—if not police protection," said Girard.[95] He believed that if Avena was sent to jail, violence in South Philadelphia would have declined.

On Monday, August 17, 1936, Police Officer Robert Weaver was standing at his beat at Sixth Street and Washington Avenue while two plainclothes officers Edward Maier and Stephen Sulvetta were to the west of Washington Avenue and Eighth Street. And between the policemen's positions at Passyunk and Washington Avenues John Avena and Martin Feldstein walked and talked. Seconds into this formation, "a sedan roared by with the snout of a sub-machine gun poked from a rear win-

Philadelphia Police photographs of John Avena and Martin Feldstein, c. 1930.

dow. The gun chattered its fatal refrain and both men fell," read the newspaper report of the incident. A woman sitting on her doorstep fainted. John Avena tried to dodge but fell, hitting his head on a parked car before landing on the ground. One news article said that he died "almost instantly, his heart practically blasted to pieces by twelve bullets" while another claimed it was "four steel-jackets from an automatic rifle" that tore into his chest and abdomen. Two policemen picked up Avena and Feldstein and took them to Pennsylvania Hospital, but Avena had expired minutes after being brought into the building. Feldstein maintained the gangster code to the end and refused to tell the police who the shooters were.[96]

• • • • • • • • • •

What John Avena left was not a Family or even a group—no one considered it an "organization" or even a gang. John Avena left individual members to represent themselves, not the whole, but parts. Until Angelo Bruno became the boss in 1959, few in Philadelphia's underworld would know if anything or anyone bound the local LCN together.

• • • • • • • • •

John Avena's significance became official when the Philadelphia FBI on at least three occasions interviewed confidential informants who confirmed Avena's membership in the Philadelphia-South Jersey Family and that he was the "former boss."[97]

Was this another betrayal?

• • • • • • • • •

URBAN ARCHIVES, TEMPLE UNIVERSITY

Group outside of crime scene 726 South Eighth Street, where Pius Lanzetti had been shot just hours before on December 31, 1936.

Chapter 6
JOSEPH BRUNO

Pius Lanzetti once "...dreamed I got out of my car and was waiting to see someone...And all the time I waited, I was sure someone was watching me, someone was pointing me out, someone was saying, 'That's the one you want...' And suddenly I knew what it was—I was on the spot. I was going to be killed. And that instant I heard a gun and felt the bullets hit me. I could feel my body sway as they thudded into me...And all the time I knew that the bullets didn't hurt. It surprised me. I always figured it would hurt terribly. And I'd always thought that when the time came to die I'd see people—dead people—and yet there was nothing at all but a funny sensation as though I were sinking down into a gray mist. I said to myself what a fool I was. Here was something I'd run away from, hidden from, paid money to be protected from—and it was just like this—dying was as easy as this..."

"I woke up, soaking wet with perspiration."[1]

Actually, Pius had spilled soda on his gray tweed suit and lavender shirt when a spray of buckshot went into his body. Still clutching the bottle of soda that was supposed to ease a hangover, Pius Lanzetti went into the gray mist in seconds.

Joseph Bruno made Pius' dream come true.

One newspaper reported that Pius' death was the work of "members of the 'Greasers,' a gang newly risen to power. All of them were supporters of Big Nose John Avena and Marty Feldstein...And instead of making peace with Lanzetti, police say the 'Greasers' were only pretending to make peace—fattening him up for their revenge..."[2] To hear one of Joseph Bruno's soldiers, Harry Riccobene, tell the story, the death of Pius Lanzetti was not revenge—it was to take down this gang boss because Pius took down his gang's boss, John Avena.

Simply understood, Pius died to balance out underworld injustices. And most likely, Joseph Bruno acted on ordering Pius' death solely upon the advice of Philadelphia's senior Mafiosi who were born into the Mafia Tradition. Unlike these men, Joseph Bruno was from eastern Sicily, an accidental member of La Cosa Nostra by choice not by custom or family.

• • • • • • • • • •

Born on February 11, 1889[3] the man who became Joseph Bruno was born Mario Giuseppe Dovi in Barcellona Pozzo di Gotto, in the province of Messina, Sicily. The town's birth register documented that a forty-six year old shoe cobbler named Salvatore Dovi and his wife Angelina had this child and that she survived the delivery of her third son. Almost one thousand infants were born there in 1889, not an unusually remarkable number, but indicative of the town's population growth.[4] Two older brothers, Antonio and Santo completed the Dovi family on via Villa in this town between the mountains and the Tyrrhenian Sea.[5] Barcellona is about five miles inland, about twenty-eight miles east of the largest nearby city, Messina. Neighboring townspeople described Barcellona's residents as "knife wielding...people who would kill you for looking the wrong way." An old term for Barcellonesi was "*malacarne*" ("bad meat"), a word that used *carne*, something dead to suggest that the people were a worthless lot. Another popular saying for the natives of Barcellona was that they were, "*carne che no cuocere*," unpalatable. Barcellona was not as small nor as remote as many of the Sicilian mountain villages who rarely had visitors. Travelling west from Messina to Palermo, one rides past Barcellona and neighboring Camporeale whose castle testified to the Catalans' presence here in the early fourteenth century.

Whatever the consensus' view of Barcellona's reputation, the Dovi family bore none of their *paesani's* less than desirable traits, said those who knew them.[6] Mario Giuseppe, or just "Giuseppe," was schooled and literate, as his father and brothers were. He also received training in cabinetmaking as a teenager by the time his older brother Antonio (Anthony) had left Barcellona for the United States at the age of fourteen in about 1900. Labor recruitment in Sicily, as in Italy, was active at this time, perhaps aggressively because Italian workers were in demand for both unskilled and skilled employment throughout the U.S.[7] Landing in New York City, Antonio Dovi, possibly for a job, went to a small town south of Syracuse, in New York called Cortland. This town offered to immigrants employment in the railroad or in the Wickwire's Company, making chicken netting and various types of wires. The county's history named a Vito James "Jim" Adessa from Bari, on the mainland of Italy, as one of the first of Italian ancestry to act in the role of a *padrone* to find workers for the local industries. He was paid a fee for each new hiring and then acted on behalf of the newcomer when translation was needed. Most of Cortland's Italians were from Campobasso, Italy, but "eighty to ninety percent of the Sicilians" originated from the Lipari Islands off Sicily's northeast coast, not far from Messina.[8] Others, though not many from Barcellona, had gone to Cortland; by 1907, "Anthony" Dovi's parents and brothers left Sicily to share in the benefits their son had written about here.[9] The family had travelled hundreds of miles north to Naples, Italy to board the passenger liner called the "Gloria Rubattino" on August 24, 1907. By September 5th, the Dovi family underwent immigrant processing at the Port of New York.[10]

From his arrival in Cortland, Giuseppe Dovi began working as a "case maker" or cabinetmaker in Cortland's piano factory. He had this steady employment, a trade and apparently with some financial means to have gotten married to Paola Cicciari, his teenage sweetheart from Barcellona. She had gone to Cortland before him; they were married by the time they had turned nineteen years old. Theirs may have been a life of few comforts at first because as "Joseph" now, the husband became a father in 1909 and was renting a place for his family that increased every two years with the birth of another child.[11] Directories in Cortland listed "Joseph Dovi" in succeeding years as a "laborer," then again as a "cabinetmaker" then as a "fruit dealer" while he was making his Declaration of Intention and Petition for U.S. citizenship.[12]

There was with Joseph Dovi, already by 1915, some contradictions to what criminologists postulated as foundations for a life in organized crime. He was reasonably educated, had a skill, was lawfully employed, was married before the age of twenty and intended to support his wife and children in a stable family unit. Dovi also had no criminal record as a youth, was religious and observant of his

Roman Catholic faith and cared nothing of exploiting others in any way, how ever slightly. What made his character so remarkable was that Dovi possessed none of the fundamental qualities noted in the urban Italian gangsters who graduated from juvenile delinquents to junior racketeers, trying their hand at anything illegal and not complying to social norms. *"The Ethnic Succession Theory"* of criminology certainly did not apply to someone who patiently worked in a lawful profession.[13] Francis A. J. Ianni's *"Kinship and Social Control Theory"* also had no bearing on one not from western Sicily and the Mafia Tradition, as it was with Salvatore Sabella and his *paesani*.[14] Joseph Dovi would become one of the cornerstones of why the Philadelphia-South Jersey La Cosa Nostra's case provided a singular history, so much in contrast to other Mafia-La Cosa Nostra venues.

Dovi's life featured other elements not conducive to one oriented towards organized crime: he had both parents in a close relationship near him; he migrated to a rural area; and he intended to continue what was socially acceptable in the community. Information from Cortland has a Joseph Dovi who was a responsible man looking to support his wife and four children well and no indications of anything marginally "gangster-like" in his habits or behavior. Dovi relatives today claimed that they carried the same religious fervor as Joseph's brothers, and that Joseph was remembered for having high standards.[15]

Nevertheless, at the age of twenty-seven in 1916, with an immediate and extended family close by, Joseph Dovi began working as a bartender during some times when the war, temperance and increased immigration added to unusual stress upon non-Americans. Dovi stood at five feet nine inches tall and weighed about one hundred and fifty pounds with a dark complexion, black hair, brown eyes and features which many of Cortland's natives found too foreign.[16] One of Cortland's historians had written on the town's attitude to the growing number of outsiders to the community borne especially in the police department "against all Italians...lots of allegations of crimes against them [Italians]."[17] Efforts at fulfilling his intention to become a U.S. citizen and his financial independence crossed while as a bartender when Dovi had a "serious criminal charge lodged against him," tainting his character and diverting him from what he so desired.[18] Despite this, prominent dry goods merchant John Kennedy remained as one of Dovi's witnesses for citizenship. But the weight of the criminal charge seemed to prevail upon the Italian colony in Cortland and Jim Adessa, the influential businessman and leader, withdrew to vouch for Dovi's reputation. Dovi was said to have been so shamed and furious over the matter that he left Cortland by the fall of 1917, abandoning his entire family. "Salvatore was always very vague on why Joseph had problems. He *was* a good man," said a Dovi relative. One of the Cicciari family members still remains mystified over the 1917 incident in which Joseph also was alleged to have punched an officer: "He had changed so much from the person he was in Cortland...he had that problem with the law and ran out of the Courtroom and kept running...he changed. He would stay away from home for many days," leaving Paola and her mother to care for the four children.[19]

After ten years in the U.S. with four children born as citizens in New York, Joseph Dovi scotched any idea to become what his children attained at birth. Sensing the negative impact of what "the Americans" did to him with the criminal charge in Cortland, Joseph Dovi assumed the surname of his sister-in-law, Carmela Bruno. Joseph's son, whom he had baptized in name after his father Salvatore was now called, "Charles" possibly after Charles H. Moshier who had been loyal to him and his brother, Tony.[20]

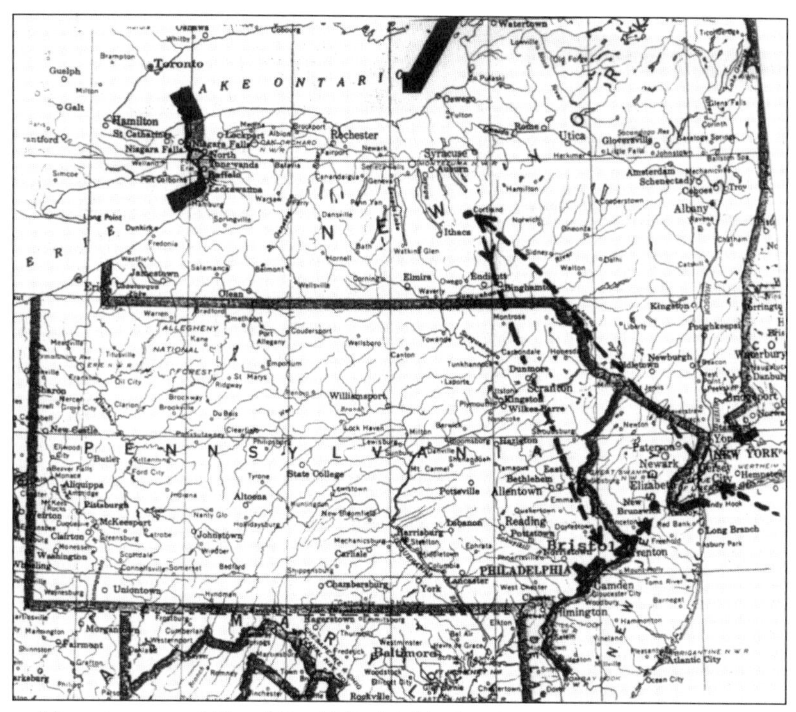

Map shows mobility of the Philadelphia-South Jersey La Cosa Nostra boss, Joseph Bruno upon his arrival in New York to his final days in a New York City Hospital. Sites point to Bruno's longterm residences.

Priorities in Joseph Dovi's life now altered his intentions with a single claim of criminality. He would still be a husband, father and provider for one family, and a son, brother and uncle to another family whose backs were turned to him for whatever reason they feared. He would be cut from them in name and association.

The widespread effect of the criminal charge seemed to bear quite differently upon the parents and brothers for the family not to have supported Joseph better. Joseph never discussed this incident with his own children; Dovi relatives in Cortland felt uncomfortable to disclose why the family failed to unify at such a critical time when shame hung vilely upon Joseph, implying that the nature of the offense may have been sexual.

If the individual who now called himself Joseph Bruno sought to relocate to places where fellow Sicilians lived, he had a number of choices: Syracuse, Rochester or Buffalo, all not too far from Cortland. Instead, Joseph Bruno crossed the New York border to Pennsylvania, passed the western Sicilian colonies in the Pittston and Wilkes-Barre area to go to a sleepy, industrial town in lower Bucks County called Bristol. Named after the place where many left with William Penn in seventeenth century England, these colonists founded Bristol on the Delaware River before Philadelphia, about twenty-five miles to the south. No one in the Bruno family knew why they moved to Bristol after Joseph settled down there. "No one would have known Bruno here. You can get lost here without getting attention," said a long-time resident. Bristol had its share of immigrants from Italy and Sicily who found work in the mills, factories and the like. Many Sicilians were from Campobello di Mazara in the Province of Trapani. Together with some Palermitani and other western Sicilians in Trenton, New Jersey, less than ten miles over the river, there had been Sicilian Mafiosi working in legitimate businesses, some sidelining in immigrant services at least since 1905. One individual, a reputed "Man of Honor" in Bristol who was born in Campobello was similar in character to "Zu Ninu" in Norristown in that he quickly learned to read and write the English language, had some skills, then a professional office and used his energies to assist other Sicilians to settle in the area. A quiet, unassuming gentleman, he was the typical business owner of means, buying and selling property and working with others at Bristol's Roman Catholic church. Also like "Zu Ninu," this individual had no criminal record and had none of the gangster-type traits as a loiterer or idler, was not suspected of immoral conduct or had any anti-social habits.[21] It would take a few years for Joseph Bruno to connect with these Mafiosi in Bristol.

The criminal proceedings from which Joseph Bruno fled had divided his family and caused a separation from his wife. Paola's mother was with her and tried to unburden her daughter from the locals' looks and sneers that she now had to bear because of her husband's alleged offense. Struggling for a few more years, Paola had to raise her children with a broken heart without Joseph. He was working somewhere in Bristol as a "Hotel Keeper," using his new name and living in a low-income area as a boarder in a home on Market Street. While there, Joseph Bruno claimed he spoke no English and was a bachelor in 1920, as he laid low from law enforcement.[22] His explanation for the single twenty-one year old homebound Italian woman living with him: "cousin." She gave her name as "Ange." She spoke English, was literate and came to the U.S. in 1904. She remained in the adjacent building all day, not admitting to any occupation. She told people that Joseph financially supported her.[23] What communications that Joseph Bruno had with his family still in Cortland were unknown, except that shortly after 1920, Paola and the children apparently were reunited with him. But their lifestyle and circumstances were not much better with Joseph on the lam: in August of 1921, Joseph and Paola's ten year old daughter "Jennie" (Giovanna) died and she was placed in an unmarked grave, a telling sign of the family's struggles.[24] What happened to "Ange" and their living arrangement was also unknown; later the family became aware of a woman named Ann Nelson who was Bruno's "business partner" from the time they had met in Bristol. Thereafter, Ann Nelson and Joseph Bruno would remain entwined for the rest of their lives.

Ann Nelson became the only female who was in full complicity with Joseph Bruno's criminal affairs. They were lovers and she assisted him, apparently since his arrival in Bristol, in prostitution. There had been some question about Ann's initial encounter with Bruno in Bristol. She was young, of Neapolitan ancestry and had been married to a fellow with the surname of Nelson. Her finest quality was that Joseph Bruno implicitly trusted this blue-eyed young woman to run his "business," which might lead one to believe that she may have begun their relationship as a prostitute for him, then as a bordello manager.[25] Harry Riccobene explained that in the post-war years, that many women of Italian ancestry became prostitutes. "Especially in the early '20s, for economic reasons, some girls reverted to that and got put out of their homes by their parents. Or their boyfriends conned their girls and made them prostitutes. Men would use an excuse like they were in trouble and needed money fast, so these 'crumbs' turned to their girls to be prostitutes and to make money for them." Riccobene said that many men and gangsters likewise were pimps for their Italian girlfriends from the 1920s to the mid-1930s, and many of the pimps ended by marrying the girls who had worked for them. "They were often very good wives," he said referring to an LCN member who was in that situation. Riccobene also confirmed another example of an Italian gangster who was a pimp, Sam Rugnetta, the brother of LCN member Joseph Rugnetta. Tying in the violence with the time and place, Riccobene said that Rugnetta was killed because of his role in prostitution. He was shot ten times on the 1100 block of South Seventh Street in South Philadelphia in 1928.[26]

Reconciling why prostitution, a mistress and underworld types entered their family was difficult for the Dovis and Cicciaris. One of Paola's relatives believed that Joseph loved Paola, his wife, his first love, "...but the other one [Ann Nelson] gave him what he wanted—she was a whiz in business. This Ann wouldn't be any good if she was in that life [prostitution]. She destroyed the family and the life they had."[27] But Riccobene, Bruno's soldier in the 1930s and

1940s witnessed the love between his boss and Ann Nelson and remembered her as the woman "whom the boss really loved, not his wife. She [Ann] did anything a woman would do for him," Riccobene remarked in his usual ambiguous way.

The veil of prostitution clung to Bruno and his "rep" was made in Bristol. Living in this town brought people from many walks of life ready to enjoy the vices in a place where law enforcement was lax. Besides its industries and growing immigrant population from all of Europe, Bristol attracted a tourism trade with vacationers who resided along the banks of the Delaware River. "Bristol was a hot town, gambling and prostitution," recalled an elderly LCN member in 2001. Some of the recreations for the well-heeled males included the "high dice" games, drinking liquor from the local stills and women brought over from New Jersey or farther. Attempting to shield his existence, not many leads pointed to what Joseph Bruno was doing in Bristol as a husband and father who was still in contact with Ann Nelson. Moving about in this level of the underworld for a time and establishing himself as one who was involved in white slavery might have brought him to the attention of others in gangland's upper echelon.

Bristol's proximity to Trenton brought bootleggers, their money and criminal activities to the town above Philadelphia where they also had their "connections to the guys downtown." Indeed, the timing of Prohibition worked well with discouraged, frustrated immigrants tempted towards an American dream scheme in illegal alcohol or in using fast, drunk women who gravitated towards these rich bootleggers for high-priced sex.[28]

Feeling rootless in this society, a desperate individual such as a Joseph Bruno in Bristol would have taken risks where he could have kept local police at bay. The Bruno children and Paola eventually learned that Joseph's income in Bristol came from the vice crimes, especially from women. "Everyone knew about Ann—it wasn't a secret," said one relative. Another of Paola's relatives believed that it was during the 1920s that Bruno "found some people in the Mafia and wanted to make money like them." Whether it was in Bristol or in Trenton where Joseph Bruno met the Sicilian American Mafiosi by the mid-1920s, the Philadelphia-South Jersey Family was next in line to introduction.

Western Sicilians migrated to Trenton contemporaneously as in other areas, bringing Mafiosi as workers. However, these Sicilians' network system tied with the Sicilian Mafiosi scattered throughout the Philadelphia-South Jersey region most effectively in the 1920s with the transport of bootlegged alcohol down the Delaware River to Trenton or Bristol, then to Philadelphia from upstate. It may have been this time when Bruno proved himself worthy to the sophisticated Mafiosi by engaging not in bootlegging, but in commissioned killings, thus earning him another reputation as a "hit man."[29] Violent crime soon came with such facility to Bruno that he was sent on interstate "jobs" for the Sicilian Mafiosi, enriching his "rep" as one they could trust and depend on for future use. Bruno came to provide better for his family and his "work" for gangsters and Mafiosi appeared as positive because the family's living standards were raised to a significantly higher degree of comfort. They were living in a large, corner house in Bristol; Joseph drove his own car. And best of all, no spectre of New York's police haunted Joseph Bruno—not even Bristol's law enforcement cared what Bruno was doing criminally or otherwise.

Joseph Bruno's short-term residence in Bristol was to become debated by investigators for the Pennsylvania Crime Commission in the 1960s. The "Report on Organized Crime" released in 1970 named Bruno as the boss who succeeded Sabella in "1927," with "his headquarters...first centered in Bristol, then in Trenton." A few years later, more investigating by the Pennsylvania Crime Commission produced a report on gambling in Bucks County, building upon the 1970 "Report's" facts. This publication stated that "on New Years [sic] Eve, 1928, one of his [Bruno's] racket associates was murdered, and shortly thereafter he moved his residence and headquarters to Trenton..." Citing a "Mr. A." and "various public sources" that were not named as their references, this Pennsylvania Crime Commission Report of 1970 had not known that it had missed quite a few more reliable sources that documented Joseph Bruno's rank, or lack thereof, in the local Mafia as well as where he had called home.[30]

Familiarizing himself with New Jersey in the mid-1920s through his growing Sicilian American Mafia contacts in Bristol and Trenton, Joseph Bruno gradually came to meet with some of New York's underworld. His family was moved to New Brunswick, New Jersey, a midway point for him between Philadelphia and New York before 1927 and they came to accept his brief stays at home. Joseph Bruno may not have seen his teenagers mature, but the children attended good schools and were compensated for his absence with gifts. Meanwhile, the Sicilian American Mafiosi tested him repeatedly as an associate, using him as an alleged gunman for more bootlegging warfare in either Philadelphia or elsewhere in Pennsylvania and in New Jersey. By the beginning of 1927 police in New Brunswick said they told Joseph Bruno they wanted him "out...and to stay out" because of his criminal reputation,[31] an unlikely response expected after a few years of breaks in arrests in Bristol and certainly none in Philadelphia, thanks to Salvatore Sabella. Bruno probably met the Philadelphia-South Jersey *rapprisentanti* between 1925 and 1927, when the liquor wars and the Lanzetti brothers were out of control in Philadelphia. His activities in New Brunswick, however, irritated local law enforcement who repeatedly cited him for various offenses in which he evaded imprisonment. New Brunswick, nevertheless, did seem to have been his homestead and scene of enough criminal interests by 1926 for Bruno to have had a number of fellow Mafia associates nearby as a crew.

Salvatore Sabella had told Joseph Bruno and a few others to meet him in Philadelphia for some work on May 30, 1927. That evening the crew was driving on South Eleventh Street when they stopped to see the Philadelphia Police bringing out Sabella, John Scopolitti and A. Domenico Pollina. The police and detectives had been inside the grocery store of Friend Philip Pollina when they saw the men "feasting on chicken and wine...in high humor." The Mafiosi and Scopolitti laughed when they were told that they were under arrest. As the men left to go outside, the car with Bruno and three others came to a halt. The police approached them and asked why they were there to which one of the crew said that they were "goodfellows out for a holiday." The persistent police refused a bribe and arrested them for a minor traffic offense, suspecting that they may have had something to do with the murders of Joseph Zanghi and Vincent Cocozza a few hours before. Joseph Bruno was arrested along with Nick Messina, John Marco and Norman Marsella and brought to see Anthony "Musky" Zanghi at City Hall. Zanghi told the police that two weeks before the murders, while "he sold a café known as 'La Tosca Hotel' to a friend of the Scapelliti [sic] crowd" he was told that he was a "marked man."[32] These four, said Zanghi, were "brought here to participate in the killing," that they were "hired assassins...brought from New Brunswick." Musky added to the foursome's other underworld activities: "They work with the others...they run women back and forth from here to New

Brunswick." Zanghi spoke of "organized gangs for running dope between Philadelphia and cities in New Jersey. According to him, there is an organized syndicate that traffics in women, running them from one city to another..."[33] A "reliable source" for the FBI later detailed that one of Joseph Bruno's "ventures had been a house of prostitution located off Route 130 in New Brunswick...this house was raided back in the 1920s." The informant further said that Joseph Bruno "was assisted by Joseph Ida and another individual from Philadelphia after some heat had been put on them in Pennsylvania during the early 1920s." These were places in the Bristol area, one of which was reputedly a large tavern in Falls Township. The FBI source added that Bruno and Ida "moved their activity to central New Jersey..." validating the moves that the families had made from Pennsylvania to northern New Jersey.[34]

There were no inconsistencies in the facts and specifics of Joseph Bruno's life by 1927—much of what his "rep" was based on now was laid bare to law enforcement in New York, New Jersey and Pennsylvania and his crime resumé included the most grievous of felonies, without prison time. Joseph Bruno may not have seen much of his family in the 1920s, but these were years in which he bloomed as a gangster, became trusted by the Philadelphia-South Jersey and Trenton Sicilian Mafia Families, and enjoyed a camaraderie that was obsessed with power and wealth.

If there was a trade-off for the material gain that Bruno could have only obtained through gangland activities, Bruno's family seemed not to have experienced any lack of moral sensitivity. The children and wife were unaware of whom Bruno associated in the underworld because he kept one side of his life separate from the other. His Livingston Street home was on a corner lot, near a synagogue and school in New Brunswick and was elegant and finely furnished. His son attended a private Catholic college at a time when only the privileged could afford to. Bruno's eldest daughter had a grand wedding with no expense too much for her. And his wife, though alone for most of this period, had furs, jewelry and anything to substitute for him. "My mother adored her father and he adored her as much—no one could compare to him," said one of Bruno's granddaughters. When he did come home, he was greeted warmly. He was allowed to relax, to sit by the radio and smoke his cigarettes. Bruno got along well with his son-in-law, whose family was from western Sicily. The son-in-law had pursued the daughter of the man with the reputation in New Brunswick as a "hit man" despite some apprehension. But it was Joseph Bruno who approached the young suitor, approved of him and gave his daughter at the altar to him. This son-in-law would be the father of Bruno's first grandchild, who for many years, had his sole attention and love.

Joseph Bruno was taking in life as a first time grandfather in the summer of 1936 when something happened in Philadelphia. No one had figured that John Avena would be killed—he, a boss of one of the many "Italian gangs" whom the Philadelphia Police knew ran the alcohol and vice activities since 1925.[35] But no one in the local underworld broke the silence kept by at least three in the Lanzetti gang, plus the female in attendance.[36] Avena had brought the Family to prominence by successful relationships with associates in New Jersey and with the Jewish mobsters who had three states tied in the numbers rackets. But no one in the LCN got tipped off to Pius Lanzetti's planned, contracted hit, leading others in gangland to wonder how much respect and power that Avena's Family actually had. The Lanzettis took Sabella's Sicilian American Mafia for granted, presuming these men were just another gang staking out clientele and an area for their operations. Leo Lanzetti's murder by Sabella proved inconsequential to future interactions with the Sicilians. Then after Sabella, Avena was brought up to representative level almost at the same time as Pius was leaving prison, with the intercession of some legal maneuvering by Judge McDevitt. Pius Lanzetti saw in John Avena nothing less than one blow against him after another, mounting in the competition in the gambling rackets. The apparent schism in Avena's Family between the non-Sicilians and the Sicilians betrayed the indifference under the veneer of trust and loyalty. For how difficult it was to teach what respect, honor, decorum and the other customs of the western Sicilian culture were to those not of a Mafia Tradition, it was more difficult for the western Sicilians to grasp that no one in the Family was close enough to the local underworld's rumor mill to reveal Pius' intentions to them.

Avena was buried by Friends in a Family of turmoil. This type of incident never happened before to a representative of a Family—a sitting boss slain without the Mafia's knowledge. But how fitting the death of Avena, the first La Cosa Nostra Family leader was in relation to the new Organization who swore by the gun and knife! His death established how the trend towards greed and treachery surmounted any elite aura the local Mafiosi believed they only possessed. All of what South Philadelphians considered in "The Protective Society" was lost on thugs like the Lanzettis,[37] and perhaps on some of Avena's own members whom he had recommended to become Friends. The more tragic scenario was Grace Avena and ten year old Salvatore. When she supposedly went to one bank to claim her deceased husband's holdings, the banker was said to have looked at the widow and asked, "What money?" The mother and son soon left Philadelphia for New Jersey and a new life.[38]

The Philadelphia-South Jersey Family, in accordance with the five New York Families, "voted unanimously" on

Joseph Bruno to succeed Avena in 1936 said Harry Riccobene, the soldier who was pleased to have worked under someone who was so agreeable to him. Bruno and Riccobene grew closer, with the soldier to remain within Bruno's immediate circle. Riccobene honored Bruno as his superior, but more for how Bruno handled Family matters in his fast rise from brief soldier status to boss. Bruno was fairly less constrained and more openminded than Sabella and his fellow western Sicilians who were far too conservative for Riccobene. Bruno trusted Riccobene, which translated to "Little Harry" as making him feel important and with authority. Months after Avena's death, Bruno reciprocated the sentiments of Riccobene and allowed Little Harry and two others to assess what had to be done from the losses incurred to the Family because of what Pius Lanzetti was doing. By then, Focoso and Gallo had vanished.[39]

Joseph Bruno had grown in reputation and wealth by 1936. He had been brought into the Philadelphia-South Jersey Family just before or just after 1930, supposedly recommended by John Avena who may have felt some affinity towards someone near his hometown in eastern Sicily. The Sicilian American Mafiosi apparently stopped Bruno from anything more in the white slavery trade because it went against their cultural beliefs. He got "straightened out," the same as with Avena. Bruno's reputation was shaped by his personality which was one of politics and some sincerity. He had mastered the "poker face" expression of Mafiosi and when his wife questioned him about things, he said that it was better that she knew less. He was protective of Paola and especially of his two remaining daughters and son. No one ever used strong words that would characterize him as one would think a pimp or hitman would be. "I remember him as being a tall, very handsome, elegant, refined soft-spoken, respectful person. You wouldn't think he was capable of such things," recalled one female relative. Another said same, but added that when Bruno and his men were in town, "These guys towed the line with him. Everyone was in awe of him when he went into a room...he never acted like a big boss." A discreet elderly LCN member in Philadelphia described Joseph Bruno as a man who was "pretty 'heavy,' a lot of 'juice,'...had men under him" though he was at a distance from the Family he represented. A now deceased LCN associate of Riccobene's had stated that Joseph Bruno as a boss was known best in Philadelphia as someone reliable to kill, citing the underworld's long record of reputed deaths at Bruno's hand. In Bristol, one older gentleman admitted that "when Joseph Bruno was in town for the gambling, the men with the tommy guns were posted and the kids were told to stay away. People used to come from all over...Philly, Camden, for the games...anyone with money when Joseph Bruno was here." A longtime resident in New Brunswick said that "people here knew that he was a big shot in the mob, that he had power." The FBI called Bruno a "prominent hoodlum" and "rackets leader," to which Harry Riccobene would laugh and add, "Joe Bruno was a degenerate gambler!"[40]

Like other gangsters, Bruno became adept at creating a mindset where he could be the family-like gentleman with a wife, children and grandchildren, or one of the mob's wise guys with the mistress, or "many women—I'm sure he had plenty of other women," and an entourage of men that included a chaffeur.[41] One of his men was "Fats," who watched over Paola and kept a male presence in the home while the boss was away. "Fats was a doll!" said everyone who remembered the jovial man who came and went from Bruno's house in New Brunswick. Joseph Bruno, before he had become boss was important enough within the Sicilian American Mafia to have been regarded as someone whom LCN opportunist Joseph Valachi invited to his wedding in 1932 with such underworld luminaries as Albert Anastasia and Carlo Gambino.[42] The Mafia association kept Bruno out of prison, which not only empowered him, but cast him as a player who was dependable and not arrogant, dutiful and not superfluous. One relative said that Bruno eventually got to know all of the police and politicians in New Brunswick and that "the police would close their eyes to a lot of things there." Bruno relatives also nod when certain names of state-wide politicians were said because they were known and had met with the boss.

Bruno could fully appreciate his role in the shadows of the Philadelphia-South Jersey Family, appearing rarely in South Philadelphia and lurking confidently behind his underboss and captains who seldom mentioned his name as a threatening force. One heard the name of "Marco Reginelli" instead, giving rise to the myth that Reginelli was the boss, not Bruno. In New Brunswick in the 1930s, Joseph Bruno's reputation as a "hitman" instilled fear to those uninformed of how Sabella's Sicilian American Mafiosi taught Bruno to appear unlike what the prejudice held. Bruno's adaptive persona assumed some of the Mafiosi gentlemen's mien, albeit he did not use a business front or have a daily working routine as the Mafiosi with stores, factories or legal diversified interests. In the 1930s, gangsters were tolerated more, and it was common to see men out of work, lounging outside or on street corners—less arrests as a "suspicious person" or "disorderly person" or "loiterer" appeared on the police blotters. Men such as Avena or Bruno were seen positively as providing entertainment and income by the gambling and numbers to the isolated row house residents. Consequently, when law enforcement arrested gangsters, politics or non-legal issues were given as reasons, not for the integrity of the offense. However, Joseph Bruno learned well how to keep Philadelphia's corruption-prone criminal justice system content enough not to interfere through another mob war in the late 1930s.

Harry Riccobene, one of Bruno's most loyal and reliable soldiers said that for about one year that he lived in Upper Darby with his boss. Riccobene evaded anything implicating this time as a "retreat" or "hiding" from the breakout of drive-by shootings that took down Anthony Piccarelli, Nicholas Bartilucci, Danny Day and Frank Piccolo, among other casualties. Riccobene hinted that the "war" was only among the local LCN Family, not between other gangs in the city. He cited "New York" as the cause for making further changes within the Family and that this "war" was considered an extension of the Castellammarese Wars, if not the Wars' legacy. The LCN as an Organization was still evolving, said Riccobene, adding that the new rules mentioned in 1931 were not fully implimented by 1939.

Riccobene said that while his function was to protect his representative, Joseph Bruno, in Upper Darby that Bruno had his mistress, Ann alongside of him throughout the ordeal. Riccobene was close to his boss and Bruno entrusted "Little Harry" to take care of matters, as in Pius Lanzetti's demise. Riccobene's relationship with Bruno was far more congenial than with Bruno's two predecessors. Riccobene would smile more, his eyes would brighten and his words were less measured when he spoke of Joe Bruno. The soldier seemed not to have had the moments of glory in the local war of 1939 as he had experienced in the Castellammarese Wars in New York, but his times with Bruno in the "safe house" were memorable because of the intimate bonding he had with a boss whom he truly liked. Bruno's role in the war was not identified and his actual position was not clear except that Riccobene and another LCN member, Charlie Scarpa were there to keep him alive and to see to his needs.[43] Joseph Bruno perhaps stayed until matters would resolve themselves because the war's activities were centered in Philadelphia, not in South or North Jersey, and because New Brunswick's distance was now at a disadvantage. Danny Day's link with the white slavery was the public reason for his killing, while Frank Piccolo's death two months later was related more to revenge. Both men died by buckshot from a twelve gauge shot gun while riding in vehicles, their heads nearly severed off their necks.[44] Piccolo's life of violence was recorded to 1918; he also had long associations in illegal narcotics going back to the early 1920s.[45]

By the end of 1939, Bruno was said to have been finished in Philadelphia, leaving his underboss and captains to resume their activities without any impediments. At the top of the list in "housecleaning chores" for Bruno was in ridding the area of the Lanzettis. Teo Lanzetti, the youngest brother, finally got a conviction for interstate drug sales that imprisoned him with the uncompromising federal authorities. Willie, whom many never considered as too criminally aggressive, nonetheless had been com-

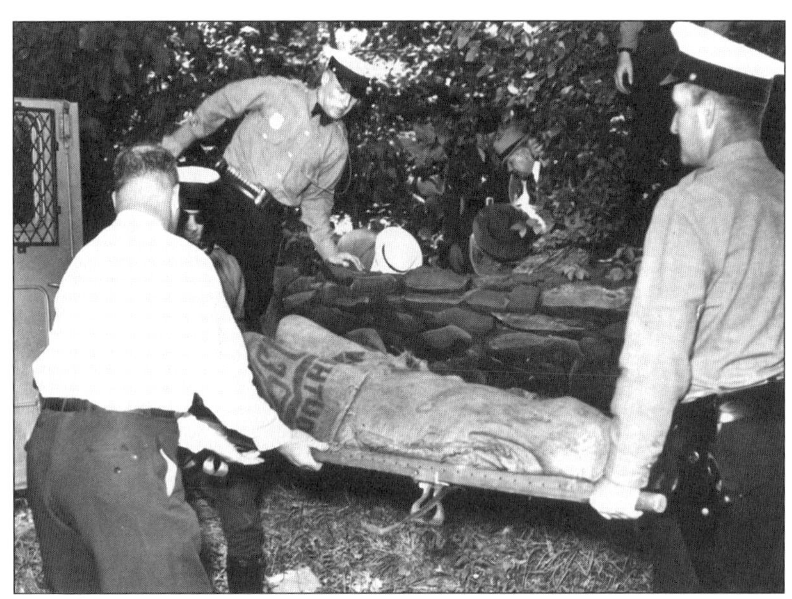

URBAN ARCHIVES, TEMPLE UNIVERSITY

Lower Merion police removing Willie Lanzetti's body.

plicit in John Avena's death and met his fate without defense.[46]

Police figured that Willie was in Philadelphia on June 30, 1939 when he encountered some people whom he knew and went off with them. On the morning of July 1st, deliveryman Charles Williams jumped the wall to the Ashton estate in Wynnewood, Montgomery County, in suburban Philadelphia, and fell near a large burlap sack. Williams looked, and pulled out his pocket knife to see what was inside. "Out popped," Willie Lanzetti's bloody head, "swathed in a heavy piece of cloth." Willie had a merciful execution by traditional Sicilian Mafiosi, a private death where without struggle he saw his end quickly with a single shot behind his right ear. It was a pure Mafia *modus operandi,* balancing underworld justice without the eyes and ears of the Little Italy community, traumatizing no one with the sight of an end so violently. Willie's body was found fully clothed and his head was delicately swaddled in a thick absorbent towel. He was sewn with great care into two dry burlap bags with copper wire, a deliberate, but respectful process between Willie's killers and his corpse.[47] The county physician pulled a single .25 caliber bullet from Willie's brain that caused his only fatal wound. Willie's death spoke of another time in another place where the ending of life by another carried less of the emotional weight of the empassioned slayer. So artful was the process of having Willie submit to his own end when he was "penniless,"[48] yet still a Lanzetti with a life to give for a life taken. There was no resistence, no torture, no symbols but the chilling sterility of Willie's body left alone, enveloped from the elements, hidden in the darkness.

Willie's death suggested a calmer, mature and confident Joseph Bruno, so unlike the person who made his dêbut as boss by avenging John Avena's death with Pius Lanzetti's. This killing was gangster-type violence at its best, taking down two other men after shoving an innocent lady and then spraying the gangster, Pius with pellets of buckshot. Children were outside—the Campbell-Lyons School was across the street—why did the hitmen want the young to see this? Disrespect for one as despised as Pius overrode all other reasons. When area residents remember back to December 31, 1936 to when Pius died, they shake their heads still and say, "Why?" to trying to figure their roles in a private, gangland matter. Pius himself had said, "It's too bad men have to be killed...Because in the underworld there are things that merit death. Sometimes the only way you can make a guy understand is to kill him...If you could just stand him up and shoot him and say, 'Now don't do it again,' wouldn't it be swell?"[49]

Buckshot hit Pius in his left check through into his brain. He had a defense wound in raising his left hand to the attack. Other gun shot wounds were in his throat, shoulder (after cutting through his suspender strap), and under his heart.[50]

• • • • • • • • • •

Joseph Bruno's life in New Brunswick did not change much in the 1940s. His family realized that he was not around all of the time. "The time away from her [Paola] was more and more as the years went by," said a relative. His fast life of gambling and horses took up some of his time aside from running from one residence to another in Philadelphia, Trenton, New Brunswick and points around. He enjoyed eating with other LCN members at "Patsy's" in New York City. "Fats," "Albie" and Joe Ida were his close companions. "Big Lipped Louie," the Jewish gangster was another in his intimate circle who used to stop by the house with Paola cooking. "Joe Bruno used to sit at the table on the holidays, and joke with my father. Joe loved snails and *cassata*. 'Just bring me those two things and I'll be happy'

Joe would tell us," said a relative. Bruno's only son graduated from college and he was now a grandfather to two little girls. The eldest granddaughter born in 1936 laughs to memories of when jockeys would come to her grandfather's home: "I would put my feet next to the jockey's and see how big theirs were to mine." Excitement followed Joseph Bruno—not only did he frequent horse racing tracks all over the East Coast, but he often went to Washington, D.C., said a cousin. Why? "To meet with the politicians." In New Jersey, the most powerful of policy makers in government "were in his pocket," claimed a Bruno family member.[51] Wartime activities for the Philadelphia-South Jersey Friends had gambling and the numbers still as priorities, and Bruno preferred to let this source of the Family's income remain in the hands of those in the lower ranks. His influence was felt in Philadelphia when some of his more active members got pinched and needed his help, as in Angelo Bruno's case.

Angelo Bruno, as a soldier in the LCN, had a number of arrests during Joseph Bruno's tenure which added to his overall criminal record that had some guilty pleas, some acquittals, but did, nonetheless, dab more color to his character portrait. In 1937, Angelo was arrested for "disorderly conduct" at Castor and Erie Avenues in North Philadelphia, to which he paid a $10.00 fine and costs. Then in 1940 Angelo was "charged with setting up and maintaining a lottery" of "50,000 number plays" and was found guilty. His cousin from Trenton, John "Johnny Keys" Simone also was involved. Three years later, the same John Simone was running "Atlas Sanitation Service" from Trenton and was arrested on suspicion. He told police that he lived in Philadelphia, giving the address of LCN member, Joseph Lagana, a rather clean gangster who laid in the background of active Family matters. Federal law enforcement noticed that Simone "went every month to the

Trenton Police Department to remove roaches from certain sections of the police department..." accompanied by Sam DeCavalcante, who later became implicated with Angelo Bruno in an early FBI organized crime sting operation.[52]

The Philadelphia police and detectives added more arrests to Angelo Bruno's rap sheet in 1944 which showed broadened interests in his criminal career. In one arrest at his home on South Broad Street, police cited Bruno for "receiving stolen goods and violation of the Witkin Firearm Act." Local police found silver fox furs and a loaded .38 in Bruno's bureau drawer. He was found not guilty. The same year federal agents noted that Angelo Bruno "was a member of the MATTEO mob, engaged in illegal liquor traffic and the handling of prostitutes..." an allegation with little support from other sources. What seemed more in line was another bit of information the same law enforcement agency wrote: "Matteo and Bruno were running a telephone baseball gambling racket...at Seventh and Morris Streets."[53]

Most of Joseph Bruno's Family members who were arrested in the 1940s were charged in gambling-related offenses; likewise, when men such as Sabella, Scopolitti and others got insignificant arrests at this time, the crimes were non-violent ones, and these were customarily discharged, if an agreement was reached with local law enforcement.[54] Joseph Bruno's scope of influence at this time furthered his Family's power as he made the politics of crime his primary focus during his tenure. Whereas Sabella was dependent on his *paesani* in New York to assist him in law enforcement and political corruption outside of Philadelphia, and Avena had yet fewer contacts, Joseph Bruno saw the importance of widescale interstate networking to include more criminal gangs, law enforcement in the local and state offices and politicians from all three levels of government. Bruno then used the proceeds from criminal

Artist's rendering from family photograph of Joseph Bruno, taken in early 1940s, is one of only two photos existing of the former LCN boss of Philadelphia and South Jersey.

activities to unfetter the many impediments that the criminal justice system could use to hamper the progress of the LCN's activities. And apparently, Joseph Bruno's personality was well suited to work with those in higher government positions because he was very successful during these years of the Second World War.

While Bruno was in New Brunswick, another LCN associate-turned-member left Philadelphia and moved near him. Joseph Ida, living across New Brunswick in Highland Park, would have much of his personal and professional life in the LCN involved with Joseph Bruno. The latter's relatives knew Ida as a "business partner" in unspoken underworld activities who was a frequent visitor to the Bruno home. So close was their relationship that Ida's wife, Mamie was the godmother to one of Bruno's granddaughters. The arrangement between Bruno and Ida had greater meaning however, because Ida was not of Sicilian ancestry and represented an element in the faction in Avena's

Family that often caused dissent over cultural diversity. Ida was born in Calabria, mainland Italy,[55] and stood by his Calabresi *paesani* like Joseph Rugnetta, Marco Reginelli, the Piccolo men, Joseph Lagana and a few others who bought their place in Sabella's, then Avena's Family during Prohibition. They were associates at that time and only after the summer of 1931 when the LCN was formalized were these non-Sicilians given recommendation for LCN membership, based on their reputations as bootleggers or hired guns for the Sicilians. The ethnic factor had no impact on Joseph Bruno who, like Avena, was in the same category as the Calabrians as coming from a non-Mafia cultural background. Bruno and Ida were viewed as gangsters or "connected guys" not as "The Sicilians in the Protective Society" as people in South Philadelphia's Little Italy called Sabella and his ilk. The Bruno-Ida relationship was considered politically good for the Philadelphia-South Jersey Family and their friendship was equally well-meaning. Under these men, the "gangster code of silence" was better understood than *omertá*; more corporate-type of businesses colored the Organization as "American," than underworld.

There was no information obtained to verify if Joseph Bruno participated in any importing of blackmarket products, food stamp fraud or any of the pedestrian crimes associated with the restrictions imposed while the nation was at war. Bruno was an infrequent visitor to Philadelphia in its part as a major city with a Navy Yard and port of entry during World War II. Bruno's interests and goals were much higher, directed to New York or Washington, D.C. as places where his status increased just by his presence. He was said to broker deals in construction and in the waste management industries in which many Sicilian Americans in northeastern and southeastern Pennsylvania had already been involved legally, but looked to expand.[56] Still remaining inconspicuously in the background, Joseph

Bruno as boss never bore the wrath of anyone in law enforcement or in politics as his contemporaries Frank Costello, Meyer Lansky, Vito Genovese and "Lucky" Luciano in New York City. Bruno's passion for horses and horseracing perhaps brought him in contact with many of same interests, like the FBI's Director J. Edgar Hoover who undoubtedly knew that betting and the numbers rackets, with the common street number depended on this sport. From an underworld point of view, Joseph Bruno was at the top of his game and was not only a major player, but a smart player.

One of Joseph Bruno's granddaughters once asked, "But if he was a boss, where's the money?" Joseph Bruno was wealthy, but not greedy. He kept his wife and children in comfort, though not in extreme luxury, as if he were a magnate like Moe Annenberg. Riccobene said that Bruno spent more than he won at the tracks. Joseph Valachi recalled an instance when his horse beat Joseph Bruno's, despite that the race had already been fixed.[57] "Those treacherous jockeys!" Riccobene said grinning. He explained that the LCN members were always trying to get the jockeys to make certain horses win. Some jockeys unexpectedly would fall off their horses while some horses sometimes could not be controlled, so the jockeys claimed. Riccobene said that the jockeys also often pitted LCN members against each other on whether the right horses were slated to win or whether there were high stakes or not. Joseph Bruno owned many horses, basking and mixing in the company of those whom a former cabinetmaker, bartender, pimp and hitman would never imagine. His polished image as a wealthy gentleman gambler was the last "rep" he would have when he gradually was taken ill with heart problems.[58]

Joseph Bruno was admitted to a New York City hospital in October of 1946. His ten year old granddaughter came to see him frequently and would gaze at the man who so fascinated her. She told of a time when her beloved grandfather had pneumonia, yet he had left his bed to get her medicine when told she had polio. She could not forget that. At Joseph Bruno's bedside was a glass basket filled with homemade candies. "Take it," he told his little granddaughter, as a tangible memory of him. A few days later he quietly died at the age of fifty-seven of natural causes, prompted by heart failure.[59] "Nearly 400 floral pieces were received" for his funeral, carried in fourteen cars with another one hundred and forty (140) cars following his casket to burial.[60]

• • • • • • • • • •

If Joseph Bruno's importance as the Philadelphia-South Jersey boss was brushed off by previous organized crime experts, they did not review how under his leadership this Family surmounted the obstacles which Sabella and Avena had yet to overcome on a more national level. In effect, Joseph Bruno had decentralized his role while his members moved forward in more non-violent criminal activities, after considerable bloodshed and after political tactics were used to achieve control on all sides. What Joseph Bruno succeeded in best was in not having the taint of the western Sicilians' Mafia affect the integrity of the LCN as a wholly new criminal entity. Bruno's choice of maneuvering corruption was more akin to Tammany Hall, not to western Sicily, though there were similarities. He was never called a "Greaser," yet he shared the same foreign nativity and migrated as a young adult as did Sabella and Avena.

But Bruno had more in common with Avena in that no strong cultural influence encumbered him—it was a matter of accepting temptations at times when the western Sicilians refused directness. Bruno, like Avena learned and interpreted from the western Sicilians, and his own model was formed on what the LCN would be for him and his Philadelphia-South Jersey Family. The mere existence of a thriving LCN Family from 1936 to 1946 confirmed that Bruno exerted an influence at a time in which to solidify his members' standing when it was most in question. Bruno's most impressive work as boss of the Philadelphia-South Jersey Family was in establishing its position while the Lanzettis fell, while the Jewish Mob continually was hustled with arrests and while the New York and Chicago LCN Families became the pawns of aspiring politicians. Though the Philadelphia-South Jersey Family was considered in these years as passive and insignificant to those outside of law enforcement,[61] by underworld standards, Joseph Bruno's tacit upheaval to reorganize his Family's internal problems allowed key members to expand criminal interests under the eyes of a subordinated criminal justice system.

Factually, what Joseph Bruno created during his years as boss provided LCN members such as Angelo Bruno with a blueprint in which to bring the Family to yet higher levels.

This would be the mysterious Joseph Bruno's legacy to the La Cosa Nostra in the Philadelphia-South Jersey area.

• • • • • • • • • •

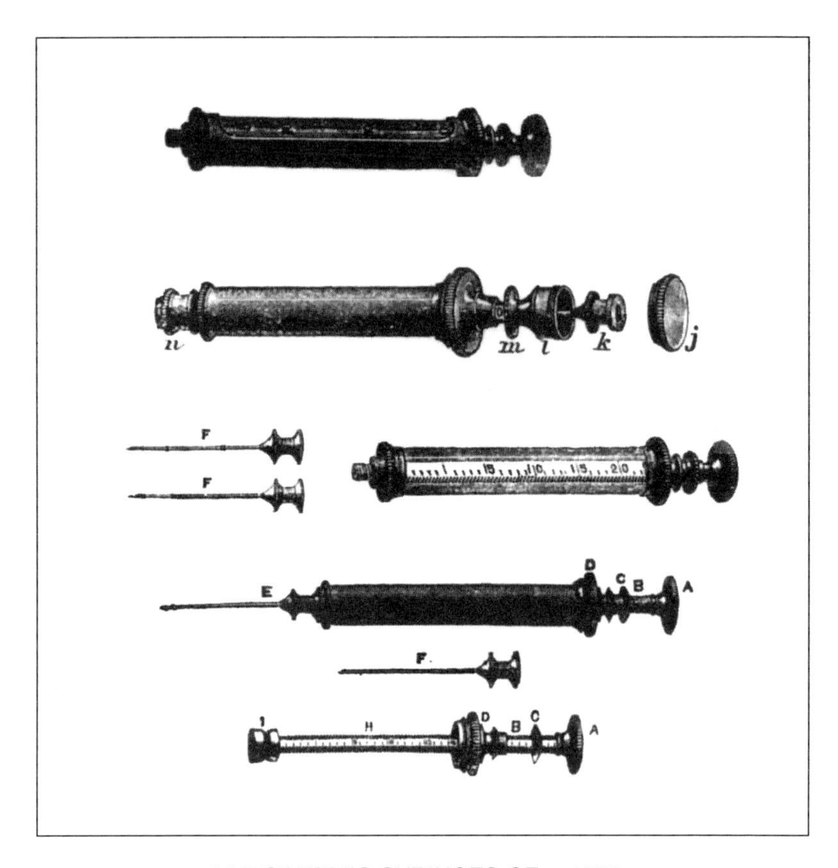

HYPODERMIC SYRINGES OF c. 1880.

These were made of glass and metal. The metal types, shown above, were made by Codman & Shurtleff of Boston. They were air-tight, "of even calibre, easily cleansed, and strong enough to withstand any ordinary blow without injury."

Needles were of plain steel, gold-plated or of pure gold.

H. H. KANE, M.D. 1880. *THE HYPODERMIC INJECTION OF MORPHIA: ITS HISTORY, ADVANTAGES & DANGERS*. NEW YORK: CHARLES L. BERMINGHAM & CO., 1880.

Chapter 7
NARCOTICS: The Future For The LCN

Hypodermic syringes used to be fashioned of metal, making them heavy and a bit cumbersome to handle for a drug addict in the early 1900s. No need to find a vein, any area will do just as well as long as the junk, whether morphine or better, heroin, got into the body. When asked about his earliest memories of narcotics in the first years of Prohibition, the boy who would be a Mafioso by 1927—that would be Harry Riccobene—has that look as if he experienced that mellow feeling of the junkies' high. Riccobene smiles and shrugs his shoulders as if illegal narcotics was nothing of particular interest. Yet, he could fully explain what kind of sensation that each drug, depressant or stimulant, caused to the user.

None of Riccobene's elders in Philadelphia's Sicilian American Mafia would be able to articulate the same. Riccobene's street experience, hanging with truants, delinquents and other teenagers who had exhausted their survivor skills in the pits of South Philadelphia was a world apart from the Mafiosi who already ran the local Family. These Mafiosi were businessmen, most born of middle class families of like values who looked upon the teenage Riccobene's peers with disgust. What did these driven men have in common with listless "dopers"? Some of the individuals selling alcohol for the Mafiosi were apparently also dealing in narcotics. During Prohibition, some salesmen found many customers with complimentary weaknesses in the vices. In time, and in times of loyalty, dealers in dope found growing, closer relationships with Sicilian American Mafiosi, the kind of relationships that were only formed and contained with common financial interests. How meaningful illegal narcotics had become to Philadelphia and to Mafiosi by the early 1930s was based on this association.[1]

Understanding why the Philadelphia La Cosa Nostra chose to become involved in what had been for the Sicilians an ideologically predatory activity was a matter of opening its options in relation to other underworld groups. The fact is that no organized crime group operating in Philadelphia in 1931 would have dismissed illegal narcotics sales because the demand for dope or "junk" had been escalating during the early years of Prohibition.[2] And the banality of human emotions in the 1920s with the parallel rises of alcohol and narcotics use was never repressed. Pleas to the federal government to criminalize the "evils" of the cocaine habit in the "Tenderloin District of Philadelphia" in the early years of the twentieth century were never heard.[3] Consequently, there was neither a legal nor a moral reprieve for actions to benefit the good of the future.

Philadelphia's nineteenth century social history of narcotics use contributed much to the results borne out in the twentieth. At least seventy years before the underworld organized a narcotics syndicate and industry, unregulated dispensing of what were supposed to be controlled substances, plus the unenforced drug laws led to widespread recreational and some misunderstood medical uses of narcotics. Well before any organized crime enterprise developed anywhere in Philadelphia, the city in 1848 was one of only six ports in the United States where inspectors checked, before distributing, the only narcotic then in demand, opium.[4] The Federal Drug Import Law, perhaps the earliest effort to identify narcotics as anti-social and, in the wrong hands, deadly, fell in the same path as other laws with noncompliance. Just as in many other American cities, opium had dual purposes in Philadelphia—as an anesthetic within the medical practice, or in "opium eating" for bored Philadelphians. Both uses fostered a gradual increase in imported opium from mostly Smyrna: in 1870, the U.S. Customs noted 254,609 pounds imported while in 1880, the annual stash rose to 533,451 pounds and "rapidly increasing in America."[5] At the same time, some Chinese in Philadelphia owned private opium dens above or below their legitimate businesses and continued a cultural practice which became adapted by white Philadelphians. Eventually, before 1900 Caucasians in the city's "Tenderloin" districts of North and South Philadelphia were found to hold their own opium sites for the mere convenience of not venturing into Chinatown and having access to the drug more directly.[6] "Hop smoking" was called a "diversion," although it was, like its derivative morphine, a depressant, a sensation not usually sought-after by the lower economic class, the typical nineteenth century narcotics user apart from the other type of user, those in the medical profession.[7]

Contemporary nineteenth century medical and recreational acceptance of the narcotic morphine ran alongside of opium in our city by the Civil War years. Doctors S. Weir Mitchell, W. W. Keen and George R. Morehouse tended to the war's wounded in Philadelphia hospitals while experimenting on gun shot wounds and performing some elementary forms of neurological surgery.[8] By 1865 they were ready to publish their findings in *On the Antagonisms of Atropia and Morphia*[9] about the use of hypodermic injections of morphia as an analgesic. The Christian Street Hospital in South Philadelphia provided to the doctors the most patients who from 1862 to the war's end had their wounds directly injected with morphine (morphia) from unsterile syringes and under unsanitary conditions. By the late 1860s, other doctors began to publish papers on using needles and narcotics;[10] nothing yet prevented the public from acquiring both and using them indiscriminately, if not haphazardly. Infected abscesses and gangrene began to appear by the 1880s on the bodies of addicts who were ignorant of cleaning the apparati and locating a proper site for injections.[11]

In Philadelphia's Victorian underworld, narcotics was also linked with prostitution, as some records from the local Magdalen Society cited difficult young females who were customarily injected with morphine to consent without their senses and to desensitize their consciences.[12] Asbury wrote that in New York a similar practice occurred; but when women were abducted for use in prostitution, they were given chloral or morphine or "drugged liquors" and then they were put out to work.[13]

Though not unique to Philadelphia, narcotics use in many urban areas in the U.S. by the 1860s had risen with word that morphine's effects could be constructive in a variety of legal and illegal activities. The medical profession dispensed with morphine to menopausal women or unruly children. Some doctors kept morphine-filled syringes in their pockets for immediate use on the unstable. Nonetheless, infuriated pharmacists cringed at the government's indifference to nostrums sold to the public such as "Dr. Bull's Cough Syrup," or "Mrs. Winslow's Soothing

Syrup" because there was no law to regulate the amount of morphine per bottle. Tolerance of morphine, a non-addictive narcotic, meant increased dosages for the desired effect.[14] By the 1890s, local newspapers ran advertisements on the treatment of "morphinism" for those who sought the drug's effects continually.

Social dilemmas led to some changes in social reactions to the broadly interpreted therapeutic uses of opium and morphine by the beginning of the twentieth century. Cocaine was then added to the list of artificial escapes used by the skilled and unskilled in all strata of society. New words, such as "doper," "dope fiend," "junk," and "junker" implied negative, degrading and even "evil" connotations to users and the products. "Physicians should guard against its unnecessary use in any form, as its influence is so charming...there is no walk in life where its victims are not found," said one Congressional report.[15] While opium and morphine mellowed users, cocaine use in the 1890s provided a different experience. One source described a gang in New York, "The Hudson Dusters," led by Red Farrell as "90%...cocaine addicts, and when under the influence of the drug were very dangerous, for they were insensible to ordinary punishment, and were possessed of great, if artificial, bravery and ferocity."[16]

Various laws were never enforced and penalties never deterred anyone involved in narcotics sales or use in the nineteenth century. The U.S. Government's endeavors proved at most, capricious. From the 1848 Drug Import Law, the Department of Agriculture was the enforcement agency; later the Department of Revenue and individual state Public Health departments were to assume some jurisdictional basis, documenting information on Philadelphia addicts and local strategies to curb availability.[17] Though ineffective, the data revealed what the new era of social reform reflected. Report after report confirmed a serious narcotics crisis in the U.S.'s major cities that needed to be addressed. But no one was certain whether the criminal justice system or the medical profession should resolve the problem of growing addictions.

What is important here is that while Sicilian American Mafiosi were in the area occupied in other matters and not narcotics, the drug problem in Philadelphia surged.[18] Who or what group was responsible is not known. But the junkies were given more choices in narcotics. Heroin now joined opium, morphine and cocaine to numb. Created in 1898, introduced into the U.S. by about 1901 and used to treat morphinism, heroin was said to be three times stronger and more deadly than morphine.[19] Some explanations that early twentieth century Philadelphians gave for their attraction to drugs were curiosity, peer pressure, or "...through association; that is not only by frequenting the company of dissolute tenderloin characters, but by association with fellow workmen and men met in pool rooms and saloons." Addicted married couples, families and individuals identified themselves as narcotics users and were hooked on injecting morphine or heroin. They were Protestant, Catholic, Jewish, mostly Caucasian and lower to lower-middle class, some employed as domestics, as factory workers, in sales, in entertainment and aged mostly between fourteen to thirty. Some of these addicts in 1915 claimed to use from only two to about twenty-four syringes per month.[20] *The Narcotic Evil in Philadelphia and Pennsylvania,* published in 1916 still left society wondering what to do with this social problem which was unlike those contemporary issues of immigrant assimilation and discord throughout Europe and Russia. The federal Harrison Act of 1914, primarily an Internal Revenue law, and the state Anti-Narcotic Act of 1917, interpreted more as a "public health measure," had failed. These acts established that narcotics was considered then as immoral, but not yet as a criminal activity to be controlled through the courts.

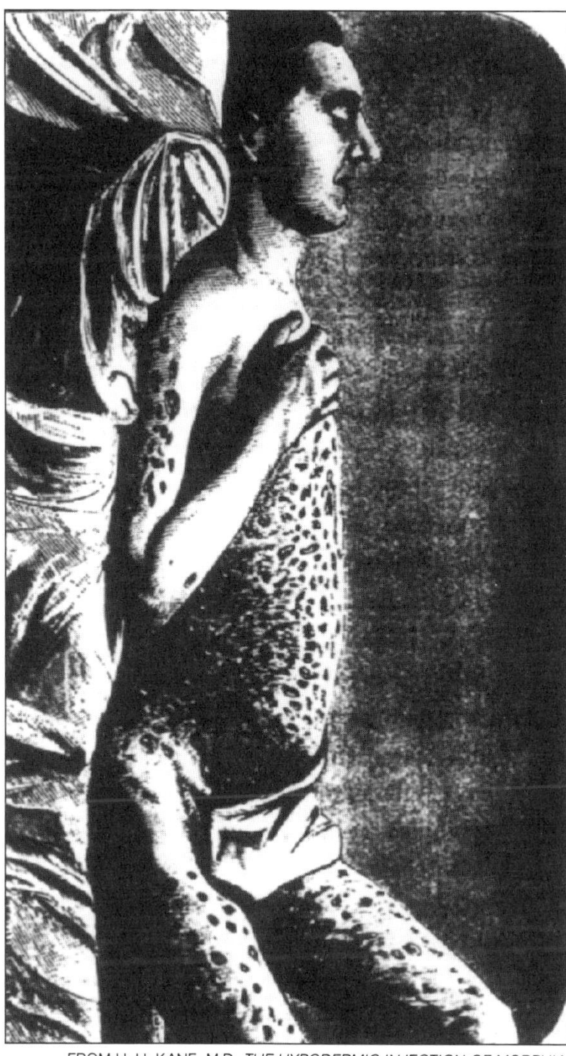

FROM H. H. KANE, M.D. *THE HYPODERMIC INJECTION OF MORPHIA: ITS HISTORY,ADVANTAGES & DANGERS*. NEW YORK: CHARLES L. BERMINGHAM & CO., 1880

This male nurse from Belleview Hospital in New York used to steal physicians' needles to maintain his addiction. Abscesses resulted from each injection; later, infection. Dr. H. H. Kane used this woodcut to emphasize the dangers of morphia addiction. Opposition to Kane's study blamed the invention of the hypodermic syringe for not just drug addiction, but to deaths from gangrene, tetanus and other infections from the unsterilized instruments. The reason why so many infected abscesses appear on this man's torso is because it was believed that drugs were absorbed faster by an injection to the abdominal area. Later, injections to the arms and legs were made. Rarely were injections given to the largest muscle, the gluteus maximus in Victorian America.

This individual was the typical (male) morphia addict of his time: most addicts were in the medical profession, notably doctors. Dr. Kane wrote that this male nurse died shortly after this woodcut was made, but did not indicate the cause of death.

During this pre-World War I period when some Philadelphia homicides attributed deaths to narcotics' influence, one "Drug Fiend" named Carl Kenlock shot an innocent Anna Phillips in the chest; a few years later in 1917, "John Ford took George E. Tangway [to Eleventh and Lombard Streets] and he asked Ford for some dope Ford pushed a needle in his arm and Tangway was taken to said hospital unconscious..." The cause of death: "Poison from Heroine [sic]." Some months later, another homicide involved a female who pled guilty to involuntary manslaughter before Judge John Monaghan for killing James Murphy by "Dose of herroine [sic]." According to the police report, "Murphy asked her to get some Dope for him which she did and gave it to him by useing [sic] a syringe and he collappesed [sic] and was sent to said Hospital where he died 11^{30} PM."[21] These fatal incidents may have highlighted the desperation and anxiety overlaying the seediness of drug addiction at the time by so many who were exposed to them.

Enslavement to an artificial substance, alteration of one's senses and loss of self-control were personally repulsive to Sicilian American Mafiosi. On another level, Mafiosi, and generally, the western Sicilians of the middle class were at odds with any impediment to progress in the advancement of wealth and material gains. The ordinary drug addict was usually not driven to much in his/her non-combative, passive, vulnerable mood and as a source of income from narcotics sales, the user was unreliable if unemployable.[22] Depressants seemed to have more followers in the 1920s, although cocaine enabled many to function well after a sniff. Overall, narcotics were viewed as a low-end market, but the potential for greater sales came with the rising numbers of users and addicts.[23]

In the early years of the twentieth century a black market and underworld assumed more control of drug sales for profit but it is unknown if distribution was by a single criminal or a criminal entity. Such doubt about non-legal narcotics sales in Philadelphia led to some investigation on how drugs came into the city. Narcotics were found to have been mailed to addicts; the Postal Service never followed on leads on who were the senders.[24] Otherwise, the Commonwealth of Pennsylvania enacted regulatory statutes to standardize record-keeping by anyone with legitimate reason to requisite and to dispense narcotics, hence the beginning of the prescription pad and registered identification of doctors, dentists and veterinarians.[25] But the attempt to create a paper trail was of brief interest because many doctors did not want to disclose any evidence of prescription narcotics whether it was for a patient's therapeutic use or continued addiction. Apparently, within the medical community the development of criminal activity for narcotics use and sales began at this time.

By 1919, the U.S. Department of the Treasury estimated that there were one to four million drug addicts residing in the nation.[26] Recognizing these findings and the "criminal type of addict" identified by the early 1920s pressed law enforcement to establish its first Narcotics Squad in the Philadelphia Police Department. Here, narcotics use and crime suddenly become synonymous. Drug offenses in 1921 ranged from elementary use to possession to "peddling," which differed from "dealing" and from "selling." (Refer to chart, p. 192.) And if police only suspected drug use, peddling or possession, there would be an arrest. Needless to say, users garnered the most arrests. But sometimes the user under the influence was subject to the substance's effects to commit serious crime. This was the case when Patrolman Charles Brendley intercepted a drug sale between two white males at Ninth and Christian Streets in 1919. One individual put a revolver to the officer's abdomen,

NARCOTICS ARRESTS IN PHILADELPHIA IN 1921	HELD	DISCHARGED
Dealer in drugs	3	1
Drugs	124	125
Illegal selling of drugs	11	10
Illegal possession of drugs	44	1
Illegal possession of narcotics	3	1
Opium smoking	2	
Peddling drugs	5	2
Possession of drugs	128	26
Selling dope	18	6
Suspicion of selling drugs	2	4
Suspicion of using drugs	20	24
Suspicion of peddling drugs	1	3
Suspicion of possession of drugs	7	10
User of drugs	179	110
TOTAL	547	323

ANNUAL NARCOTICS ARRESTS IN PHILADELPHIA	1920	1921	1922
Narcotic drugs, selling and possessing	269	331	352
Narcotic drug users	524	448	683
ANNUAL TOTAL	793	779	1035

Source: Report Crimes Survey, published by the Law Association of Philadelphia, 1926.

but the officer fired first and killed the user/dealer.[27] Another homicide in 1921 occurred when one white male in South Philadelphia while injecting himself was brutally stabbed by his male roommate. Philadelphia policemen found the tragic crime scene—blood-splattered drug paraphernalia and the corpse lying in the waste it created.[28]

There were some sources which refer to the Jewish mobsters as organizing an early narcotics sales network on the East Coast that would have included Philadelphia. Asbury wrote on Monk Eastman and others who sold and used narcotics, though not exclusively; then Block and Chambliss followed with this information and found several Jewish gangsters forming cocaine "trade networks" to

Philadelphia and other cities on the Atlantic seaboard before Prohibition.[29]

These accounts served more as findings based on ethnic cohesion, not necessarily gang dynamics, which was the case in Philadelphia. Assumptions along ethnic lines can be too much of an oversimplification. In Philadelphia, immigration, settlement and acculturation was uneven at this World War I period because the course and flow of immigration by eastern and southern Europeans was constant from about 1875 to 1930, a very long time frame in which to reckon economic, social and political developments. The place and time of settlement then, would seem to indicate how and if there was commingling of ethnic groups and the formation of criminals into gangs for the purpose of living off illegal activities.

In Philadelphia, while there may have been ethnic majorities in some neighborhoods, such as “Little Italy,” no community in the north, south or west of Center City had true ethnic homogeneity. Philadelphia’s census records of 1900 and 1910 most clearly proved the diversity of races and foreign origins of Philadelphia row house residents, allowing for some acceptance of each’s cultural background. Residential mobility, as Warner had shown, also accounted for more heterogeneity.[30] Likewise, the case in Philadelphia denied any one criminal group, whether ethnically-based on the surface or not, to control local narcotics distribution and sales. *Narcotics Education*, a compilation of data from local and some international drug enforcement agencies opened the eyes of many in Philadelphia to this world-wide problem of addictions and availability to illicit drugs. Some of the city’s most noteworthy justices addressed what they encountered in the courtrooms: Judge Harry S. McDevitt, along with then-judge John Monaghan, had in the early 1920s waged their continuing battles against users and drug dealers with “hundreds of convictions.” McDevitt in fact mentioned without referring to any group in particular that a "well organized" drug ring in Philadelphia "kept books on when addicts were committed and discharged..." He added that one of the goals to this local narcotics monopoly was targetting private, public and parochial school children as young as six years old.[31] Judge McDevitt dryly commented to those at the 1926 Narcotics Conference that in Philadelphia drug addicts were of all ages, colors and creeds, and further, "...the public does not cooperate; they do not care...and they don't want to know" about the dope or junkies. Sergeant Francis J. Dunn of the Philadelphia Police's Narcotics Squad named two certain sites in the city where narcotics activity was the heaviest: at Eighth and Vine Streets, and at Eighth and Christian Streets. Dunn claimed that "...if a drug addict alighted from a trolley car and walked the corner there was a gun battle over which peddler would sell the man narcotics."

This was in the mid-1920s, when the illegal narcotics use represented "...a steady increase at an alarming rate" throughout the United States. As part of the Sesquicentennial Celebration in Philadelphia, the convention of politicians, law enforcement and corrections officers concluded that "...the country...is absolutely asleep to the evil of drug addiction."[32] Philadelphia General Hospital's doctors had spent years with "reduction" techniques or substituting veronal or luminal pills to patients who were addicts in lieu of the harsher substance. Despite the doctors' efforts to research whether narcotics had either a physiological or purely a psychological effect on the addict, the drug dealers were ahead.[33]

One of Judge McDevitt's more memorable convictions was of "dope peddler" Hyman Cohen and three of the Lanzetti brothers in 1923. Cohen purportedly made a confession that a "dope syndicate" was operating in Philadelphia which included the Lanzettis. Leo Lanzetti had been arrested in 1921 for narcotics offenses that failed to steer him or his brothers from future narcotics use and sales. By 1924, the Lanzettis were taking turns going up to New York every Monday, Wednesday and Friday to get dope for "hop heads."[34] Though possibly the most publicized dopers and junk peddlers in Philadelphia, the Lanzettis were major players in what were mass arrests: Judge McDevitt claimed to have tried over two hundred drug sellers and one thousand addicts in only two months in 1922.[35] By 1926, there was an estimated 30,000 to 40,000 addicts living in Philadelphia.[36] Exaggerations made by the local press called the Lanzettis the "principals in a dope-selling ring," and the 800 block of Christian Street in Little Italy was called, "Dope Row."[37] In fact, the 800 block of Christian was where the Italian Provincial of the Augustinian Order had their church, Our Lady of Good Counsel, the rectory, convent and school which held about two thousand children.[38] Priests and nuns, pushcarts and shoppers—how these scenes of the 1920s often were confused with Prohibition's deadly high risk players in crimes and substance abuses was extraordinary, to say the least. But throughout the city the silent cries about narcotics' sleaziness, its withdrawal effects, injecting or snorting, the sores on junkies' bodies...few could attach the fun and gaiety of drinking liquor to the moroseness of heroin, morphine and opium.

The 1920s in Philadelphia were years of change for all organized crime groups and of course, a pivotal time in which the Sicilian American Mafia slowly fell to the influence of the local underworld. While Salvatore Sabella and his Friends or peers were too occupied with Family, family and business affairs, no one gave too much thought on who would comprise the next generation of Mafiosi. Whereas in western Sicily there was concern for the perpetuity of the Mafia, in Philadelphia, the priority was in making substantial monetary gains, which to Mafiosi wives made more sense than the foreign Tradition. Far more mobile and less stabilized in local society in the Philadelphia-South Jersey area than in Sicily, the Sicilian American Mafiosi felt the pressure of the New York axis powers to maintain a working, high income-producing Family during Prohibition. Gentile wrote that all of the Mafia Families in the U.S. had agreed during Prohibition to become involved in alcohol sales and distribution, not with narcotics, even as an ancillary income.[39]

Given that the senior Mafiosi in Sabella's Mafia Family were more removed from the common gangsters and the rest of the city's underworld, the same could not be said of the youngest Friend. "I was the only one [in Sabella's Family] to foresee a market for drugs," mused Harry Riccobene. He knew who in South Philadelphia was doing and dealing junk. "Teo" Lanzetti, "was the worst drug user" of the Lanzetti brothers, Riccobene said. Teo shot heroin, while his brother, Willie often chose, "the pipe," i.e., opium. Riccobene remembered narcotics use in Philadelphia during his adolescence in the 1920s as "very widespread." He recalled the morphine and heroin users secreted their spoons and needles in pockets or in little pencil box-type cases. Pimps and prostitutes, as well as the wealthy in Philadelphia chemically clouded their minds with narcotics brought down to the city from New York. At the same time that streetwise Riccobene was maturing to adulthood, drugs began to be peddled throughout Philadelphia, now for a profit.

Riccobene may have been able to stave off any narcotics arrests during Sabella's tenure as boss because both were in New York for about twenty months to fight in the Castellammarese Wars. However, in 1932 under LCN boss John Avena, the Philadelphia police collared twenty-two year old Riccobene who nixed any compromise, remaining incarcerated for two years at Holmesburg Prison on what would be the first of many narcotics offenses.[40]

This incident may have been a point of reference for some Philadelphia Mafiosi who were traditionalists, and they were few. Riccobene, who was a member of the Philadelphia Family for at least five years before his arrest, was in "battle" with Sabella for almost two years and was pinched by the local police actually "took a rap" without the fear of shame. Unlike other Friends in the Philadelphia-South Jersey Family, Riccobene, the youngest, had a growing criminal record which he did not seem to mind. He had an attitude as the Italian American gangster who scoffed at jail time. In Avena's Family, Riccobene found similar characters though from mainland Italy, the new recruits, the gamblers mostly, who had dealt with narcotics or had indifferent opinions about drugs. During Prohibition, these mobsters noticed that those who preferred opium and morphine were occasional users, considered as non-addicts and partook of drugs sporadically. Heroin though, was reputed to have long term, exclusive use. Many of the heroin addicts in the 1930s most likely became addicted when there was a rise in drug use throughout Philadelphia between 1910 and 1915.[41] Though it became the "...leading and most dangerous drug of addiction" by the mid-1920s, Philadelphia physicians noted the relative ease of trafficking in heroin, more than any other narcotic.[42] By the 1930s both underworld figures and doctors realized that heroin addicts were "hopeless."[43] But these dopers, such as George Benz, born in 1897 and using heroin with his friends since 1914 claimed fifteen years later that he still enjoyed the drug's effects.[44]

Local law enforcement's arrests on drug dealers correlated to arrests for alcohol offenders by the late 1920s: with very little attention from whatever agency had jurisdiction over narcotics sales, there was easy entry into the city, making Philadelphia an open market for many drug lords to govern.[45] National law enforcement by the mid-1930s had been identifying narcotics smugglers and ports of entry for the contraband, but again, Philadelphia did not rank with New York or even New Orleans as a point for investigation, at least with importation. An opportunity for some individual or group to organize illegal narcotics sales and distribution in Philadelphia arose by the early 1930s, but John Avena was not interested. A. Domenico Pollina "told my father to stay away from the Lanzettis and drugs," said the boss' son, Salvatore J. Avena, Esquire, although Riccobene, Peter Casella and Frank Piccolo ranked among Family members with narcotics convictions. In Avena's tenure as the first LCN boss of the Philadelphia-South Jersey Family, there was not a full, complete transition from a Sicilian American Mafia to an American Mafia. Rather, some acceptance of illegal activities, such as narcotics represented the more progressive direction of the new type of criminal organization. Thus began at this time some LCN members who were drug dealers and the narcotics as sources of some profit.

Angelo Bruno, an initiate under Avena was certainly aware of narcotics sales by his fellow Friends who in the 1930s were no less respected and called "men of honor" just as he. Bound by the same oaths as the LCN members-drug dealers, Bruno had to accept this development as a fact of the Organization. Angelo Bruno's personal views on narcotics sales as a source of profits therefore, had to be put aside in order for the greater advantages to affect the Family's economic power and prominence within the local underworld. That Bruno claimed to have "kept drugs out of Philadelphia" was a fallacy—he was a part of this new American Mafia in the early 1930s which at the inception had to acknowledge what other Families in the U.S. had at the same time. Bruno saw that Friends contributed drug profits to the Family in the 1930s and he allowed the same when he was a boss thirty years later. Narcotics profits were in Angelo Bruno's LCN heritage—why would he have discouraged anyone in his Family from making money that would eventually have gone to him?[46]

Avena's execution confirmed that gambling and bookmaking were the bases of his operation and the chief sources of the Family's power. Why some of his LCN members sought diversification suggested that perhaps there was more simplicity in supplying drugs to a middleman for fast money. Or, there may have been a connection with some of Avena's newer members and those involved in prostitution, or white slavery. Nevertheless, in the 1930s in Philadelphia, there were no significant arrests of gangsters for narcotics as there were in New York with Luciano, Vito Genovese and Jewish mobster Louis "Lepke" Buchalter. While there was national recognition of narcotics together with criminality, the law succeeded with more creative arrests that combined narcotics with homicide and prostitution offenses. But nothing like this happened in Philadelphia. This does not mean however, that the Philadelphia-South Jersey Family was not on par with the other Families in the United States. On the contrary, while gambling may have been more popular than narcotics in the 1930s, the break with the "past," i.e., the Sicilian American Mafia, was realized in the high price of a commodity with the illegal status which narcotics had. Mafioso Joseph Bonanno had written on the Mafia's ethic concerning drugs: "My Tradition outlaws narcotics. It had always been understood that 'men of honor' don't deal in narcotics. However, the lure of high profits had tempted some underlings to freelance in the narcotics trade."[47] He described this as the attitude of the consensus of his peers in 1956, when about two decades before, Sicilian-born Mafioso Nick Gentile implied that *trafficanti di stupefacenti* (drug dealers) had relieved him immediately of a dwindling cash flow with fast, large sums of money.[48]

The Philadelphia-South Jersey Family under Avena, then under Joseph Bruno never showed signs of resistance to the involvement of narcotics in the 1930s to 1940s. The pressure on local LCN members came from efforts to make an appearance to conform to what other Families were doing, especially in New York with their contemporaries and with the Jewish gangsters. There was a perception that LCN members were only involved in gambling while multi-criminal activities such as narcotics and prostitution, like loan sharking, were tangential to most of the Philadelphia-South Jersey men who rose from gangster to LCN member. Gambling was less stigmatizing of course, but the dicta of the New York axis Families persuaded the "men of honor" to become involved in narcotics as a product. Sworn to obey the Organization, LCN members dared not to deny the Family any potential earnings from narcotics. Stalling this command then became the focus for anyone from the local Family in the 1940s through the 1990s.

• • • • • • • • • •

On the surface it would seem that during the period 1931 to 1946, the history of the Philadelphia-South Jersey LCN would be consistent with the history of the New York and Chicago Mafias, especially within the context of the immigrant's role in major crime. Philadelphia ranked third in the United States in its Italian-born population by the beginning of the twentieth century. But this city had particular problems with the newly arrived from Italy and Sicily not found to exist in New York or Chicago, and that influenced the character of its La Cosa Nostra Family.

Violence at will, by and against those of Italian ancestry, came early and stayed late with this ethnic group. This issue ran through this discourse of the Philadelphia-South Jersey LCN to mark the position that this Family held among its contemporaries in the U.S. Italian crime and criminality first were distinguished to emphasize identifying traits and origins, whether foreign or native to the U.S. The Italian offender, as viewed distinctly from the Sicilian Mafioso had risen in criminality in Philadelphia similarly in typology to the mid-nineteenth century Irish American Catholics. They were from the same neighborhoods and challenged their own people through victimization, a quality not shared by the Mafiosi. Such intraethnic violence by all immigrants responding to problems in assimilation would seem to validate the "Ethnic Succession Theory" in criminology. However, this concept alone does not explain why a majority of one particular ethnic group such as the Italians would not fall into criminality when presented with various adversities, disadvantages and inabilities. In the Philadelphia case, this theory also cannot answer why there was a very lengthy term of intraethnic violence in the Italian colony that spanned generations.

The Italian and Sicilian-born offenders generally found support from local government and its criminal justice system in Philadelphia. This characterization though, should not be construed so simply. The Philadelphia case's history was not without references to the still-developing police department, to new social services for immigrants, to the city's handling of the effects of Prohibition and to the corrupt District Attorney and judges who were ruled by local politicians. Moreover, no group, ethnically-based or otherwise, dominated the underworld in the city at any time, which left the organizing of criminal activities in a vacuum, open for competition and additional serious crime.

Certainly, economics was the primary reason why the violence occurred in Philadelphia among Italians and Sicilians who may or may not have pursued criminality as a profession. But class differences, social attitudes and values also contributed to intraethnic violence in the city. There was a notable absence of what types of crimes that the western Sicilian-born Mafiosi may have been engaged in the 1880 to 1920 period because of their standing in mainstream society and legitimate work. Unlike the Mafiosi, the Italian-born, then later the Italian American criminal was described as a former idler and street corner lounger who willfully chose low level criminal activity in order to earn income. Groups of these men then emerged to form gangs who became involved in more complicated crimes.

Clearly, the relationships that Mafiosi held within their social sphere, as well as outside, with Philadelphia's criminal justice system, was at odds with the singularity of the early generic Italian criminal who affected the behavior of the rootless common thug. Without a large, strong and specific colony of Italians or Sicilians in Philadelphia, the newcomer in Little Italy could act without the shame imposed by fellow *paesani*. The criminal typology of the gangster, however, represented what kind of member would be taken into the local LCN while the Mafiosi resigned themselves to more socially responsible and legal endeavors. The LCN member would prevail in the Philadelphia-South Jersey LCN Family and cause the organization to continue to fall behind other major organized crime centers as the years followed.

The LCN bosses in this book, John Avena and Joseph Bruno represented quite a change from Salvatore Sabella's Family. In effect, Avena, the first LCN boss of Philadelphia, and his successor, Joseph Bruno, advanced their careers based on intraethnic victimization, and then later, mostly from the non-violent offenses of gambling and narcotics. Focussed in the blue-collared neighborhoods of Philadelphia and surrounding communities, gambling especially took a higher death toll than illegal alcohol. Ambiguously perceived by the local residents as either providing recreation or escapes from their boring lives, underworld types under Avena and Bruno cultivated the vices of gambling and narcotics to be used as income-generating means in the neighborhood culture. In the Philadelphia case, gambling kept the LCN Family intact within the confines of Little Italy's row houses, where the gangster-turned-LCN member reigned. Also during the tenures of Avena and Bruno, the Philadelphia neighborhood residents acquired the "fear-respect" response to the new image of the Italian American gangster who offered some relief to the disadvantaged when the rest of society failed during the Depression and its aftermath.

Though not as important as gambling within the Philadelphia-South Jersey LCN, narcotics was silently condoned by Family members at this early date. Friends Harry Riccobene and Peter Casella were convicted on narcotics offenses, yet were never reprimanded or ostracized for their activities or viewed with less esteem by their peers. Illegal drugs eventually proved to be an option in the wider scheme for profits in which the Philadelphia-South Jersey Family was instructed to participate, if only as a condition to sustaining itself in the national LCN network for the future.

• • • • • • • • • •

Notes

Introduction Notes

1. Please refer to HUMBERT S. NELLI'S *The Business of Crime: Italians and Syndicate Crime in the United States.* Chicago: The University of Chicago Press, 1976; MARK H. HALLER'S "Organized Crime in Urban Society: Chicago in the Twentieth Century" in *The Journal of Social History,* Volume V, pp. 210-234, (1971-1972); DONALD CRESSEY'S "The Functions and Structure of Criminal Syndicates," in the *Task Force Report: Organized Crime, U.S. President's Commission on Law Enforcement and Administration of Justice,* Washington, D.C.: U.S. Government Printing Office, 1967, and *Theft of the Nation: The Structure and Operations of Organized Crime in America*, New York: Harper & Row, 1969; and DANIEL BELL'S article, "Crime as an American Way of Life," in *The Antioch Review,* 13, 1953, pp. 131-154.
2. FRANCIS A. J. IANNI was best known for applying the "Ethnic Succession" theory to his work in examining cultural aspects of various ethnic and racial groups in relation to criminal activities for economic gain. Refer to his *A Family Business.* New York: Russell Sage Foundation, 1972; "New Mafia: Black, Hispanic and Italian styles," in *Society*, Volume 2, March–April 1974, pp. 23-36; *Black Mafia: Ethnic Succession in Organized Crime*, New York: Simon & Schuster, 1974.

Notes to Chapter I

1. Philadelphia Police Homicide Unit's indices, Volume 1, 3 to 9, 1892 to October 7, 1933 cover violent deaths in each page.
2. Because crime history is still essentially an area deserving of more exploration, there is quite a dearth of historical writing especially in Philadelphia, where crime historiography is vague or lacking—the references to immigrants engaged in criminal activities were often found in immigration history. One of the best sources is ALLEN F. DAVIS and MARK H. HALLER (Eds.), *The Peoples of Philadelphia: A History of Ethnic Groups and Lower Class Life, 1870–1940*, Philadelphia: Temple University Press, 1973.
3. ROGER LANE, *Violent Death in the City: Suicide, Accident & Murder in Nineteenth Century Philadelphia*, Cambridge: Harvard University Press, 1979, p. 133.
4. RICHARD N. JULIANI, *Building Little Italy: Philadelphia's Italians Before Mass Migration*, University Park: Pennsylvania State University Press, 1998, pp. 134-6; 138; 214-5.
5. ROGER LANE, *William Dorsey's Philadelphia and Ours*, New York: Oxford University Press, 1991, p. 268.
6. LANE, *Violent Death*, p. 102.
7. The best source which argues on the foundation of a negative Italian stereotype is in RICHARD GAMBINO'S *Vendetta*, New York: Doubleday & Company, 1977. Gambino also provided a substantial

amount of historical data on the Italian response to the American Government's indemnities to the lynchings of Italian-born and Italian Americans in 1891.

8. LANE, *Violent Death*, p. 53.
9. *Ibid.*, p. 27.
10. ROGER LANE, *Murder in America: A History*, Columbus, Ohio: Ohio State University Press, 1997, p. 188.
11. Philadelphia Police Homicide Volume 3.
12. These words were found in the homicides of May 13, 1910, June 12, 1910, August 5, 1910, September 18, 1910, July 4, 1911, July 16, 1911, August 8, 1911 and many more in Volume 3.
13. Philadelphia Police Homicide record of March 12, 1910, Volume 3. *The Philadelphia Inquirer,* May 9, 1910.
14. All information on the detectives and doctors of Italian ancestry were noted in the Philadelphia Police Homicide Volumes 3, 4 and 5.
15. Please refer to GOPSILL's Business Directories of Philadelphia; BOYD'S Business/City Directories; POLK'S City Directories; and the Philadelphia City Directories from 1900 to 1910. Gopsill's Directories are at either Temple University's Urban Archives or at the Historical Society of Pennsylvania, as the others.
16. RICHARD VARBERO, *Philadelphia's South Italians in the 1920s*, in DAVIS & HALLER'S *Peoples of Philadelphia*, pp. 255-275.
17. *Ibid.*, pp. 262-264.
18. STEFANO LUCONI, "Bringing Out the Italian-American Vote in Philadelphia," in *The Pennsylvania Magazine of History and Biography*. Volume CXVII, Number 4, October 1993, p. 282.
19. CAROLINE GOLAB, "The Immigrant and The City: Poles, Italians, and Jews in Philadelphia, 1870-1920" in DAVIS AND HALLER, *Peoples of Philadelphia,* pp. 214-5.
20. LANE, *Murder in America,* pp. 235-6.
21. According to the Philadelphia Police Homicide index, eight (8) deaths occurred to residents of North Philadelphia, seven (7) of the deaths were of South Philadelphia residents all of whom but one were of Italian ancestry. Of the eighteen (18) total arsenic deaths, five (5) were of non-Italian ancestry. Of those indicted who pled guilty were Herman Petrillo of Langhorne, Pennsylvania; Carina

Favata and Agnes Mandiuk of North Philadelphia; Morris Bolber; Joseph Swartz of West Philadelphia; Grace Giovanetti and Providenza. Micicce of South Philadelphia.

22. As cited in STUART PALMER, *The Psychology of Murder*, New York: Thomas Y. Crowell Company, 1960, p. 4.

23. LANE in *Murder in America* cited Professor H. C. Brearly's homicide figures in the U.S. in the 1920s to average 8.4 deaths per 100,000. "Only the provinces of southern Italy had higher rates than the overall U.S. average, but even there the 22.0 (rate) for Sicily was topped by the 30.0 for the state of Florida." p. 229. On page 239, Lane opined that Brearly's statistics may have been "flawed," depending on Brearly's sources and what type of death description was reviewed.

24. *Ibid.*, p. 258 cited from MARVIN WOLFGANG'S *Patterns of Criminal Homicide*, (1957). Wolfgang found that the 1920 murder rate in Philadelphia was 9.3 per 100,000 while in the years 1948 to 1952 the rate was 5.7 per 100,000.

• • • • • • • • •

Notes to Chapter II

1. DAVID R. JOHNSON, *Policing the Urban Underworld: The Impact of Crime on the Development of the American Police, 1800–1887.* Philadelphia: Temple University Press, 1979, p. 79.
2. *Ibid.*, pp. 88-89.
3. LANE, *Murder in America*, pp. 158-9.
4. Please refer to the work which became the foundation for the "Bowery Boys" series, HERBERT ASBURY'S *The Gangs of New York: An Informal History of the Underworld.* New York: Capricorn Books, 1927, in addition to the studies of JOHNSON in *Policing the Urban Underworld* and MARVIN WOLFGANG'S *Patterns in Criminal Homicide.* Philadelphia: 1958, upon which this composite was drawn.
5. Scopoletti's rap sheet included arrests noted in the Philadelphia Police Homicide indices of April 24, 1917 and October 3, 1920; Department of Justice, Federal Bureau of Investigation records noted an arrest by Atlantic City Police on September 1, 1917, File PH 92-445 of August 28, 1958, p. 11.

   Joseph Ida was arrested by the Philadelphia Police as a "suspicious character" on August 7, 1915. FBI File NK 92-381 of April 21, 1958, p. 5; FBI File NK 92-381, of September 21, 1963, p. 2, as "Giuseppi Iddie."

   Joseph Bruno's arrest record dates before the 1920s. His Petition for Naturalization from 1917 cited a "serious criminal charge" which cannot now be determined because no records currently exist to confirm what the felony was. Bruno's criminal record expanded when he went to Pennsylvania, then to New Jersey in the 1920s on.

John Avena's first arrest was in Philadelphia in about 1914. Source: Massachusetts Department of Corrections, File #15775.

Marco Reginelli's first arrest, quite late at age 22, was by the Philadelphia Police as a "suspicious character" on January 12, 1920.

6. These were only some of the motives or reasons behind the Italian-on-Italian homicides where noted on the indices from 1892 to 1899, then again from 1909 through the 1920s. Source: Philadelphia Police Homicide Records Volumes 1, 3 to 5.
7. LANE, *Violent Death*, p. 102.
8. Refer to 5n; the narcotics and gambling charges against future LCN members occurred in the 1920s and 1930s as recorded in the same FBI files.
9. CAROLINE GOLAB, *Immigrant Destinations*, Philadelphia: Temple University Press, 1977, p. 58.
10. The BOYD'S and POLK'S City Directories and Philadelphia City Business Directories note the professionals and store owners from the "laborers" in Little Italy in the 1880s through to the 1930s. These directories also list whether the store owner lived atop his business or elsewhere outside of South Philadelphia.
11. GOLAB, *Immigrant Destinations*, p. 58.
12. Sources include the FBI files of Joseph Ida and Angelo Bruno, Philadelphia Police Homicide Records, Volumes 1, 3 to 9 and the Philadelphia Police Records of Arrest, c. 1913 to 1930.
13. Philadelphia Police Homicide Record of June 25, 1919, August 26, 1919, September 7, and September 15, 1919, Volumes 4 and 5.
14. *Ibid.*
15. BOYD'S City Directory of 1915; Philadelphia City Directory of 1919–1920. Quite a few men not identified as Sicilian American Mafiosi by law enforcement also appear: George Catania, a "grocer," George Catanese, "Grocer," Joseph Maggio "Cheese," and Sebastiano Restuccia, "Grocer," all Mafiosi and all businessmen. Their identities were verified by another Mafioso. Directories found in the Historical Society of Pennsylvania, Philadelphia.

16. WILLIAM J. FLYNN, *The Barrel Mystery*, New York: The James A. McCann Company, 1919, discussed the Giuseppe Morello Mafia networks with the counterfeiting, fencing and theft ring—Morello also had contacts in every major U.S. city in the East, Midwest and South, as well as in Canada, alleged Flynn. Morello's operational base was in New York City. Philadelphia was also one of Morello's network cities, but there was no Mafioso or gangster in Philadelphia who had a comparable illegal business network. The quote was from p. 97.

17. See FLYNN'S *Barrel Mystery*, NICK GENTILE'S *Vita di Capomafia*, Milan: Editori Riuniti, 1963, and JOSEPH BONANNO'S *A Man of Honor: An Autobiography*, New York: Simon & Schuster, 1983.

18. These men supported these churches in South Philadelphia's Little Italy area and their names sometimes appeared as benefactors.

19. HUMBERT S. NELLI, *The Business of Crime*, gives a breakdown of some Sicilians' financial holdings in New Orleans, pp. 270-1, 6n and 7n; GENTILE in *Vita*, pp. 25, 38-75; IANNI, *A Family Business*, p. 177; MORELLO, *Before Bruno, Book 1,* pp. 8, 12, 16-17, 124-5. "Zu Ninu" was one of my great-grandfathers; other Norristown Mafiosi who were identified were checked through the Montgomery County business directories for their employment status.

20. Refer to individual cases found the *The New York Times* indices from 1902 to 1912.

21. GENTILE, *Vita,* pp. 24, 55-57.

22. Refer to the demographical studies of Phildelphia and the residential mobility of the immigrants from the 1880s to 1930s in SAM BASS WARNER'S *The Private City: Philadelphia in Three Periods of its Growth* (Second Edition), Philadelphia: University of Pennsylvania Press, 1968; THEODORE HERSHBERG'S *Philadelphia: Work, Space, Family, and Group Experience in the Nineteenth Century-Essays Toward an Interdisciplinary History of the City*, New York: Oxford University Press, 1981; and WILLIAM G. CUTLER, III'S and HOWARD GILLETTE, JR.'S, *The Divided Metropolis: Social and Spatial Dimensions of Philadelphia*, 1800–1975. Westport, Connecticut: Greenwood Press, 1980.

23. Frank Piccolo was one of the Piccolos cited in Philadelphia law enforcement records as "associates" and/or "members" of the La Cosa Nostra Family. All were of mainland Italian (Calabrian) ancestry. The cases cited were from February 23, 1917, September

28, 1918, November 7, 1918 and January 24, 1919. An LCN member confirmed that Gaetano Bruno was a Mafioso in Philadelphia at that time.

24. Though not noted in the homicide report in the list of arrests in this April 24, 1917 death, a twenty-seven year old John Scopolitti was named in *The Evening Bulletin's* account of the murder. Battaglia was convicted of second degree murder and sentenced from nineteen to twenty years on February 17, 1922. Falcone, also known as "Mickey Britt" also received a long sentence. Source: Philadelphia Police Homicide Record of March 20, 1919, Volume 5.

25. David R. Johnson, *American Law Enforcement: A History,* Arlington Heights, Illinois: Forum Press, 1981, p. 115.

26. Philadelphia Police Homicide Record of May 31, 1921, Volume 5 and the two deaths that occurred on August 2, 1926, Volume 7.

27. These incidents were many, such as in this information written in the "Remarks" of the homicide of Peter Olsen on September 24, 1920: "William Forsberg and Peter Olsen were In the Saloon Drinking And Got Into an Argument..." and on October 17, 1920, "Manuel Mendez went into the Saloon of Rokus Gaubas...Mendez Order Drinks for the 4 men then refused to pay For Them..." Then, on October 15, 1921, the "Remarks" read: "Joseph DeSauter, who is employed as Bartender at the Saloon of James McKewon...John Grainer and James McDade Enter the Saloon and called for Beers was Served..." A March 17, 1924 homicide report read: "During an altercation in Saloon..." (Volume 6) One particular tragedy verified most Philadelphians' attitudes towards Prohibition: On February 24, 1927, at 8:30 AM, both Patrolman Robert McGarvey and Patrolman James Leigh "in full uniform, went into saloon, played pinochle and about 11 AM McGarvey was shot and killed by Leigh..." Leigh was found "not guilty" by Judge Potter. Sources: Volumes 5 to 7 of the Philadelphia Police's Homicide Records.

28. Pius Lanzetti's first arrest was as a suspect in larceny and receiving stolen goods, which was later discharged; Willie Lanzetti's first arrest was on attempted larceny of a mink coat, then on unlawful possession and sale of narcotic drugs; Ignatius' arrest record began in 1923 also with the illegal possession, sale and use of narcotic drugs, which later was discharged. Source: Criminal Records of the Lanzetti brothers from the Department of Public Safety, City of Philadelphia.

29. Confidential informants. Philadelphia Police Homicide Records, Volumes 6 and 7. *The Evening Bulletin* of November 23, 1925. *The Philadelphia Record* of May 31, 1927.

30. Philadelphia newspapers of January 25, 1925. Philadelphia Police Homicide Record of January 24, 1925, Volume 7.

31. Boyd's Philadelphia City Directory of 1915. The Philadelphia City Directory of 1919–1920. Polk's City Directory of 1925.

32. *The Evening Bulletin*, August 19, 1925. Philadelphia Police Homicide Records of August 19, 1925, August 22, 1925, May 9, 1926 and May 26, 1926, Volumes 6 and 7.

33. Though none of the alcohol violation arrest records exist from the early 1920s, the five major newspapers in Philadelphia wrote on the numerous raids of non-Italian alcohol violators at this time, if not for the propaganda and publicity for Butler.

34. Philadelphia Police Homicide Record of September 10, 1928 and April 24, 1929, Volume 8. *The Philadelphia Daily News* of August 1, 1929 wrote: "...members of a South Philadelphia racketeering gang who faced murder charges in connection with the slaying of Vincent Coccozza [sic] and Joseph Zanghi, younger brother of 'Musky' Zanghi, gang leader at Eighth and Christian streets on Memorial [sic] day, 1928 [sic]."

35. Special Grand Jury of August, 1928, p. 48. *Papers of the Committee of Seventy*. Temple University Urban Archives, Philadelphia.

36. Documentation on Jewish gangsters and eastern European Jews in organized crime may be found in ASBURY'S *Gangs of New York;* GENTILE'S *Vita di Capomafia*; BONANNO'S *Man of Honor*; NELLI'S *Business*... Also refer to ALAN A. BLOCK and WILLIAM CHAMBLISS in *Organizing Crime*, New York: Elsevier, 1981, pp. 51-59.

37. GOLAB, "The Immigrant and the City," in *Peoples*, p. 206.

38. WARNER, *Private City*, p. 182.

39. GOLAB, "The Immigrant...," p. 214.

40. Pennsylvania Crime Commission Report of 1990, pp. 104-5.

41. GOLAB, "The Immigrant...," p. 214.

42. Refer to GOLAB, *ibid.*, as well as complementing findings in VARBERO in *Peoples of Philadelphia*; RICHARD N. JULIANI in *The Social Organization of Immigration: The Italians in Philadelphia*, New York: Arno Press, 1980; and, LUCONI, *Bringing Out*... pp. 251- 285.

43. U.S. Senate, Special Committee to Investigate Organized Crime in Interstate Commerce, "Investigation of Organized Crime in Interstate Commerce," Washington, D.C.: U.S. Government Printing Office, 1951, pp. 744-4, (otherwise known as the "Kefauver Investigation.")

44. Philadelphia Police Homicide Records found in Volumes 6 to 8.

45. Among the publications, foremost leading this fiction was the Pennsylvania Crime Commission's Reports of 1970, 1980 and 1990, the last of the decade in summary before disbanding in 1994. In *Before Bruno, Book 1,* Appendix II presented some discussion on the reliability of the Commission's "histories," pp. 131-135. GARY W. POTTER and PHILIP JENKINS in *The City and The Syndicate: Organizing Crime in Philadelphia,* Lexington, Massachusetts: Ginn Press, 1985 also do not sufficiently divert from what the Crime Commission wrote, despite the inconsistencies in the 1970 to 1990 Reports. An example of this is in the omission of John Avena in the 1970 Report as the successor of Salvatore Sabella and as the first La Cosa Nostra boss of the Philadelphia-South Jersey Family.

46. *The Evening Bulletin,* March 6, 1951. Confidential informants. Interviews of Harry Riccobene (1910–2000) from 1992–1999, (hereafter, "Riccobene Interviews.")

47. *The Evening Bulletin,* August 19, 1925.

48. *The Evening Bulletin,* March 6, 1951.

49. Criminal record of Pius Lanzetti from the Philadelphia Police. *St. Louis Post-Dispatch,* Sunday Magazine, December 1, 1935, pp. 4-5.

50. Philadelphia Police Homicide Record of January 24, 1926, Volume 7.

51. *The Philadelphia Daily News,* August 5, 1929.

52. Philadelphia Police Homicide Record of August 5, 1929, Volume 8.

53. *Ibid.,* and homicide of September 1, 1930, Volume 9.

54. Philadelphia Police Homicide Record of July 13, 1929, Volume 8.

55. *The Philadelphia Daily News,* August 5-6, 1929.

56. Philadelphia Police Homicide Records of September 5, 1929, July 19, 1930, July 29, 1930 and December 28, 1931, Volumes 8 and 9.

57. Interview of Robert Montgomery, born in 1912, formerly a reporter with *The Evening Bulletin* in the 1930s.

58. "Fats" was John Focoso; "Doc" was John Amato; and "Pickles" was Anthony Piccarelli who was related to Dan "The Hook" Piccarelli.

59. The full citation is: LEOPOLDO FRANCHETTI, *La Sicilia nel 1876: Libro Primo—Condizioni Politiche e Amministrative*. Florence: Vallecchi Editore, 1925; SIDNEY SONNINO, *La Sicilia nel 1876: Libro Secondo—I Contadini*. Florence: Vallecchi Editore, 1925.

60. Refer to the social history provided by DENIS MACK SMITH in his volume, *Modern Sicily After 1713*, in the series, *A History of Sicily*, New York: The Viking Press, 1968, Chapters 49 through 55, pp. 445-512. CESARE LOMBROSO'S classic is, *L'Uomo Delinquente*, Milan: Hoepli Press, 1876.

61. WALTER WHITE, *Rope & Faggot: A Biography of Judge Lynch*, New York: ALFRED A. KNOPF, 1929, pp. 121, 165. Nelli in *Business of Crime* cited an economic justification, p. 64. Gambino's *Vendetta* blamed contemporary xenophobia through his work. A more recent historical review was taken on by MARCO RIMANELLI and SHERYL L. POSTMAN'S (Eds.) *The 1891 New Orleans Lynching and U.S.-Italian Relations: A look back*, New York: Peter Lang, 1992.

62. J. ALEXANDER KARLIN'S arguments appeared in "The New Orleans Lynchings of 1891 and The American Press," a condensed version of the issues published by *The Louisiana Historical Quarterly* 24, January, 1941; and as "The Italo-American Incident of 1891 and the Road to Reunion," in *Journal of Southern History 8,* May, 1942 both based on his unpublished doctoral dissertation.

63. *The New York Times* publicized Black Hand activities from 1902. Black Hand crimes and homicides in Philadelphia continued until 1926 when the last deaths were recorded in Volume 7 of the Philadelphia Police Homicide Records.

• • • • • • • • •

Notes to Chapter III

1. WALTER B. MILLER, "Lower Class Culture as a Generating Milieu of Gang Delinquency," *Journal of Social Issues*, Volume XIV, 1958, no. 3, pp. 5-19, (hereafter, "MILLER, *'Lower Class Culture...'*")
2. *The New York Times*, Indices of 1877, 1882, 1890 to 1915, article on September 24, 1911.
3. LANE, *Murder in America*, pp. 158-9.
4. MORELLO, *Before Bruno: The History of the Philadelphia Mafia, Book 1*, pp. 19-20, 27, 39, 43, 53 and 76.
5. *The New York Times*, February 11, and February 25, 1907, and March 25, 1907. Refer to Gentile, *Vita di Capomafia*, pp. 38, 69-70, 128-134, 141-4 and 148.
6. *Ibid.*
7. THOMAS MONROE PITKIN & FRANCESCO CORDASCO, *The Black Hand: A Chapter in Ethnic Crime*. Totowa, New Jersey: Rowman & Littlefield, 1977, Bibliographical Note, pp. 247-259. Also refer to the Index listings on Morello and Saitta.
8. *The New York Times*, August 4, 1908.
9. *The New York Times*, September 26, 1909.
10. Confidential informants in Norristown, Pennsylvania interviewed in 1997.

11. *Ibid.* and in the *The New York Times* Indices of listings under "Black Hand." PITKIN also on the newspaper sensationalism in *The Black Hand*, pp. 250-254.
12. *The New York Times*, June 14, and June 28, 1908. PITKIN, *The Black Hand*, p. 215.
13. *The New York Times*, June, 14, 1908, July 8, and July 12, 1908.
14. DENIS MACK SMITH, *History of Sicily—Modern Sicily*. New York: Viking Press, 1968, pp. 464, 506. MARTIN CLARK, *Modern Italy, 1871–1982*. Singapore: The Print House (Pte) Ltd., 1984, pp. 88, 104.
15. *The New York Times*, July 12, 1908.
16. Oral histories of Little Italy residents taken from 1992 to 2001; *The Philadelphia Inquirer*, December 3, 1903.
17. MORELLO, *Before Bruno, Book 1*, p. 53.
18. *The New York Times*, February 8, 1908.
19. Riccobene interviews. Interviews and conversations with confidential informants from 1982 to present.
20. GOLAB, *The Immigrant and the City*, pp. 214-5, 224-6. LUCONI, *Bringing Out...*, pp.251-285. VARBERO, *Philadelphia's South Italians*, pp. 255-272. Philadelphia Police Homicide Records.
21. Confidential informants in Little Italy, Philadelphia.
22. Riccobene interviews.
23. GENTILE, *Vita di Capomafia*, pp. 45 and 93.
24. These dates were cited by GENTILE in *Vita,* p. 102. Joseph Bonanno did not give precise dates of the Castellammarese Wars, but otherwise devoted an entire section of *A Man of Honor,* pp. 61-143. Riccobene interviews confirmed dates of the war.
25. Riccobene interviews. Many of the myths about the Castellammarese Wars began in the 1950s with the Kefauver and McClellan investigations. Joseph Valachi's testimony to the U.S. Senate in 1963 also added more hearsay to the myths, although his version has often been invariably interpreted by others such as HOWARD ABADINSKY in *Organized Crime*. Boston: Allyn & Bacon, Inc., 1981, pp. 51-2; and STEPHEN FOX'S *Blood & Power: Organized Crime in Twentieth Century America*. New York: William Morrow & Company, 1989, pp. 67-70.

26. GENTILE, p. 25.
27. *Ibid.*, pp. 115-6.
28. Riccobene interviews.
29. Department of Justice, Federal Bureau of Investigation, File PH 92-444, December 26, 1957, pp. 2-3.
30. PINO ARLACCHI, *Men of Dishonor: Inside the Sicilian Mafia*. New York: William Morrow & Company, Inc., 1992, pp. 74-8.
31. Philadelphia Police Arrest Record of Harry Riccobene of 1932.
32. *Ibid.* and Philadelphia Police Arrest Record of Angelo Bruno; Riccobene interviews; FBI File PH 92-444, December 26, 1957, p.7.
33. MILLER, *Lower Class Culture...* p. 13.
34. Riccobene interviews.
35. E. J. HOBSBAWM, *Primitive Rebels*, Manchester, England: Manchester University Press, 1959, pp. 30, 37-9; MACK SMITH, *Modern Sicily*, p. 448; HENNER HESS, *Mafia & Mafiosi: The Structure of Power*. Saxon House-Lexington Books, 1970, p. 54; BONANNO, *A Man of Honor*, pp. 148-9, 154-6, 162-5; ARLACCHI, *Men of Dishonor*, pp. 38-41; Riccobene interviews.
36. Riccobene interviews.
37. Bruno family (relatives) interviews, 1982–2001; FBI File PH 92-444, December 26, 1957, pp. 2-3.
38. Riccobene interviews. Confidential informants.
39. Riccobene interviews. ARLACCHI, *Men of Dishonor*, pp.21-23. GENTILE, *Vita*, pp. 11-12. Bonanno, pp. 40-1, 148-165.
40. PHILIP V. CANNISTRARO, *Generoso Pope and the Rise of Italian American Politics, 1925-1936*, in LYDIO F. TOMASI (Ed.) *Italian Americans: New Perspectives in Italian Immigration & Ethnicity*. New York: Center For Migration Studies of New York, 1985, pp. 264-288.
41. LUCONI, "Tempi e dinamiche dell'imperimento dell'elettorato italo-americans nella coalizione rooseveltiana: il caso sul voto delle comunità di Filadelfia e di Pittsburgh." (unpublished doctoral dissertation) Third University of Rome, 1995, p. 165.
42. Riccobene interviews. Confidential informants.

43. WALTER LICHT, *Getting Work: Philadelphia, 1840-1950*. Cambridge, Massachusetts: Harvard University Press, 1992, Chapter 2, pp. 17- 56.

44. NELLI, *Business...*, p. 168.

45. GENTILE, *Vita di Capomafia*, p. 104.

46. *The New York Times*, September 11, 1931. Also, refer to some rather contemporary works by BURTON B. TURKUS, former assistant District Attorney in New York City and SID FEDER of the Associated Press, *Murder, Inc. The Story of the Syndicate,* New York: DaCapo Press, 1951; and HICKMAN POWELL'S *Ninety Times Guilty* or *Lucky Luciano: The Man who Organized Crime in America*. New York: Barricade Books, 1939.

47. *The Philadelphia Record*, September 9, 1935.

48. *Ibid.*

49. Cugino is buried in Fernwood Cemetery, just outside of Philadelphia. *The Philadelphia Daily News* and *Philadelphia Record*, September 9, 1935.

50. Philadelphia Police Homicide Records, Volume 10.

51. Riccobene interviews.

52. LANE, *Murder in America*, p. 219.

53. Confidential interviews of individuals from Montgomery and Bucks Counties, Pennsylvania.

54. Grand Jury of 1937–1939, Presentments. pp. 270-272. Pennsylvania State Archives, State Police Records, Harrisburg, Pennsylvania.

55. *Ibid.*

56. Philadelphia Police Homicide Records, Volumes 11 and 12. Willie Lanzetti's body was found on July 1, 1939 in Wynnewood, Montgomery County, Pennsylvania and was listed in that county's homicide records, though he was believed to have been murdered in Philadelphia.

57. Riccobene interviews. *The Philadelphia Evening Bulletin*, July 1, 1939; *The Philadelphia Daily News*, July 3, 1939; and *The Philadelphia Inquirer*, July 2, 1939.

58. NELLI, Business, pp. 252-253.

59. CRESSEY, *Theft of the Nation*, pp. x, xi, 140-155.

60. WARNER, *The Private City*, p. 223.
61. *Ibid.*, p. 219.
62. Refer to MILLER'S, "Focal Concern Theory," outlined in his essay, *Lower Class Culture...*, pp. 13-14.
63. Confidential informants, including relatives and business associates of relatives' interviewed from early 1980s to present. Many of these individuals were young adults in the 1940s and were present and aware of such progressions in the local LCN.

• • • • • • • • • •

Notes to Chapter IV

1. LANE, *Murder in America*, p. 172. ASBURY, *Gangs of New York*, p. 302.
2. JAN MCMILLEN (Ed.) *Gambling Cultures: Studies in history and interpretation*, London: Routledge Press, 1966, p. 6.
3. JOHNSON, *Policing the Urban Underworld*, p. 158
4. *Ibid.*, p. 172.
5. LANE, *William Dorsey's Philadelphia*, p. 223.
6. MCMILLEN, *Gambling Cultures*, p. 13. Also refer to VARBERO in *Peoples of Philadelphia*, p. 259.
7. LANE, *Dorsey*, p. 130.
8. Philadelphia Police Homicide Volumes 4 to 9, covering the years 1914 (from August) to December of 1930.
9. ASBURY, *Gangs*, p. 87. Miller, pp. 11-12.
10. Refer to the Philadelphia Police Homicide Volumes 4 to 9.
11. LANE, *Violent Death*, p. 83.
12. VARBERO in *Peoples of Philadelphia*, pp. 256, 258, and 259.
13. WARNER, *The Private City*, p. 185.
14. MILLER, pp. 11-12.

15. As noted in the Homicide Volumes 4 to 9.
16. *The Philadelphia Inquirer* and *Philadelphia Record*, January 1, 1937.
17. FBI File PH 92-444, dated December 26, 1956, p. 10.
18. Confidential informants. Riccobene interviews.
19. Philadelphia Police Homicide Records of March 14 and 15, 1933.
20. *The Evening Bulletin*, June 13, 1933.
21. *The Evening Bulletin*, June 17, 1933 and September 29, 1935.
22. *The Evening Bulletin*, February 6, 1935.
23. *The Evening Bulletin*, June 8, 1935.
24. Confidential informants.
25. JAMES SMITH in *Gambling Cultures*, p. 107.
26. Philadelphia Police Homicide Record of December 4, 1925, Volume 7.
27. Philadelphia Police Homicide Record of October 5, 1927, Volume 7.
28. Confidential informants in Bucks, Montgomery and Philadelphia Counties in Pennsylvania.
29. MARK H. HALLER, "Philadelphia Bootlegging and The Report of the Special August Grand Jury," *Pennsylvania Magazine of History and Biography*, April, 1985, p. 233.
30. *Ibid.*
31. *The Evening Bulletin*, October 19, 1935.
32. *The Evening Bulletin*, January 8, 1937
33. Confidential informants.
34. Confidential informant who still is an LCN member, "made" in 1947 and interviewed in 2001.

• • • • • • • • • •

Notes to Chapter V

1. Massachusetts Department of Corrections File #15575 for John DiNatale, (hereafter, "MA DOC File.")
2. Confidential informants. Riccobene interviews. John Avena's dates of tenure were not documented by the Philadelphia Police or Philadelphia Federal Bureau of Investigation. The Pennsylvania Crime Commission Report of 1970 had no mention of Avena; the 1980 Report has "Joseph Avena" as boss in 1927 to 1936; the 1990 Report also has Avena as boss in 1927 after the Zanghi-Cocozzo murders. My sources gave 1931 as the year when Avena became boss.
3. Registro Civile degli Atti di Nacità, comune di Novara di Sicilia, Provincia di Messina, anno 1892. Avena believed that he was born in 1893, hence, that year in his criminal record and death certificate.
4. Foremost in the recent revisionist histories on Frederick II is DAVID ABULAFIA'S *Frederick II: A Medieval Emperor*, New York: Oxford University Press, 1988. MACK SMITH'S *Medieval Sicily*, New York: Viking Press, 1968 is no less competent and has many contemporary sources cited.
5. FRANCHETTI and SONNINO, *La Sicilia nel 1876*, Volumes 1 and 2, Florence: 1925.
6. MACK SMITH, *Modern Sicily*, p. 496.

7. JOHN L. STODDARD'S *Lectures: Sicily*, Boston: Balch Brothers, 1906, p. 109.
8. MACK SMITH, p. 496, citing Cesare Lombroso's *L'Uomo Delinquente*, Milan: Hoepli Press, 1876.
9. ANTONIO CUTRERA, *La Mafia e i Mafiosi*, Palermo: 1900. HOWARD ABADINSKY also briefly cited this in *Organized Crime*, Boston: Allyn & Bacon, Inc., 1981, p. 37. PINO ARLACCHI, *Men of Dishonor*, New York: William Morrow & Company, pp. 19, 23-26.
10. Interviews taken from 1992 to present on Little Italy residents. Interview of Salvatore J. Avena, Esquire.
11. MA DOC File on John DiNatale.
12. Interview from Salvatore J. Avena, Esquire.
13. MA DOC File of John DiNatale. U.S. Census of 1910 for Philadelphia.
14. Records of the Archdiocese of Philadelphia. Catholic Directories of 1910. Also refer to DAVIS & HALLER (Eds.) *Peoples of Philadelphia*, and WALTER LICHT'S *Getting Work*.
15. Refer to the class divisions in VARBERO'S piece in *Peoples of Philadelphia*, pp. 255-275; GOLAB, *Ibid*., p. 205. *Bulletin,* May 9, 1910. *Public Ledger* of May 16, 1910.
16. *Public Ledger*, May 16, 1910.
17. GOLAB, "The Immigrant...," p. 205, in *Peoples of Philadelphia*,
18. Full citations: *La Colonia di Filadelfia*, Philadelphia: L'Opinione, 1906; PROF. ALFONSO STRAFILE, *Memorandum, Coloniale...Vita Coloniale degli Italiani*, Philadelphia: "Mastro Paolo" Printing-house, 1910.
19. MA DOC file of John DiNatale. Interviews of Little Italy residents. U.S. Census of 1910 for Philadelphia.
20. *The Boston Globe*, March 6, 1916, p. 3. *Public Ledger,* of March 6, 1916.
21. MILLER, *Lower Class Culture...*, pp. 10-11.
22. BOYD'S Philadelphia City Directory of 1915.
23. MA DOC file of John DiNatale.
24. Massachusetts Department of Correction Files #15573 & 15574 of Conti and Costa.

25. *Ibid. Boston Globe*, March 6, 1916.
26. *Ibid.*
27. MA DOC file of John DiNatale.
28. *Boston Globe*, March 6, 1916. FBI File BU 92-8045 report dated December 11, 1964, p. 1. (Also known as PH 92-1449.)
29. *Boston Globe*, March 23, 1916. MA DOC file of John DiNatale.
30. GENTILE, p. 62.
31. Philadelphia City Directory of 1919-1920.
32. I am indebted to CHUCK HASSON and his unpublished information on Philadelphia's boxing history, as well as his published articles, one of which that was cited was "The Philadelphia Story," in *International Boxing Digest*, November/December, 1998, pp. 54-55.
33. *Ibid.* Hasson said that local newspapers provided most of the information for these facts as there has yet to be a history of boxing in Philadelphia based on any other source(s).
34. *Ibid.* p. 56. Also refer to NAT FLEISCHER and SAM E. ANDRE'S *An Illustrated History of Boxing*, Secaucus, New Jersey: Carol Publishing, 1959.
35. *Ibid.* Chuck Hasson's interview of Herman "Mugsy" Taylor appeared in an article, "The Promoter," in the June 3, 1997 fight program published in Philadelphia for The Blue Horizon Arena.
36. FOX, *Blood & Power*, pp. 88-89, citing Nat Fleischer.
37. Confidential informants. Interviews from Little Italy residents.
38. Philadelphia City Directories of 1919-1920. Riccobene interviews. Interview of A. Domenico Pollina in 1992.
39. Arlacchi, pp. 74-77. FBI File PH 92-444, report of December 26, 1957, p. 2. Bruno family interviews.
40. MA DOC file of John DiNatale. CHRISTOPHER MORLEY, *Travels in Philadelphia,* Philadelphia: J.B. Lippincott Co., 1920, pp. 19-20.
41. Letter by Henry A. Higgins, Acting Chairman, Commonwealth of Massachusetts Department of Corrections Board of Parole to William D. Hendry, Warden, State Prison in Charlestown, Massachusetts, dated March 6, 1923, File # 15575.
42. MA DOC file of John DiNatale.

43. Special Agent in Charge, Philadelphia FBI Office, File 92-1449 "Memorandum" dated December 29, 1964, p. 1. Philadelphia Police Number 20397.
44. *The Public Ledger*, *Philadelphia Inquirer* and *Bulletin*, all dated May 10, 1923.
45. Riccobene interviews. Arlacchi, pp. 21-22.
46. Confidential informants. Riccobene interviews. Bonanno, p. 162.
47. Interview from Salvatore J. Avena, Esquire. *Bulletin*, June 2, 1927.
48. *Bulletin*, July 29, 1926. *Inquirer*, *Public Ledger* and *Bulletin* of July 30, 1926.
49. *Public Ledger* and *Record,* January 25, 1926. Philadelphia Police Homicide Record of January 24, 1926, Volume 7.
50. *Ibid.* This later became the "softdrink store" and place where Avena admitted to bringing in the bootlegged liquor in May, 1927.
51. Leonetti was most likely an associate of Sabella and the other Mafiosi, one without much of any type of record for reference.
52. Philadelphia Police Homicide Report of January 24, 1926, Volume 7.
53. *Public Ledger*, March 11, 1927.
54. *Bulletin*, *Inquirer* and *Public Ledger*, July 30, 1926.
55. *Bulletin* and *Public Ledge*r, March 11, 1927.
56. *Ibid.*
57. *Public Ledger*, May 31, 1927. Similar accounts were noted in the *Inquirer*, *Public Ledger* and *Record,* June 1, 1927.
58. *Inquirer* and *Record*, May 31, 1927.
59. *Bulletin*, May, 31, 1927. *Inquirer* and *Record*, June 1, 1927.
60. *Record*, June 1, 1927.
61. *Bulletin* and *Record*, June 1, 1927.
62. *Bulletin*, June 2, 1927.
63. *Inquirer*, June 15, 1927. *Bulletin*, June 17, 1927.
64. *Ibid.* *Record*, June 16, 1927.
65. *Inquirer* and *Record*, June 19, 1927.
66. *Bulletin*, June 17, 1927. *Record*, June 18, 1927.

67. *Commonwealth of Pennsylvania versus John Avena, et al.*, May Sessions, 1927, #1528 et seq. now lost. Refer to *Before Bruno, Book 1* Appendix III, pp. 139-144.
68. *Ibid.*
69. *Bulletin*, August 18, 1936.
70. BONANNO, pp. 154-156.
71. FBI File PH 92-445, report of June 4, 1958, p. 33 read: "Antonio and Philip Pollina had a grocery business in Riverside New Jersey from about 1926 to about 1937...They had granted credit to a great many individuals in the town during the depression and had much uncollected money on their books."
72. MA DOC file of John DiNatale.
73. Confidential informant. *Record*, January 1, 1937.
74. The Philadelphia Police's Department of Public Safety's record on Pius showed mostly "poss. and sale narcotic drugs" in 1923, after two arrests for larceny. The March 19, 1924 arrest for rape ("F&B") somehow had its sentence to run concurrent with the April 7, 1927 arrest and conviction of Aggravated Assault and Battery "by shooting with intent to kill & C.C.D.W. (revolver)" A confidential informant closed with that statement.
75. This is an example of how Mafia and LCN bosses do not necessarily inherit their predecessor's contacts. Each boss personalized his Family and tried different activities.
76. FBI Philadelphia Anti-Racketeering Case of Angelo Bruno, report dated December 26, 1957, p. 7, based on the Philadelphia Police's arrest of November 21, 1928, #85869.
77. NELLI, pp. 179-218. Nelli apparently recognized that many Italian gangsters and Sicilian Mafiosi were forced to socialize more with the "Americans" during Prohibition, but this socialization did not alter the Sicilian American Mafia's hierarchy, rules and function—substituting Sicilian American Mafiosi with gangsters with mainland Italian origins or no Mafia Tradition in their background caused a considerable breakdown in the Mafia's form and function.
78. PETER LUPSHA, "Individual Choice, Material Culture, and Organized Crime," in *Criminology*, Volume 19, Number 1, May 1981, pp. 3-24. His "Table I" paralleled Nelli's text but is filled with errors. He would have had a stronger argument separating those from a Mafia Tradition, such as Bonanno, Gambino, Maranzano,

etc....from home-grown Italian gangsters, then placing them within the appropriate time frame and environment. Lupsha dealt with at least two generations and different times of migrating to the U.S., or not migrating. He stressed "choice," but the table does not prove anything definitive.

79. ADRIAN LYTTELTON, *The Seizure of Power: Fascism in Italy: 1919-1929*. New York: Charles Scribner's Sons, 1973, p. 199. CHRISTOPHER DUGGAN, *Fascism and the Mafia*. New Haven: Yale University Press, 1989, pp. 186-187. Gentile, pp. 94-95.

80. BONANNO, pp. 161-163. GENTILE, pp. 23, 163.

81. GENTILE, p. 112. If only he could have said it in fewer words: "...era di raggiungere uno stato di cose nel quale non si sparasse più."

82. Gentile wrote about it before Bonanno, though much terser on pp. 118-119, then interspersed in succeeding chapters. Bonanno devoted an entire chapter on "The Commission," alluding to the old "Fathers" stepping down for new ones who represented the new "Order," on pp. 141, 145-204.

83. Riccobene interviews. Confidential informants.

84. *Ibid.*

85. The 1891 hangings in New Orleans set off law enforcement and news media to this Mafia, the "first" sources for this information. which were indicative of the times and sentiments in the U.S. Previous chapters cited revisionist historical literature.

86. *Before Bruno, Book 1* explored some of this within proximity to Philadelphia with the Montgomery and Luzerne Counties' Mafia Families, typically considered as rural Mafia sites. But Philadelphia's Mafia still had no documentation with which to compare with other urban centers.

87. NELLI, pp. 270-271, 2n-8n. *The New York Times* pieces on the arrival of Raffaele Palizzolo in June, 1908 reveal an upper class of wealthy and professional Sicilians, most likely from western Sicily who were from the Mafia culture that bore the likes of a Raffaele Palizzolo.

88. Gentile wrote of this transition as very difficult, but something that was fated to happen. Bonanno realized that different Mafia Family locales were subject to their preferences and noted the meetings and proceedings on pp. 124-127.

89. Riccobene interviews. Confidential informants.

90. Some of the Calabrians were named; some of the eastern Sicilians included Joseph Bruno and Salvatore Testa from Giardini, Province of Messina, Sicily.
91. Confidential informant. *Record*, January 1, 1937.
92. *Inquirer*, *Public Ledger* and *Record*, August 18, 1936. *Inquirer*, March 21, 1937. *Record*, July 2, 1939.
93. Confidential informants. Interviews of South Philadelphia residents.
94. Commonwealth of Pennsylvania Department of Health, Bureau of Vital Statistics File #82185, Registered #17257.
95. *Bulletin*, August 18, 1936.
96. *Bulletin*, *Daily News* and *Inquirer*, August 18, 1936.
97. FBI File PH 92-1449 to FBI Director dated December 29, 1964.

• • • • • • • • • •

Notes to Chapter VI

1. *The Philadelphia Record*, January 1, 1937.
2. *Ibid.* Confidential informants. Riccobene interviews,
3. Registro degli Atti di Nacità, comune di Barcellona Pozzo di Gotto, Provincia di Messina, (Sicily), Italy, per anno 1889.
4. *Ibid.*
5. 1915 City of Cortland, New York and New York State Census, CTC50118 CEM & CCD. Cortland County Historical Society, Cortland, New York.
6. Interviews of Dovi relatives of Joseph Bruno.
7. Refer to Golab's studies in DAVIS & HALLER'S *Peoples of Philadelphia*, pp. 228-8, 6n, 7n and 10n.
8. Interview of LOUIS VANARIA, PH.D. author of "Settlement Patterns of Cortland's Italians: The First Generation, 1892–1925," in *From Many Roots: Immigrants & Ethnic Groups in the History of Cortland County, New York*. Cortland: Cortland County Chronicles, County Historical Society, 1986, pp. 20-35.
9. U.S. Census. Census of the County of Cortland, Cortland City, Enumeration Date, April 27, 1910, Sheet 10-A, District 117. Cortland County Historical Society.
10. *Ibid.* Also, Petition for Naturalization for Mario Giuseppe Dovi in the Supreme Court of Cortland County, New York, Declaration of Intention Number 90, Certificate of Arrival Number 747036.

11. U.S. Census of 1910, City of Cortland, New York. Interviews of Dovi relatives in Cortland, New York.
12. City and Business Directories of Cortland of 1912, 1916. Petition for Naturalization of January 10, 1917. U.S. Census of 1910. The 1915 Cortland City and New York State Census.
13. Refer to previous chapters for other examples and explanation.
14. Refer to IANNI'S theory in *A Family Business* for explanation. The Mafia's origins in western Sicily are indisputable and this fact has some of its earliest sources in Franchetti and Sonnino's 1876 work, with MACK SMITH'S *History of Modern Sicily* as one of the most recent major references. See also *Before Bruno, Book 1.*
15. Interviews of Dovi relatives in Cortland.
16. Declaration of Intent and Petition for Naturalization for Mario Giuseppe Dovi. Cortland County Historical Society, Cortland, New York.
17. Interview of Dr. Vanaria.
18. Declaration of Intent and Petition for Naturalization of Mario Giuseppe Dovi.
19. Interview of Cicciari relative from New York.
20. Business and City Directories of Cortland City, New York of 1916.
21. Interviews taken from several confidential informants in Bristol Borough, Bucks County, Pennsylvania.
22. U.S. Census of 1920, Bucks County, Pennsylvania Volume 71, #1542 for Bristol Borough, Ward 1, Enumeration District 7, Sheet 5, Lines 48 and 49. Bucks County Historical Society, Doylestown, Pennsylvania.
23. *Ibid.*, line 49. The woman may have used the word, *comare* (girl-friend) to translate to "cousin."
24. St. Mark's Roman Catholic Cemetery Records. Bucks County Historical Society.
25. Interviews of Bruno and Cicciari relatives.
26. Riccobene interviews. Philadelphia Police Homicide Record of January 24, 1928, Volume 7.
27. Interview of Cicciari relative.
28. Interviews of confidential informants in Bristol.
29. Interviews of confidential informants in New Brunswick, New Jersey taken from 1994, on.

30. Certainly a murder would have been publicized! Again, as in Book 1, the Pennsylvania Crime Commission's publications fall short on this type of fact-finding by not citing the "various public sources." The Crime Commission's end of decade report in 1970, then the 1975–1976 report on gambling were referenced for these statements made about Joseph Bruno. *The Daily Home News of Greater New Brunswick* and *The Philadelphia Inquirer*, both dated June 1, 1927 mention Joseph Bruno as from "New Brunswick" and with a criminal record there, without any specifics on what types of offenses. Bruno's FBI record has been destroyed; the New Brunswick Police's criminal files had to be discarded after a flood in the basement; therefore, few pieces of evidence remain to ascertain what the offenses were.
31. *Ibid. Daily Home News* and *Inquirer*. Riccobene interviews.
32. *Bulletin*, June 1, 1927.
33. *Bulletin* and *Public Ledger*, May 31, 1927. *Record, Public Ledger* and *Inquirer*, June 1, 1927.
34. FBI File NK 92-381, report of April 21, 1958, pp. 30-31.
35. *Inquirer*, June 1, 1927 and *Record*, May 31, 1927.
36. *Inquirer,* January 1, 1937.
37. Confidential informants in South Philadelphia.
38. Confidential informant. Interview of Salvatore J. Avena.
39. Confidential informants. Riccobene interviews.
40. Interviews of Bruno and Cicciari relatives. Confidential informants in Bristol and Philadelphia, and in New Brunswick. FBI File NK 92-381, dated September 23, 1960, p. 5.
41. Confidential informants. Bruno and Cicciari relatives.
42. Peter Maas, *The Valachi Papers*, New York: Bantam Books, 1968, p. 128.
43. Riccobene interviews.
44. Philadelphia Police Homicide records of May 29, 1939 and July 21, 1939, Volume 11. Confidential informants.
45. Philadelphia Police Homicide Record of September 28, 1918, Volume 4. *Inquirer*, July 22, 1939.
46. *Inquirer*, July 2, 1939.
47. *Ibid. Public Ledger*, August 6, 1939.
48. *Ibid.*

49. *Inquirer*, and *Record*, January 1, 1937.
50. Philadelphia Police Homicide Record of December 31, 1936, Volume 10.
51. Interviews of Bruno family members.
52. FBI Anti-Racketeerinq File, Case of Angelo Bruno, PH 92-444, report dated March 7, 1958, pp. 14, 19 and 20. FBI PH 92-444, report dated December 26, 1957, pp. 6-8. Philadelphia Police Form 75-10, Extract of Criminal Record of Angelo Bruno, prepared on October 21, 1970. *Commonwealth of Pennsylvania* v. *Angelo Bruno,* October Term, 1940, #678, Philadelphia County. Also referenced in *U.S.* v. *DeCavalcante, et al.,* U.S. District Court, Camden, New Jersey, #111-68.
53. Philadelphia Police Arrest Record of Angelo Bruno. FBI PH 92-444 report dated March 7, 1958, p. 14.
54. Refer to Sabella's arrests by the Philadelphia Police in February, 1940, September of 1943 and *Commonwealth* v. *Salvatore Sabella,* November Term, 1943, #443-444, Philadelphia County, cited in his FBI File PH 92-1377. Scopolitti's arrest record was previously discussed. Also, File PH 92-445 of May 22, 1958, p. 12 and the report of August 28, 1958, p. 11.
55. Joseph Ida's FBI File is 92-381 and stated many "Bruno-Ida" associations, chief among them in report dated June 26, 1958, p. 1 and NK File report dated September 23, 1960, p. 5, as "under the sponsorship of Joe Bruno, deceased, former New Brunswick, New Jersey rackets leader."
56. Confidential informants. Interviews of Bruno relatives.
57. Maas, pp. 181-5. Bruno's horse was named, "High Caste."
58. *Daily Home News of Greater New Brunswick,* October 23, 1946 and October 25, 1946.
59. Certificate of Death, No. 22294, Municipal Archives, Department of Records and Information Services, City of New York, New York.
60. *Daily Home News of Greater New Brunswick*, October 25, 1946, verified by Bruno relatives.
61. Confidential informants, Riccobene interviews. Refer also to *Before Bruno. Book 1*, pp. 132-3 on how Joseph Bruno's criminal career and role change with each Pennsylvania Crime Commission report from 1970 to the last in 1990.

• • • • • • • • • •

Notes to Chapter VII

1. Riccobene interviews. Confidential informants.
2. J. B. Mattison, *The Mattison Method of Morphinism: A Modern and Humane Treatment of the Morphin Disease.* New York: E.B. Treat & Co., 1902; U.S. Public Health Report of January 15, 1915, "Laws and Regulations Relating to the production, importation, manufacturing...of opium or coca leaves, their salts, derivatives or preparations;" "The Opium Evil," Message from the President of the U.S., 62nd Congress, 2nd Session of the Senate, December 1, 1911 to January 23, 1912; "The Narcotic Evil in Philadelphia and Pennsylvania," The Philadelphia Narcotic Drug Committee, 1916; "In Explanation of the Pennsylvania Anti-Narcotic Act," Commonwealth of Pennsylvania's Department of Health, Public Act #282 of July 11, 1917; "Philadelphia Committee for the Clinical Study of Opium Addiction, 1925–1929".
3. *The Evening Bulletin*, April 23, 1910.
4. Joseph W. England (Ed.), *The First Century of the Philadelphia College of Pharmacy,* 1821-1921. Published by the Philadelphia College of Pharmacy in Philadelphia, 1922, p. 132.
5. Public Law #223 of the 63rd Congress, March 1, 1915. Published by the Government Printing Office in Washington, D.C.
6. Summaries taken of Philadelphians in case studies cited in the U.S. Public Health Report of 1915, called, "condensed histories of

patients admitted to the narcotic ward" of the Pennsylvania General Hospital in the "Philadelphia Committee for the Clinical Study of Opium Addiction, 1925-1929."

7. *Ibid.* Also refer to H. H. KANE, MD, *The Hypodermic Injection of Morphia: its history, advantages & dangers*. New York: Charles L. Bermingham & Company, 1880.

8. A number of cases were noted in the volumes of *The Medical & Surgical History of the War of the Rebellion* published in Washington, D.C.: Government Printing Office, 1875 to 1883; S. WEIR MITCHELL, GEORGE A. MOREHOUSE and WM. W. KEEN, *Gunshot Wounds & Other Injuries of Nerves*. Philadelphia: J. B. Lippincott, 1864; MITCHELL, MOREHOUSE and KEEN, "On the Antagonisms of Atropia and Morphia" *American Journal of the Medical Sciences*, Volume L, 1865.

9. *Ibid.*

10. C. E. BROWN-SÈQUARD, "Lectures on the diagnosis and treatment of functional nervous affections," Philadelphia: 1868; A. Ruppaner, "Hypodermic Injections," Boston, 1865; R. Bartholow, "Manual of hypodermic medication," Philadelphia, 1869. All were journal pieces cited in *The Medical & Surgical History of the War of the Rebellion,* Washington, D.C.: 1875-1883, Volumes 3 to 12.

11. Refer to KANE, *The Hypodermic Injection...*

12. "Minutes of the Magdalen Society," 1850-1869.

13. ASBURY, *Gangs of New York*, p. 256.

14. EDMUNDS & GUNN (Revised), *A Text-book of Pharmacology & Therapeutics or the Action of Drugs in Health & Disease.* Philadelphia: Lea & Febiger, 11th edition, 1936, p. 388.

15. Report of the Public Law #223 of the 63rd Congress, March 1, 1915.

16. ASBURY, p. 256.

17. "The Narcotic Evil in Philadelphia and Pennsylvania," The Philadelphia Narcotic Drug Committee, 1916. "Philadelphia Committee for the Clinical Study of Opium Addiction, 1925-1929." College of Physicians. "Report Crimes Survey..."

18. "Narcotics Education," pp. 17-21, 221 and 223.

19. EDMUNDS & GUNN, pp. 390-400. "Narcotic Education," p. 35.

20. Case summaries of Philadelphians noted in the U.S. Public Health Report of 1915 and, the "condensed histories of patients admitted to the narcotic ward" of the Philadelphia General Hospital, researched and published by the Philadelphia Committee for the Clinical Study of Opium Addiction.

21. Philadelphia Police Homicide Records, February 21, 1914, May 6, 1917 and January 3, 1917, Volumes 3 and 4.

22. Case studies from the U.S. Public Health Report of 1915. PGH patients from 1925–1929.

23. Refer to the series of Public Acts and Public Resolutions from PA #227 of 1922, PA #318 of 1922, PR #96 of 1923, PR #20 of 1924, PA #274 of 1924 and *Narcotic Education* of 1926, pp. 29, 35.

24. *The Evening Bulletin,* April 24, 1910. *Narcotic Education*, p. 227.

25. Commonwealth of Pennsylvania's Department of Health, Public Act #282, "In Explanation of the Pennsylvania Anti-Narcotic Act," July 11, 1917.

26. *Narcotic Education,* p. 17.

27. Philadelphia Police Homicide Record, December 10, 1919, Volume 5.

28. Philadelphia Police Homicide Record, October 3, 1921, Volume 5.

29. ASBURY, *Gangs of New York*, p. 296. Block and Chambliss, pp. 51- 59.

30. WARNER, *The Private City*, p. 182.

31. *Narcotic Education*, p. 221.

32. *Ibid.*, pp. 25-6.

33. *Ibid.*

34. *The Evening Bulletin*, March 19, 1924. Philadelphia Police Arrest records for Leo, Pius, William, Ignatius, Lucien and Teo Lanzetti. A "hop head" was an opium smoker.

35. *Narcotics Education*, pp. 221, 223. *The Evening Bulletin,* September 24, 1924.

36. *Ibid.*

37. *Bulletin*, September 24, 1924. *Inquirer*, September 14, 1925.

38. Catholic Directory for the Archdiocese of Philadelphia of 1920.

39. Riccobene interviews. Confidential informants. GENTILE, pp. 59-64, 67-70, 81.
40. Riccobene interviews. Philadelphia Police Arrest Record of Harry Riccobene.
41. PGH records of 1925-1929. *Narcotics Education*, pp. 21, 32.
42. *Narcotics Education*, p. 32. EDMUNDS & GUNN, pp. 390-1.
43. *Ibid.*
44. PGH records of 1925-1929.
45. *Report Crimes Survey Committee.*
46. Confidential informants, one of whom worked as an undercover federal agent within the Bruno Family.
47. The local newspapers were consistent in naming a motive for Avena's and Feldstein's deaths. *Inquirer*, *Bulletin*, *Daily News* and *Record*, of August 18, 1936. BONANNO, p. 209.
48. GENTILE, p. 150.

• • • • • • • • •

Acknowledgements

Friends, relatives, friends and associates of the bosses of the Philadelphia-South Jersey La Cosa Nostra Family have my heartfelt appreciation for their assistance in constructing this very difficult history. In particular, I would like to thank Attorney Salvatore J. Avena and the Bruno, Cicciari, Dovi and Montgomery families for their courage in reliving memories which I am sure elicit many questions about the men whom they loved so dearly. I also wish to acknowledge the following individuals who provided valuable information, written or otherwise: Cathy Barber, Betty Bonawitz, Kathy Bouras, J. Michael Comeau, Anthony Constantini, Reverend Francis Crupi, Joseph Cuttone, Joseph DiMino, "Elizabeth," Danny Falcone, Berenice Giarratana, Pasquale Ingenito, Jr., Katie Maloney, "Mr. M.", Thomas D. Montalbano, Rebecca Mullaney, Mr. Charles Santore, Sr., Sergeant Robert W. Tagert, Mr. Lawrence Tornetta, Mr. Vincent Villone, Frances Waite; and remembering those who passed during my research: Mr. Harry Riccobene, Mr. Orlando Puppo, Mr. DeRogatis, Mr. Calogero "Uncle Charlie" Morello, Mr. Rosario "Uncle

Russell" Morello, and Albert Copeland. And I remember, always with thanks, Albert C. Wicks, former Assistant Chief of the U.S. Attorney's Office's Organized Crime Strike Force in Philadelphia.

Book 2 introduced more comparative data to isolate the Philadelphia case of the Sicilian American Mafia and La Cosa Nostra which was made possible through the use of the homicide indices of the Philadelphia Police. Thanks therefore to former Commissioners Willie Williams and Richard Neal for their permission, and to now-retired homicide Inspector Jerrold Kane who from 1992 to 1996 allowed me to compile my information at their offices. More recent thanks and acknowledgements go to homicide Inspector James M. Boyle and Detective Francis T. Kerrigan whose smiles and support surmounted the present restrictions to curtail my research by Philadelphia Commissioner John F. Timoney. Hampering such work was not constructive but rather added suspicion to the overall effort to fill the void in local crime history.

Nevertheless, I do thank the Philadelphia Police Department without Timoney, as well as the police departments of Camden, New Jersey and Boston, Massachusetts for their photographs that seize upon those brief glimpses in the history of law enforcement and organized crime. Other photographs are credited to the College of Physicians in Philadelphia; the Free Library's Map Collection with help from Mr. Richard Boardman; the Urban Archives at Temple University with Ms. Margaret Jerrido and Mrs. Brenda Galloway-Wright; the City Archives; and Mrs. William (Loretta Coffaro) Montgomery.

The construction of this book involved many individuals who were guided by nothing less than a duty towards thoroughness. I give my most sincere thanks to Mr. Joseph Casino, of Villanova and St. Joseph's Universities for his careful eyes that kept my writing to professional technical standards. James J. Greenfield, Esquire suggested a few comments to the text which I heeded. Jefferies and Manz, Publishers' staff, which included Shirley Flaville, Rita Marsden and Frank Szerbin produced a visual concept consistent with the historical account. At my request, Mr. Szerbin created a look to reflect the 1930s and did his job well.

Finally, I cannot thank enough my gracious friend, John F. Seidler, Vice President of Jefferies and Manz, for his unlimited assistance which in so many ways meant his belief in my work. He will be remembered as a man of truth...with great honor.

• • • • • • • • •

Index